Dancing in the Forest

Dancing in the Forest

KOREAN SHAMANS
IN THE UNITED STATES

Helen Hong

PICKWICK *Publications* · Eugene, Oregon

DANCING IN THE FOREST
Korean Shamans in the United States

Pickwick Publications
An Imprint of Wipf and Stock Publishers
199 W. 8th Ave., Suite 3
Eugene, OR 97401

www.wipfandstock.com

PAPERBACK ISBN: 978-1-6667-4147-6
HARDCOVER ISBN: 978-1-6667-4148-3
EBOOK ISBN: 978-1-6667-4149-0

Cataloguing-in-Publication data:

Names: Hong, Helen, author.

Title: Dancing in the forest : Korean shamans in the United States / Helen Hong.

Description: Eugene, OR: Pickwick Publications, 2022. | Includes bibliographical references and index.

Identifiers: ISBN 978-1-6667-4147-6 (paperback). | ISBN 978-1-6667-4148-3 (hardcover). | ISBN 978-1-6667-4149-0 (ebook).

Subjects: LSCH: Shamans—Korea (South). | Women shamans. | Shamanism. | Confucianism. | Ethnology—Korean immigrants.

Classification: BL2236.S5 H71 2022 (print). | BL2236.S5 (ebook).

This study is gratefully dedicated to my late advisor
Professor Karen McCarthy Brown,
Professor Emeritus Herbert B. Huffmon,
and anyone who is interested in religion.

Contents

Acknowledgments

IT IS MY HONOR to acknowledge all those who have inspired me on the long and bumpy journey to give birth to this ethnography. This work is an amalgamation of my academic achievement, including relentless challenges and an unexhausted craving for knowledge that has yielded tears and laughter in each associated time, space, and person I have met along the way. My heartfelt gratitude is offered to all of them. Among them, first of all, I would like to honor my late teacher and advisor, Karen McCarthy Brown, who inspired me to begin this project by emboldening me to challenge stereotypes lodged unconsciously in my life while opening to me to a multidisciplinary approach. Professor Brown passed shortly after my defense on March 4, 2015. I would also like to honor the late Professor Otto Maduro who had become my new advisor after Professor Brown had to step aside but who then passed at the beginning of May, 2013. My thanks collectively and individually go to my committee members who offered thoughtful evaluation and warm encouragement in the process until the completion of this dissertation: Professor Laurel Kearns in sociology and religion and environmental studies, Professor Emeritus Philip Peek in anthropology, Professor Young-chan Ro as the chair of the Religious Studies department at George Mason University, and Professor Hyo-Dong Lee in theological philosophy. Special thanks go to Professor Emeritus Herbert B. Huffmon, my initial academic advisor at Drew University, who has been a champion of unmeasurable encouragement in supporting my project from the beginning to its completion. My thanks also go to Drew University, particularly to the graduate division of religion and its chair, Professor Stephen Moore. Finally, my deepest thanks go to my late mother who passed in January 2013 before the completion of my dissertation. My special acknowledgment also goes to my daughter, Yun-Hwa, who gave up her chances for play, often patiently sitting with drowsy eyes in my night classes and winning the nickname of "little theologian."

1

Introduction

Korean Shamanism with and beyond the Migration

1. Introduction to Korean Shamanism

Shamanism

THE NOMENCLATURE OF SHAMAN was first recognized by the Russian Orthodox priest Avvakum. His note, produced during the period of his exile to Siberia from 1653 to 1664, included the term *shaman* in a description of the Tungus diviner's ritual performed for a Russian officer (DuBois 2009, 19–20).[1] Similar inscriptions could have already been produced elsewhere prior to the note of the exiled Russian Orthodox priest, but it was only after the term shaman kindled and solicited academic interest that various aspects of shamanism in globally distinct traditions were brought to attention, producing innumerable studies to this day (DuBois 2009, 12–18).

These studies have demonstrated that shamanism is culturally shaped and ethnically located by introducing a variety of distinct ritual forms, assorted materials, and ritual contents itemized particularly in each shamanic tradition. The Chukchee shaman in the northeast terrain of Siberia, for example, perceives the world through the animistic belief

---

1. His note designated shaman as a male diviner who conducted a divinatory ritual in a state of spirit possession with a living ram.

system that "all that exists lives" (Halifax 1982, 9). In the Ob Ugarian shamanic tradition located along the northwest edge of Mongolia, spirits of the deceased are identified as disembodied shadows (Michael 1963, 9). The Putumayo Indian shamans on the border between northern Peru and Colombia can travel unrestrictedly into and back through the space of death, i.e., the world of spirits (Taussig 1987, 449). Furthermore, in the tradition of Korean shamanism, spiritual apparitions are identified with the presence of dead ancestors or, as natural spirits, are considered to be a superhuman agency with superpower and therefore are served by as many rituals of loyalty and filial piety as those found in cultural observations of hierarchy.

Mircea Eliade highlighted "the archaic technique of ecstasy" (Eliade 1964, 19) as an essential definition of shamanism after his encounter with an odd religious phenomenon of spiritual flight accompanied by the state of possession trance in a shamanic performance (Eliade 1964, 5). Yet, as also noted by Eliade, there are certain features commonly shared as universal traits among distinct shamanic traditions.

Over a century ago, Edward B. Tylor determined the religion of the present day was the survival of an animistic belief that he considered "the origin of the belief in spiritual beings" (Tylor 1958, 446), whereas Eliade determined shamanism was "the archaic repetition of hierophany" (Eliade 1964, 19). Shamanism was regarded as a degenerative form of religion by both Eliade and Tylor (G. Harvey 2003, 19). This deterioration theory as a typological discussion of shamanism is buttressed by the discourse of the hunter society regarded as the origin of human culture, from which modern scientific society has evolved. Fading away from the civilized world, shamanism is recognized as a folk practice, as it continues being replaced by forms of institutionalized religion, modern science, and advanced technology, according to this discussion. It sounds seemingly rational to determine that shamanism is disappearing as the general society advances, particularly when comparing the conventional forms to the modified or newly added ritual segments in current shamanic practice in progressive cultural contexts.

The discussion of the origin of shamanism is largely speculative, despite prolific research for many decades on its geographically distinctive history (S. N. Kim 1998, 40). Whether the shamanic tradition primarily derived from the northern hunter culture, the agrarian society of South Asia, or both, its root is still in dispute. Moreover, certain topics such as spirit flight or spirit dialogue in the state of possession and trance in the shamanic practice have occasioned many discussions in the field of social science, yet still remain too enigmatic to understand. Simply, these phenomena have been interpreted only with each culturally specific meaning but are not scientifically clarified yet. In this regard, the fundamental inquiry into the essence of shamanism noted by Eliade, "the archaic technique of ecstasy," still remains puzzling, while inviting curiosity as to how it happens and what it is truly about.

The prototypical shamanic calling is generally received when something "happens" to the shamanic candidate, when that person is disturbed by various life crises, including physical, mental, relational, and/or economic anomalies, which are believed to be unilaterally caused by the condition of spirit possession. Interestingly, this stereotypical, passive form of shamanic calling has been extended by the rise of neo-shamanic movements, from being "called by spirits" to a fabrication of an "experience of spirits" broadly open to anyone interested in shamanism. Some training institutes of shamanism (Michael Harner at the Foundation for Shamanic Studies) attempt to artificially create the experience of spirits, not as a way to be passively, selectively called and possessed but as a way to experience actively, voluntarily calling for spirits. By open access through these training institutes, people in general can be involved in the esoteric experience in spirits of the shamanic world, without going through the traditional route of pain and gain that is the customary procedure to become a professional shamanic practitioner. One of the representative institutes is Michael Harner's (Harner 1968; 1972; 1973).[2] The front page of Michael Harner's Foundation for Shamanic Studies makes a reference to accessing "another reality" in the experience of spirits by intrigued modern seekers exploring a mystic, intangible reality beyond this palpable world.

The world of shamanism seems now to be undergoing a paradigm shift through moving along the spiritual currents of this age, by being cross-culturally reconfigured, professionally reconstructed, and conceptually altered to the seekers' passage of "experience." But traditional forms of shamanism still actively survive, often as an alternative to institutional religions at local and global levels of the ethnic "dialectic of hierophany" (Eliade 1964, 12). If culturally determined, shamanism will hardly be disappearing soon but will be modified to continue enlivening care and cure

---

2. Michael Harner, an anthropologist, has engaged in extensive fieldwork with native Indian shamans.

in a this-worldly reality, which provides a *raison d'être* for the continuance of fieldwork in shamanism.

Korean Shamanism: The Cultural Role

The impulse of Western cultural intervention associated with the Christian worldview cannot be minimized, when considering that it has largely contributed to misrepresenting and denigrating the legitimate value of folk belief systems in the non-Western hemisphere. Counteracting the institutional mainstream religions in this era through the effort to recapture a new awareness of folk belief systems' value, the postmodern curiosity in spirituality includes various subterranean topics on roles and ritual phenomena in the shamanic practice, such as healer, medicine man, magician, possession, trance, etc. (Noel 1997, 21).

Shamanism is a culturally entrenched, spiritually animated, and ritually negotiated belief system, which is acknowledged as a long-standing belief system in Korea. One of the essential features underlying this folk belief system is the binary contrast between unfortunate life experiences and the call for good fortune, identified as *gibok* ("remedies") in Korean. Remedies or comfort to fix unwanted life situations can be obtained by ritual compliance, along with the outward behavior of filial piety and loyalty toward the spirits, just as a breach of this compliant manner can bring about resentful actions by the spirits that are dissatisfied.

Shamanic tradition in Korea retains some interesting and profound cultural influences from the neo-Confucian world,[3] particularly visible in the form of shamanic deities or spirits bearing a resemblance to prototypical figures and personae of the power structure in the early Joseon dynasty. Alongside ritual props and attire, the illustrated characters in the shamanic ritual are recognized as authoritative personnel in military uniforms who carry weaponry of the privileged upper-class personae in the Joseon dynasty. The active role of deceased family members summoned forth in ritual is also shared by a combination of Confucian ancestral worship and the shamanic ritual in seeking remedies or good fortune.

In the course of ritually tranquilizing or appeasing discontented spirits in order to fix undesirable life conditions or acquire fortune, bargaining for a requisite remedy develops (Yu and Phillips 1983, 146; C. Kim

---

3. The neo-Confucian or Joseon regime prevailed in Korean history from 1392 CE to 1910 CE.

2003, 38). Accompanying this ritual enactment is a multifaceted form of entertainment, including a monetary offering, a rich food table, music, instruments, chanting, dance, persuasive pleading, constant kowtow-ing, etc. The shaman plays an imperative role in ritual as the one calling for spirits, falling into the state of possession and trance, and mediating between deities or spirits and the living kin. Moreover, through behavior-ally, emotionally, and verbally impersonating a particular character or spirit in ritual, only the shaman can aid in acquiring good fortune or an effective remedy for the client. The success associated with ritual repeti-tions is the ultimate sanction of this act.

The shamanic ritual, named *gut* in Korean, is very much like a play that encases a collection of performances such as esthetic dance, unflag-ging chanting, colorful ritual costumes, satirical humor, mocking narra-tives, drenching tears, and enthralled joys (C. Choi 1989, 235–49; Y. Yoon 1996, 188–91).[4] The shaman's body becomes a medium for facilitating a dialogue between the dead and the living in the state of spirit possession and trance, which is a climactic feature in each shamanic enactment (C. Kim 2003, 38; T. Kim and Chang 1998, 20; Yu and Phillips 1983, 146; Pai 2000, 11). Not only as a supernatural agent but also as a negotiator, the shaman detects the broken bonds between the living and the spirits. In so doing, the shaman is able to assist with healing or a remedy from misfortune in the lives of living kin.

The purpose of Korean shamanic ritual is similar to that of the prac-tice in other folk religious traditions. Each ritual is predetermined by the particular demand of each client, which enables the shaman to enact and thus achieve a particular remedy. Shamanic rituals vary in distinctive forms and goals, such as the *gut* for initiation of shamanic novices, the *gut* for healing of illnesses, the *gut* for good fortune, the *gut* for sending off the dead or the spirit of the dead to the other world, and so on. With regard to the role of shamans, rituals can be categorized briefly as either for shamans or for common people (Haeoe Gongbo-Gwan 1997, 128).[5] There are two types of initiation rituals: one called *naerimgut, immuje,* or

4. The ritual performance of *gut* has often been circumscribed in Korea. A course of intense political hostility, particularly under both the neo-Confucian regime and the military dictatorship of Chung-hee Park in the 1980s, officially prevented its prac-tice in public. Moreover, the arrival of Protestantism in Korea began promoting hostil-ity towards shamans and their practices since the 1800s.

5. Scholarly approaches differ in grouping shamanic rituals in reference to either a deity or spirit, a shaman or people, or the living or the dead.

shingut, which is quintessential for the charismatic shamanic novice who undergoes a shamanic illness, *shinbyeong*;[6] and one called *cheokshinje*, which aims at "greeting deities" and is performed for the neophyte inheriting her or his shamanic profession from her or his family members rather than being individually called in spirit possession (Haeoe Gongbo-Gwan 1997, 128).[7]

The types of shamanic ritual are also differentiated with regard to life or death, whereas the ritual setting is differentiated by its purpose, particularly as to whether it is familial or communal.[8] Two distinct forms of rituals are carried out on behalf of the dead. One is the memorial ritual performed right after death, called *ogwigut* or *neokgut*, and the other is the ritual for a deceased adult who is unmarried, called *jinogwigut* or *honnyeong-gut* (T. Kim and Chang 1998, 20). An unusual feature presented in *jinogwigut* or *honnyeong-gut* is the wedding ceremony performed for the deceased, unmarried adult. In order to match the deceased person with a bride or a groom, it is often the case that another deceased person of the opposite sex is searched for, so as to take part in the wedding ritual (Huhm 1980, 12; Kister 1997, 50–51).[9] In observing the unique content of *jinogwigut*, it is apparent that the cultural significance of the rite of passage is accentuated in the form of the ritual. Simply put, the unaccomplished human progress—culturally expected—is still morally ascribed to the deceased even after death. The intended beneficiaries of the completion of the rite of passage for an unmarried adult are the surviving kin. The underlying belief here is to fulfill the passage of the deceased person and to create a positive path to good fortune for the living kin.

Three sequential segments constitute the ritual procedure of Korean shamanism, namely "invoking, communicating with and entertaining, and sending off the deities and spirits" (Haeoe Gongbo-Gwan 1997, 127; T. Kim and Chang 1998, 20). These three ritual steps also contain

6. A form of involuntary shamanic illness occurring to chosen individuals in the state of spirit possession. In becoming shamanic candidates, they undergo the initiation ritual to serve the deities or spirits.

7. Two types of shamans are represented in Korean shamanism: the charismatic shaman, involved in spirit possession, is rooted geographically in the northern regions; whereas the hereditary shaman, within a family heritage, dominated the southern areas of Korea.

8. Ritual forms and sizes in Korean shamanism are distinctively linked to either individual or communal requisites.

9. A spirit bride or groom is often searched out for the wedding by the shaman or family members.

elaborate, distinctive enactments that are individually called *gori*, an episodic segment. Commonly comprised of a collection of theatrical acts, each *gori* plays a specific role for each deity served in the tradition of shamanism, with regional variations of the rituals (J. Kim 1996, 196; Huhm 1980, 13).[10] Out of these three steps, the second portion, communicating and entertaining, is the most dynamic and pivotal part of the ritual as a dialogic stage, involving the shaman and the deities or ancestral spirits.

Korean Shamanism in the Immigrant Community of the U.S.

The practice of Korean immigrant shamanism has been primarily underground in the history of Korean immigration, because the Korean immigrant community is dominated by the robust success of Evangelical Protestantism in the U.S.[11] Compared to the abundance of ethnic scholarship and educational activity made available to the immigrant public, there has been very little research dealing with Korean immigrant shamanism in the U.S.[12] A major difficulty is even being able to trace the presence of Korean immigrant shamans in the East Coast and to gather appropriate statistical data, for which the primary sources are the various versions of the commercial business directories that are circulated among the Korean immigrant community. Precise quantitative data or the history of Korean immigrant shamans is not a feasible research goal, partly due to the heavily protestantized environment of the Korean immigrant community in the U.S. Another difficulty is the absence, as noted, of serious study of Korean immigrant shamanism. Many modest academic endeavors have been produced in regard to indigenous forms of Korean shamanism and are indeed helpful in demonstrating an awareness of immigrant shamanic practice. However, these studies do not offer any

10. As the formal shamanic ritual involves twelve *gori* in traditional Korean shamanism, each *gori* also varies the components and ritual references in connection with the representation of each distinctive spirit.

11. The first group of the Korean diaspora, numbering 203, were loaded in a ship heading for the Hawaii sugar plantation as laborers in 1903.

12. The subject of Korean shamanism has been mentioned in various studies in connection with specific issues of ethnic identity, the status of women, and its ethos in Korean culture; but it has not been the focus of any published academic research in terms of its function and ritual character in the Korean immigrant community of the U.S.

significant comparative study, nor do they contribute much to the understanding of the fundamental interplay of traditional shamanic practice with a new and very different cultural context.

For example, in New York and New Jersey, having the second largest population of Korean immigrants in the U.S., of the 50 fortune-telling businesses and about 790 immigrant Protestant Korean churches listed in the 2011 commercial directories,[13] only 12 are identified as traditional shamans (Y. Kwon 2011).[14] Most Korean shamans are located in the metropolitan areas,[15] and the majority of the fortune-telling businesses in the directories are actually *Yi-Jing* or *I-Ching* practitioners.[16] Though the actual number of shamans is doubtlessly higher than the twelve listed in the directories, given that unlisted and underground Korean shamanic practitioners are active in Korean immigrant communities, the number of shamans is a relatively small group compared to the demographics of the immigrant Korean community within the multiple immigrant Protestant Korean churches in the metropolitan area.[17] Tolerance of shamanic practice seems to be more a feature of Korea proper than of the Korean

13. The most populous center of the Korean diasporic communities in the U.S. is the so-called K-town in Los Angeles, with an official Korean immigrant population of 451,892, as of the 2010 Korean American census. In New York and New Jersey, which rank next after California, the Korean immigrant community had grown to about 234,673, according to the 2010 U.S. census, an increase from the 150,000 cited in the 1990 U.S. census (Budiman 2021). The research of N. Kibria also offers a good overview of statistical data about the Asian American population of the past (Kibria 2002, 23).

14. Among the fifty listed members in the category of destiny and Oriental fortune-telling of the Korean business directory, the majority are fortune-tellers, while geomancers and psychics are also included (see Y. Kwon 2011).

15. The list also shows two geomancers and two Western psychic readers. Out of the twelve shamans, seven are *bosal* and five *baksu* (see the Jung-Ang Ilbo Yellow Book 2010 for the source list). *Bosal* refers to Bodhisattva addressed as female Buddhist shamans, while *baksu* means the male shaman. For more information on shamanic terminology, see C. Kim 2003, 23; S. N. Kim 1998, 43; Jung Lee 1981.

16. *Yi-Jing* or *I-Ching*, the Chinese philosophy based on the Book of Change, provides fortune-telling through each individual's four birth pillars: the year, month, date, and time of birth. See Jung Y. Lee 1994, 17–40.

17. For convenience, *underground shamanic practitioners* designates either initiated shamans who professionally practice shamanism or shamanic novices who are serving a shamanic apprenticeship, the practice of which is rarely visible in public. All shamans are entitled to a shamanic kinship such as goddaughter, *shinddal*, or godson, *shinadeul*, to the shamanic teacher as a godparent, the title of which is gifted to the shaman in the Korean tradition of shamanism.

immigrant community of the U.S.[18] More notable is that, according to demographics, the professional shamans in the New York and New Jersey areas (those with the second largest Korean immigrant community) occur at the ratio of one for every group of 4,693 Korean immigrants. In South Korea, the ratio is about 500,000 shamans in the current population of 50,219,669, meaning roughly one shaman for every one hundred persons (*Chosun Ilbo* 2022; Song 2020).[19] So, there is an impressive contrast in the ratios between the Korean homeland and the heavily Christianized Korean immigrant population in the U.S., suggesting that the shamanic practice is rather minor and probably contextually suppressed by the protestantized Korean immigrant community of the U.S.

The testimony of a male shaman who is one of my shaman informants—identified as M. Doryeong—is striking. He describes himself as being desolate and secluded in his practice within the immigrant context, a minority within a minority:

> Neither shamanic association nor my own Korean community exists to me. I am a male shaman. In the atmosphere where even the shaman is unwelcomed, I am a male shaman.[20]

His brief testimony constituted a lament, offering a glimpse of the conflict that he encounters in the culturally modified and religiously sanctioned ambiance of the protestantized Korean immigrant community. However, his testimony seems to retain a sense of uncertainty as to how his largely unsought services might attract clients in the context of the male-dominant, protestantized Korean immigrant community.

In traditional Korean society, the shaman often functioned as communal mediator. Yet, this seems to be to no avail in an immigrant context in which the Protestant Church dominates Korean immigrant community as well as provides resourceful aid for the survival of immigrants (Ministry of Culture 1996, 133; Min 1996, 41–42). Moreover, the Korean

18. Yet, allegations of shamanic fraud and even virtual blackmail have often come to public notice and have led to concerns by the Korean public and ordinary Korean shamanic clients about shamanistic extortion. Shamanic frauds are often connected with sexual abuse, financial extortion, blackmail, or violence (J. A. Lee 2012).

19. The current trend of the shamanic practitioner in Korea is shifting to fortune-telling, thereby diminishing occasions for rich rituals (see the Korean Statistical Information Service [KOSIS]; *Chosun Ilbo* 2022; Song 2020).

20. My informant practices shamanism on the edge of an immigrant Korean community in the East Coast. He resides in a small apartment room that contains his own shamanic altar.

immigrant church assists in promoting solidarity through providing cultural practices alongside religious gatherings, while preserving spaces and supporting relationships. In so doing, the Korean immigrant church also supports Korean immigrants by reinforcing their ethnic self-identity through a sense of belonging that is religiously aware. As the new context demands different needs and values that are satisfied primarily through the Protestant church community, the role of the shaman in the absence of its own organized, shared community is considerably disadvantaged. Thus, the role of shaman should be understood differently in this context. Nonetheless, the religious shift in the makeup of the immigrant community does not seem to completely do away with the cultural nostalgia of Korean immigrants in the U.S. An interesting parallel is found in the preservation of the shamanic tradition during the religious segregation of the Joseon dynasty; a culturally constituted superhuman agency continues to gain the attention of the Korean immigrant cultural mind, particularly in cases of urgency for remedies and/or good fortune, along with a special sense of otherness in the immigrant context. Lee Bosal, a female shaman who is another important informant of mine, offers a brief sketch of her clients: "The majority of my clients go to the Protestant church. They are careful to avoid the attention of others in case of visits or calls to me."[21] Her remarks allow a glimpse into the current situation of Korean immigrant shamanism while conveying how the condition of secrecy preserves a route for cultural agency without gaining the attention of the protestantized Korean immigrant community of the U.S.

Korean Immigrant Shamanism:
Shamanic Rituals in the Immigrant Context

The ritual environment is important for the practice of Korean shamanism, particularly in the immigrant context. Since the shamanic ritual performance includes the use of instruments and chanting such as shaking charms, banging a drum, and beating gongs, even the lesser noises that come with a simple practice may easily upset neighbors in residential areas and often do result in warnings by police summoned to stop noises. Particularly in the case of M. Doryeong, whose altar room is a tiny space in a closely spaced apartment complex, his brief rituals or divinations that

21. This female shaman, *mudang*, owns both Buddhist and shamanic altar rooms separately in a mansion in the forest near a big mountain on the East Coast of the U.S.

come with shaking charms and chanting often raise complaints from his next-door neighbors.[22] Moreover, it is often rather difficult for the urban shaman, particularly in the case of M. Doryeong, to find an appropriate location for the formal outdoor rituals in nearby mountains or rivers. For a ritual that is best performed in a comfortable and uninterrupted environment, shamans needs access to spaces that allow them to freely play instruments, chant and dance, set up the food table, and fall into a trance, while avoiding public attention. Meanwhile, considering the shamanic ritual exclusively in relation to the natural environment, different forms of energy experienced from the mountains and rivers in the U.S. make the immigrant shamans feel ill at ease about finding and performing outdoor rituals. In brief, it is difficult for the immigrant shaman to locate a suitable ritual space with mountains, rivers, trees, and other components in the U.S. that can provide the favorite form of spiritual energy available in the natural environment in Korea.

Lee Bosal reflected on the years that she had spent, while practicing within her urban environment, personally exploring the mountains and rivers of the East Coast region in the U.S. and looking for a suitable place to perform rituals. In her judgment, the security of her outdoor ritual location was essential for successful ritual performance, a place neither known nor easily accessible for the general public or even for other shamans. The secured location should be conserved and protected from defilement of the spiritual power, according to Lee Bosal. Each shaman looks for a place with spiritual power or energy, *qi* in Chinese, a difficult task when dealing with the dissimilar natural environment in the U.S. M. Doryeong continues to feel somewhat pessimistic about the natural features of the mountains and rivers and insists that the spiritual energy from the U.S. natural environment itself is much weaker than in Korea. Meanwhile, Lee Bosal believes that the natural world in the U.S. still has strong *qi* in some well-preserved areas that have not been "domesticated" or taken by housing projects or industrial developments. Yet, I wondered if the form of *qi* could be differently experienced by each shaman even in the same location, or if the form of each shaman's *qi* differentiates her or his experience of the natural environment in different locations.

22. My informant, M. Doryeong, told me that he attempted to continue lowering the noise levels of his voice and instrumental performance during divinations or brief rituals, following his experience of a noise warning from the police in 2006. On that occasion, a next-door neighbor of M. Doryeong made a complaint to the police when he was disturbed by the constant noise of the chanting and gonging.

M. Doryeong picked for his outdoor ritual a popular mountain close to a crowded city, whereas Lee Bosal acquired for her own practices the edge of an old forest with abundant space and wild surroundings in the metropolitan area. It still seems unclear how each shaman measures the *qi*-factor and what makes shamans determine that they have a suitable location, especially given the difficulty and the necessity of finding such a place. Nonetheless, what is clear is that any type of disruption of the ritual content or process would result in a negative *qi*-factor for either indoor or outdoor ritual performances.

Both shamans had had unpleasant encounters with state troopers or local police who interfered with their ritual performances and issued warnings to them while they were carrying out rituals in isolated river or mountain areas. In these cases, my informants said that they just moved on to another spot. Meanwhile, the shamanic ritual scene might easily lead those who are unfamiliar with such matters to feel that something strange and improper is going on at the encounter with the noise of gonging, drumming, chanting, dancing, or observing the shaman's condition of possession trance. Probably such a ritual scene would startle or unnerve Westerners who are unacquainted with this type of cultural practice. It would sufficiently provoke biases, even at best being viewed as uncivilized by those who have no experience or knowledge of shamanic rituals. M. Doryeong expresses his serious unease in regard to such a ritual environment by stating:

> The American mountains and rivers treat me like an alien though I am a citizen of the U.S. Yet, the mountains and rivers in Korea always seemed to welcome my presence. Whether dancing, chanting, or gonging, I was at ease in the Korean mountains and rivers.

Korean immigrant shamans may share a similar condition, as most of them cannot afford to own a private space for a shamanic shrine, a space that can provide unlimited access and an appropriate room and time to perform rituals, without environmental interference or external restrictions. The situation of Lee Bosal seems different from that of most other shamans, in that she may be now one of the most prosperous immigrant shamans on the East Coast. Her ownership of a large property with a sizeable personal residence provides a suitable environment and protects her shamanic practice from the potential interruptions with which other shamans routinely have to deal. Apart from her private residence and shrine in the forest, she also makes use of a separate consultation office in a big city. So, Lee Bosal no longer has to deal with obstacles to her ritual practices, except for the potential of neighborhoods straying into her forest preserve.

One concern about the environmental issue is whether the shaman, as similarly reflected by M. Doryeong, can still work effectively for clients to achieve the desired level of remedy or good fortune while working under potentially disadvantaged conditions. That is, it is puzzling if the environmental distractions and resultant distress of the shaman do not pollute or affect to some extent the ritual performance, thereby presumably upsetting the spirits and working against the success of the ritual. As an example of this potential, Kang monk shaman, my third informant, who became the husband of Lee Bosal, insists that the presence of Christians alarms the spirits in general in the shamanic ritual in Korea, and thus Christians are requested to immediately leave the ritual scene, particularly in the case that the shaman dances on a double-edged blade.[23] The risk of ritual pollution, *bujeong tanda*, is in itself upsetting to the spirits, which endangers the objective and goal of the ritual. Thus, the threat of pollution must immediately be removed from the ritual scene (Jung Y. Lee 1981, 41). Given that the proper ritual environment is critical for successful ritual achievement and that the presence of unwanted elements can pollute the ritual, as Kang monk shaman indicated, the whole shamanic ritual enterprise in the immigrant context is somewhat precarious. Problems can easily come through a Protestant presence, a neighbor's complaints, noise violations, etc., such that the spirits may be discomforted, putting the success of the ritual in doubt. In this regard, it is also puzzling as to whether those environmental issues encountered in the practice of immigrant shamans might ultimately lead to changes of significance and/or ritual forms in the shamans' negotiation with the new context. More questions can be asked in this regard, and it will be interesting to see what developments will arise to address the issue of

---

23. Dancing on a sharp blade is referred to as *jakdu tanda* in Korean. *Jakdu* implies a sharp double-edged knife, while *tanda* means "riding." Only some shamans, when they are prepared, risk dancing on the sharp blade in the full state of spirit possession in the shamanic ritual. Unless there is supernatural assurance of protection, the shaman can be badly cut and bleed extensively, according to Lee Bosal. Thus, the skill involved in dancing on the sharp blade demonstrates not only supernatural assistance but also the competence of the shaman as a professional practitioner (Jung Y. Lee 1981, 149; Covell 1986, 154–58).

environmental negotiation, potentially an explosive issue in Korean immigrant shamanism in general and in the U.S. in particular.

According to my shaman informants, about one hundred dollars is charged per hour for "standard" divination, while ritual size and purpose may lead to higher charges for other kinds of shamanic rituals, called *gut* in Korean. Since the main source of income for shamans is divination and the shamanic ritual,[24] more precise divination and effective rituals bring reputation and more clients. Shamanic skill, called *jaeju* in Korean, is primarily gifted from the *momju* spirit,[25] the spirit possessing the shaman. M. Doryeong advertises his gift for divining the cause of mishaps, whereas Lee Bosal convincingly refers to her gift for accurate forecasts of the future, her gift of clairvoyance. Lee Bosal once spoke to the shrine attendees about her experiences of forewarning visions that she had in advance of those incidents such as the Asian tsunami that calamitously swept the South Asian countries in 2004, and the collapse of twin towers in Manhattan in 2001.[26] Her widely accepted ability to predict the future often motivates clients to request ritual remedies in advance. So her shrine is mostly crowded with upper-middle-class and educated clientele who want to obtain an upscale life. The range of her clients is in major contrast to that of M. Doryeong whose main talent is for diagnosing unfortunate life situations. So, the clientele of M. Doryeong are mostly the poverty- and adversity-stricken who strive for survival in the immigrant context. Another reason that Lee Bosal has more upscale clients is the presentation of her shrine. The comfortable and well-furnished environment of Lee Bosal's practice impresses the clients and also attracts many upper-middle-class clients who are searching for a culturally suitable shaman. Whereas M. Doryeong is unable to provide a comparable setting for his clients, Lee Bosal may acquire more assets from those clients who are impressed by the environmental and religious presentation of her shrine. However, the socioeconomic status of the shamans is not a

24. The price range for a general *gut* ritual in the East Coast is from about three thousand to ten thousand dollars. The cost is sometimes over ten thousand dollars, particularly in the case of an initiation ritual, according to Lee Bosal and Kang monk shaman.

25. *Momju* literally refers to a "master of the body," as expressed in Korean. It denotes the spirit that possesses the shaman at the beginning of the shamanic call, the spirit that the shaman serves throughout the life of shamanic performance.

26. According to Lee Bosal, she had a vision prior to the tsunami in 2004, and she smelled human bodies burning at the restaurant on the top floor of the World Trade Center a week before the collapse of the twin towers.

subjective issue but is the extent to which the shamans' deities control good fortunes, according to my informants.

The food table is an indispensable part of the altar in the tradition of Korean shamanism.[27] The food table represents an important element of traditional Korean culture. It is a very visible expression of hospitality, welcoming guests with an affirmation of social relationships and creating intimacy among family members and relatives. A table that displays a variety of good food and drink conveys the host's recognition of the guests as important, whether as individuals or as a group. In shamanic ritual, the food table, similarly welcoming the spirits and deities, is in a manner consistent with traditional Korean culture. Constituting a ritual threshold, the food table plays a role to bridge between the living kin, the deities, and the ancestral spirits; between the real and unreal world; and between death and life. The size of ritual is proportional to the resources of the client, and the degree of ritual that is offered to the deities or spirits is also measured by the size of the food table. The cooking and setting up of foods on the table follow a strict order in the shamanic tradition that is solely under control of the shaman. Detailed instructions accompany each ritual associated with each distinct purpose, specifying the selection of foods to either include or avoid, recipes involving specific seasonings, and arrangements to set items in the correct direction and specific place on the table. In this regard, the general belief is that the more generous and abundant the food table, the more satisfactory are the ritual outcomes granted from the pleased deities or spirits.

Considering that the preparatory cooking and the setting up of the ritual food table are never simple, the table setting is perhaps more difficult for male shamans to handle, as they mostly grow up in a traditional society where domestic chores are solely carried out by women. Moreover, the newer and younger shamans attempt to dismiss the strict traditional order of the food table, according to Lee Bosal. The shaman M. Doryeong acknowledges that he used to get help from his *shinttal*[28]

27. The food table is subsequently set up at the altar or combined with the setting of the altar. The food table contains rice, steamed rice, traditional rice wine, herbs, fish, fried meats, fruits, snacks, etc. The food components and the order of their setting on the food table are differentiated for each ritual purpose.

28. *Shinttal* refers to the spiritual daughter of the spiritual parent such as a *shineomeoni*, implying the spiritual mother, or a *shinabeoji*, meaning the spiritual father. The spiritual parent provides the initiation ritual and training for her or his spiritual daughter or son within the shamanic apprenticeship. The *shinttal* of M. Doryeong, in her late fifties, lives in a suburban area close to New York City.

(Y. Harvey 1979, 285–96; Kendall 1985, 199–21) to cook and set the food table, while often taking advantage of her house that offered sufficient room for ritual preparation.

Most of the food items are purchased at local Korean grocery markets near Korean immigrant communities. Some ritual materials are imported directly from Korea by special order, because they are ethnically and culturally specific products that are rarely found in Korean or other markets in the U.S. In the case of the food table, the subject of ritual items in the practice of shamanism is probably another issue that comes into play in the development of Korean immigrant shamanism in a culturally unconventional context.

In front of the food table, constant kowtows[29] are accompanied by expressions of obedience and reverence to deities and ancestral spirits, the model for which is similarly seen in the traditional culture of Korea in the subordination of the younger to the senior or of those of lower social standing to the superior. The shaman also calls for subsequent monetary offerings from time to time during the ritual in order to express gratitude and to satisfy the deities in accomplishing the ritual objective. Offering money to the altar implies not only an indulgent expression of respect and gratitude but also an opportunity to bargain for good fortune by pleasing deities and the ancestral spirits.

Korean Immigrant Shamanism: Gender Ambivalence

The gender identity of the shaman generally corresponds with that of the *momju* or the governing spirit. The gender of the shaman is no longer definitively determined as either female or male because of the impact of frequent cross-gendered possession of *momju*, such as a female shaman possessed by a male *momju* and vice versa. The gender states of the shaman can be portrayed thus as either "a third gender" or "on the border between sexes/genders" (Blain 2001, 129–35; Czaplicka 1914, 253).[30] In

29. Kowtow refers to an act of deep respect or submission shown by bowing on one's knees while touching the forehead almost to the ground.

30. Blain accounts for the references to the gender-crossing status of the shaman, beyond the determination of either female or male, by describing it as "third gender." In doing so, Blain supports that label by referring to the "third class" category cited by Maria Czaplicka. According to Blain, Czaplicka's reference is to "the third class as for those who are privileged to engage in deviance departed from the ordinary life" (Blain 2001, 129.)

her work *Nine Worlds of Seid-Magic*, Blain describes the indefinite gender states of the Siberian shaman, similar to that of the Korean shaman, as she comments:

> By clothing, ritual observance, or taboos, Siberian shamans might be incorporating characteristics of both males and females, holding an in-between location. (Blain 2001, 129)

The cross-gender state evident in the interplay between femininity and masculinity of the shaman and the *momju* is even more complex than the issue of homosexuality. It might be a challenge for a Korean shaman to survive in a male-dominant culture in which heteronormativity in relationship is morally demanded. This gender deviancy of Korean shamans can be considered culturally shameful and morally improper, even named demonic in the Korean immigrant community.[31]

The heteronormative moral demand of the cultural tradition—that the roles of women and of those of lower social standing are both identified with the *nae* metaphor[32] that characteristically symbolizes states of subordination, inferiority, shame, guilt, and even evil in the male-dominant Korean immigrant community—leaves the gender ambivalence of the shaman as something enigmatic, to be somehow managed in her or his encounters with the *momju* persona (Y.-C. Kim 1982, 134).

The form of the shaman's deviant gender, regardless, might be understood as the nature of "interconvertibility." For example, quickly converting from a feminine to a masculine persona back and forth, Lee Bosal often impersonates a dominant male persona, deviant from her meek personality and animated by the persona of her male *momju*. Meanwhile, M. Doryeong behaves like a docile female even beyond the ritual setting, as that seems also derived from the persona of his female *momju*. Kang monk shaman's *momju* is also female, but his Buddhist practice and unique gift intercede in his shamanic transformation, downplaying the feminine nature in the deviant gender role, according to him. The deviant gender role employed by the shaman seems odd in terms of traditional Korean culture. The shaman's gender status can also be viewed historically as a vestige of the camouflage used by the shaman for survival, as Korean shamans experienced political vicissitudes and stigmatizations

31. Graham Harvey refers to the category of indigeneity as he points out the vestige of the colonial construction toward non-Westerners and indigenous cultures (Harvey 2003, 3–8).

32. *Nae* refers to "inside," in the Chinese letter with a Korean pronunciation.

in Korean history, similar to that noted by Franz Fanon (Loomba 1998, 139). That is, the ego of the possessing deity or spirit alters the demeanor of the shaman who then deviates from her or his "normal" gender pattern. This deviation may also take on socioculturally specific forms, such as similarly seen in the Zarian ritual of the Hofriyati women of the northern Sudan (Boddy 1989). The experience of gender interconvertibility on the part of the shaman is a ritual phenomenon of spirit possession that not only engages the particularities of the cultural location to which the spirit belongs to but also deviates from the ordinary context of her or his status quo. As Boddy states, the third-gender person goes through "the anti-structure to grasp not only her own particular context, but the social context of her context" (Boddy 1989, 19).

The unique feature of cross-gender state can be observed in various ways in traditional Korean shamanic rituals. Associated with the masculinized pantheon, the majority of the ritual outfits used by the shaman originate in the masculine fashion favored in the past tradition, particularly in the early Joseon society (K. O. Kim 1992, 48–53). In turn, the male shaman often wears traditional female costumes in order to serve female deities or spirits during the ritual, while personifying the spirits by animating feminine vocalization and behavior in the state of spirit possession.

Some scholarly discussion emphasizes the interesting subject of gender interchange in respect to the cross-dressing tradition in Korean shamanism. Charles Allen Clark, one of the early Western writers about Korean culture, refers to this unusual cross-dressing feature found in the Korean shamanic tradition as having "mystic significance," drawing upon his ambiguity in the exploration of Korean cultural grass roots about a half century ago (Clark 1961, 183).[33] Kilsŏng Ch'oe, a Korean male scholar of shamanism, simply regards this cross-dressing aspect as the impact of the preponderant female population in Korean shamanic tradition (Ch'oe 1984, 227–33). Yet, Alan Carter Covell, a Western male scholar of Korean shamanism, refers to the songs of the Chou dynasty of ancient China, providing them as a reasonable resource for grasping the meaning of that cross-dressing in the shamanic tradition. As the songs express it, the cross-dressing implies a heterosexuality between the shaman and the

---

33. He also mentions other scholarly discussions on "exchange of sex" and "exchange of garment" as reflecting the Siberian influence upon the issue of dress code.

deity, with the female shaman "longing or calling for the male gods" for sexual pleasure (Covell 1983, 42). Culturally contextualizing, this poetic expression of shamanic cross-dressing provides a possible explanation of the existential condition of the shaman, mostly identified as female, whose status is traditionally and socially minor and whose life is subjected to the masculine power structure in both society and the shamanic pantheon. Masculine characters who are consecrated as deities or spirits in the shamanic pantheon may be appropriately understood as consistent with the traditional male supremacy in society that still prevails in the contemporary Korean immigrant community. Accordingly, the sexual norm is confined by traditional heteronormativity in which the female shaman with male cross-dressing fits in the stereotypical gender/sexual role within the male hegemony, and vice versa. In this regard, the male garments described in the songs of the Chou dynasty symbolically signify the masculine divinity in what was meant to be understood as "hetero-sexual intercourse" (Covell 1983, 97). Similar features of cross-dressing are widely attested in various traditional practices. Philip M. Peek, an American anthropologist, provides varied examples of cross-gender dressing featured by the diviners' practices, particularly centered on southern African regions. In his remarks, Peek notes that the cross-gender dressing symbolizes an expressive action of the African diviners for "the androgynous state" that may assist them in being aided by the paired spirits and in serving their clients, both males and females, better (Peek 1991, 196). Regardless of the reference to either the stereotypical heterosexuality or androgyny (Covell 1983, 97; Peek 1996, 197), the cross-gender dressing symbolically represents a quintessential character of Korean shamanism, namely, the shamanic union with the deity or spirit. Nonetheless, none of my shaman informants has ever given me a clear response about either sexual or asexual experiences in relation to the cross-gender dressing or possession in their shamanic practice. In this regard, the cross-gender feature in the practice of Korean shamanism still leaves room for further discussion as to whether it reflects sexual intercourse, a sexless state, or something else with other symbolic implications.

Korean Immigrant Shamanism:
Learning in a Protestant Context

The religious experience of Korean immigrants in North America has shifted to correspond to the mainstream tradition that inspires "the power of paternalism . . . and the Protestant discourse" (Jacobson 2000, 176).[34] Fumitaka Matsuoka asserts that the impulse of Christian ethical monotheism has been confirmed in history as properly normative through the marriage of the American power regime with Protestant Christian theology (Matsuoka 1995, 4). In this atmosphere, there is not only a certain sense of hostility but also a basic curiosity about the exotic that accompanies those who observe indigenous ethnic religious practices and spiritualities that persevere in the context of immigration. Implicitly, the power of mainstream Christianity blinds immigrant minds, prompting them to disrespect precious references of their own traditional cultures while becoming receptive to mainstream Western culture, as noted by Robert Young, who comments that "mimicry at once enables power and produces the loss of agency" (Matsuoka 1999, 147). Similarly, the shamanic tradition has been overwhelmed by the power of Western Protestant paternalism while managing to survive as a subculture in the collective consciousness of the Korean immigrant community.

Homi Bhabha may well represent this point by means of his postcolonial discourse advocacy of the colonized for their own "new historicity of a third world metaphor" not appropriated by "any powerful somebody" (Bhabha 1994, 238). Bhabha, in his remarks, seeks to alert the reader to the importance of an ethnic sense of self-awareness, the capacity to reevaluate and preserve one's own cultural legacy, which has been ground down under the political power of colonial normativity. The Korean ethnic community has been led by a neo-Confucian moral ethos that culturally features a strong gender and interrelational hierarchy. Moreover, the Korean immigrant community has been self-segregating in the attempt to learn to be Protestant while sharing the mainstream paternalistic perspective regarding collective ethnic solidarity. The particularity of the Korean cultural legacy, which includes the tradition of

---

34. Matthew Frye Jacobson employs this term of paternalism to portray the ambivalent face of the North American politics toward ethnic immigrants, borrowing President William McKinley's insightful comment about imperial politics toward the Philippines.

shamanism, is minimized in the midst of learning to be Protestant and Western in the immigrant context of the U.S. (Thandeka 2000).[35]

Religion can be defined more by experiences than formal theology, more by the physical than metaphysical, particularly in the context of migration. In this regard, note the radical comment by Jonathan Z. Smith, that "religion is an anthropological, not a theological category" (Smith 1998, 269).[36] Incessant global migration has relocated distinct ethnic cultural legacies into specific neighborhoods elsewhere, which often provokes a confrontation with the others in the neighborhood who represent the coexistent context of immigration. The homogeneity and masculinity harbored in religious tradition generally serves the purpose of the domineering power that carries a "self-possessive and abusive episteme against women and the other," labeling women and the other as the socially counter presence (Young 1999, 158).[37] Such an atmosphere is seemingly dominant, particularly in the Korean immigrant community in the process of assimilating to the mainstream Protestant culture, simply marking the presence of the shaman, mostly female, as barbaric or demonic.

Yet, the variety and abundance of individual and communal immigrant cultural experiences and narratives cannot be lost under the dogmatic, institutional monotheism. Routine experiences and narratives of Korean immigrants that go beyond Evangelical Protestantism are treated as a "margin of mess," in the symbolic remark of Barbara Babcock (Babcock 1978, 28). Yet, the state of the margin of mess also calls for "questions about the orders by which we live" (Babcock 1978, 28). That is to say, the presence of margins itself in society embodies questions for the reason of the very existence of margins. Experiences that "deviate from normativity" can include a richness for better understanding of life within the Korean immigrant community, providing lively footprints in

35. The phrase "learning to be Protestant and Western" is inspired by the work of Thandeka, *Learning to Be White*.

36. Smith asserts that "the singular term of religion is a scholarly construction which is not a native category," conceiving the term of religion "not as the first person term of self-characterization, but as a category imposed from the outside" (Smith 1998, 36, 79).

37. In citing the analysis of Gayatri Spivak, Young asserts that "history is not simply the disinterested production of facts, but is rather a process of epistemic violence" (Young 1999, 158). That is, history is a process in which social others are ceaselessly created. In this light, the religious domain is not an exception, naming as others those who deviate from the mainstream normativity.

the diversity of the Korean immigrant history in the U.S. (Blain 2001, 129). In this regard, "what is socially peripheral can represent something symbolically important and central" (Babcock 1978, 32).

Gaining a sense of belonging in the new contextual community is associated with the demand for evangelical loyalty to Protestantism, so that Korean immigrants early on learn to give up some of their own significant cultural, religious, and folk practices for the sake of survival and assimilation as immigrants in the U.S. Learning to be properly Protestant is achieved by foregoing or concealing interest in their own cultural assets, discarded as a "mess" of peripheral matters. As Korean migration continues, the first-generation Korean diaspora will continue to strive to fit within the Protestant legacy of their predecessors in the immigrant community, so as to redesign themselves to join in with the new immigrant context. The second- and third-generation Koreans in the U.S. make cultural exits from the lives of their parents or grandparents, because they have lost their sympathy for an ethnically cultural community (Lien and Carnes 2004, 43). In doing so, a concern emerges for the future of the Korean immigrant community as to just what should identify Korean diaspora, when the "mess of margins" is occupied by the mainstream attractiveness of learning to be Protestant (Babcock 1973, 28). In this regard, the autonomy of cultural self-awareness might be imperative for the Korean immigrant community, in order for them to be able to retrieve and document the plethora of ordinary experiences and expressions in the context of their transmigration.

2. Methodology and Research Design

The topic of my research is Korean immigrant shamanism in actual practice in the immigrant context, particularly in the East Coast of the U.S. The objective of this study is to examine how the practice of Korean shamanism is contextually negotiated in its own Korean immigrant community that is highly Christianized, as illustrated by changes in cultural references and ritual components in the new geographical and cultural location of the U.S. This is a cross-cultural comparative study within the Korean shamanic tradition itself in regard to the contextual differences that prompt changes in meaning and experience in the face of trans-national relocation. My research builds on an in-depth study of two shamanic shrines and three shamanic practitioners for over seven years from 2004 to 2011. It builds on interviews and careful observations of their routines and ritual practices in the East Coast of the U.S. It can be acknowledged, in this regard, that this study focuses on my fieldwork with only three specifically regional shamans, one female and two male shamans, and thus is unable to represent the whole range of different styles and ritual forms present in the practice of Korean immigrant shamanism, particularly in the West Coast of the U.S.

As a study of the adapted survival of cultural otherness in the immigrant context of the U.S., the retrieval of the bond with ancestral spirits offers insights into Korean immigrants, particularly in times of need. The appeal of shamanic practice is in part that shamanism functions as a culturally constituted remedial mechanism for Korean immigrants, by calling forth the superhuman power of spirits into the world of the seemingly powerless, in the experience of otherness. The Korean collective consciousness, particularly of the first generation of immigration, continues to adhere to the belief that the spirits of dead ancestors have power to provide security, resolve anomalies, adjust misfortune, and bring good fortune to their lives. In this regard, chapters 4 through 7 of this study discuss forms of ritual practice that effect remedies and healings.

Two questions are basic for my discussion of potential changes that may occur in shamanic practice in the U.S., as that practice continues to adapt to its specific context under the new cultural influence. The first question concerns whether or not the shift in context is related to changes in the objectives, forms, and content of shamanic ritual presentations. The second question, which arises from adjustments made by shamanic practitioners working within a predominantly Christianized Korean immigrant community, concerns whether shamans negotiate with the evangelical zeal that dominates the Korean immigrant community and that dismisses various aspects of the Korean folk cultural tradition as deviant and/or demonic. Will Korean immigrants continue to reach out for shamanic help in dealing with unfortunate life situations? The vast majority of Korean immigrants who have relocated to the U.S. are seeking better lives for themselves and, especially, their children. But the path to success is often elusive, in spite of hard work. So my curiosity also concerns how shamanic practices serve the life of Korean immigrants, who experience routine tension and anxiety as they seek to adjust and to build up a prosperous life in a foreign country.

While shamanic practice is not only viewed as polytheistic in character but also as individualistically adapted in the practice of each shaman, particularly in the immigrant context, Korean shamans do not have a sense of community, of networking with other shamans or professional groups; they are acting as somewhat isolated individuals. Along with the absence of an organized professional and/or lay community for survival, shamans have no resources to offer cultural belonging and social networking in meeting immediate needs, such as those resources offered by the Korean Protestant church. Nonetheless, Korean immigrants in the U.S. continue to seek out shamans, while the majority of those who seek shamanic assistance are still more or less affiliated with the Protestant church, according to my informants. The clientele comes primarily from the Christianized Korean community, which raises a critical question as to what their grassroots hunger might be. That is, what leads these immigrants to seek the "demonic" assistance of shamans, far from acceptable within the Korean immigrant Protestant community. In this, it would be more accurate to say that the practice of shamanism is less believed in than it is utilized as a remedial mechanism, in keeping with the culturally familiar supernatural assistance.

This study employs three methods: historical, theoretical, and ethnographic. The interviews, informal conversations, and extensive observations are the central qualitative data for the analysis of the practice of Korean immigrant shamanism, particularly in the metropolitan areas in the East Coast of the U.S. The historical method is employed in order to situate the current practice within the long history of Korean shamanism, so as to provide a basic understanding of my research topic. I will discuss the collective consciousness replicated in the shamanic ritual in comparison to the subjective charismatic skill acquired by each shaman in the practice of Korean shamanism. To this end, in terms of theory, I employ Emile Durkheim's theory of religion and Max Weber's analysis of charismatic authority, including a vast array of anthropological and Korean scholars's discussions on the specific topic of shamanism. My intent, in this regard, is to examine the aspect of ambivalence unfolded in the interplay between cultural collectivism, collective consciousness, and the individual practices of Korean shamanism (Durkheim 1933; 1982; 1995; Weber 1947; 1968; 1971, 1993). To put it differently, I will look into how the individual shaman's gift of charisma enables one to maneuver and confirm a culturally collective consciousness in ritual and vice versa. It will reflect a certain ambiguity in shamanic practice that mediates both individualism and collectivism. I associate this analysis with a counter discussion of the feminist discourse that articulates the power and autonomy of the female shaman apart from consideration of a social context that subordinates the practice and role of shamans to Korean traditional cultural norms (Chung 1990; Kwok 2000; Sun 1991). Finally, my ethnographic study is a reminiscence of the metaphoric prose in a poem that is shared by Chongho Kim in his fieldwork report, so as to account for Kim's focus on the cultural paradox (C. Kim 2003). He highlights this perspective through his emphasis on the aspect of ambiguity present in cultural behavior in regard to the practice of Korean shamanism. I borrow his poetic prose with the confidence that it provides an expressive means for my discussion of Korean immigrant shamanism that struggles for survival within the cultural incongruity between the ethnically Korean culture and the religiously protestantized immigrant community of the U.S.:

> Shamanism is superstitious, so it should not be used. Shamanism is not superstition, because it is actually used. Again, shamanism is superstitious, so, paradoxically, it is used. (C. Kim 2003, 12)

Breaking New Ground

This ethnographic study includes three new directions that are distinctively different from prior studies of Korean shamanism. First and primarily, this study is a fresh academic attempt that introduces forms of Korean immigrant shamanism that are practiced in the nonconventional context of the U.S. Whereas existing studies focus on indigenous forms of Korean shamanism as found within Korea itself, my own field study represents an initial effort to analyze its practice in the Korean immigrant community in the East Coast of the U.S. I have discovered only one published research dealing with this particular variety of Korean immigrant shamanism in the context of transmigration (Ha 1996). Indeed, it was somewhat difficult to locate, observe, and interview underground shamans in the Korean immigrant community. This study responds to the absence of academic research in this new and very different context in regard to Korean shamanism as the product of a dearth of theory and practice. Considering the magnitude of the critical research addressing Korean shamanism in its home context, initiated by Nŭng-hwa Yi in 1927 (N. Yi 1977), the absence of comparable research engaging the one-hundred plus years of Korean immigrant history in the U.S. is striking

(Y. Yoon 2000, 197).[38] One reason for this academic omission may be the evangelical environment of Korean immigrant community. Whereas the analytical academic examination of the Korean immigrant context in the U.S. is almost exclusively attentive to developments within the protestant-ized immigrant community, the topic of minor folk religious traditions, particularly shamanic practice, has been disregarded throughout the Korean immigrant history in the U.S. Although some minor references to shamanism are found in various interdisciplinary discussions regarding native cultural implications of Koreanness, these references, by and large, have apologetic or reductionist purposes and do not engage the ritual aspects or the religious divergence. The majority of these references are employed in exploring the cultural roots of specific liturgical elements or the faith community of the Korean immigrant Protestant church. For instance, the root of the *tongseong-gido*, the loud prayer that is culturally particular in the liturgy of the Korean immigrant church, is considered to be in the ritual chanting of the shamanic tradition (S. Kim 2010, 93). Moreover, the "excessive emphasis in sermons on the believers' earthly blessings" or "shamanic preaching" in the immigrant Korean church may be explained as the cultural influence of shamanism in the Korean collective consciousness (M. Kim 2007, 32–33). This present research, there-fore, builds on a fresh ethnographic study as well as established analyses of Korean shamanism in its original setting.

A second departure of this present study is its focus on clarifying the importance of women's presence in the tradition of Korean shaman-ism. The Korean shamanic arena has been regarded as a feminine asset, constituting an important channel for magnifying the roles of women (Covell 1983, 10; Clark 1961, 181–84; Sookjin Lee 2001, 210), as mani-fested in the substantial female presence, including both female shaman and female clientele in the traditional shamanic domain (Grim 1984, 235; Covell 1983, 11).[39] However, a discussion of the cultural impact of female shamans—a crucial aspect of the practice of Korean shamanism— is missing from some Christian feminist discourses that rose with the wave of *minjung* theology (N. Suh 1983; Ro 2014, 12; U. Kim and Choi

---

38. The work of Nŭng-hwa Yi, *Joseon Musokgo* [*A Study of Joseon Shamanism*] marked the beginning of shamanic research, according to Yee-Heum Yoon.

39. Compared to the male-dominated society of Korea, Korean shamanism has been a realm for women. Moreover, seeking out and attending shamanic rituals for the welfare of the family is conceived to be a traditionally domestic task for women.

1995; A. Park 2004, 10–15)[40] from the late 1970s to the 1990s, on the fringes, during the military dictatorship in Korea.[41] My discussion on the role of women in Korean immigrant shamanism constitutes a counter discourse to the Protestant feminist advocacy. To counter the feminist discussion, which emphasizes women's power and autonomy as secured through religious leadership and sacred roles, my focuses are more on the role of female shamans who replicate the male hegemony of the spirits through an ego-exchange.

A third fresh direction in this present study is in the difference in regard to the gender display of the research subject. In contrast to prior field research of Korean shamanism, which basically centered on the female practice such as the popular studies *Six Korean Women* by Young-sook Kim Harvey and *Shamans, Housewives, and Other Restless Spirits* by Laurel Kendall, this ethnographic study investigates the practice of two male shamans as well as a female shaman. This present ethnographic research is an in-depth study of a particular threesome of Korean immigrant shamans and claims to describe them as a new academic venture that has been carried out in an unexplored, nontraditional immigrant context in the East Coast as home to the second largest Korean community in the U.S. However, it should be certain that it is difficult to comment on how much this study can represent a comprehensive survey of the commonalities and particularities of the rather large number of Korean immigrant shamans practicing in the immigrant context in the U.S.

40. *Minjung* in Korean refers to the "common people," people who experience unjust life conditions. *Minjung* theology emerged from the Christian domain in the 1970s in response to the military dictatorship in Korea, a period when common people were undergoing sociopolitical oppression. The common people in Korea shared the experience of *han*, which represents a culturally collective consciousness of "experiencing a sense of oppression" (A. Park 2004, 10–15; U. Kim and Choi 1995). For Young-chan Ro, the concept of *han* expresses "the soul of *minjung* as the symbolic reality," and thus the significance of *minjung* or *han* should not be conceptualized but should be approached through narrative and storytelling as an empirical aspect. In this regard, Ro also emphasizes the important role of Korean shamans who represents a keen sense of *han*, because they engage with various stories in dealing with their shamanic clients in the practice (Ro 2014, 12).

41. The main military dictatorship in South Korea began with the regime of Chung-hee Park from 1963 to 1979, until Park was assassinated. The political dictatorship continued under the regime of Doo-hwan Chun from 1980 to 1987.

Ethnographic Method

The study of religion has broadened its scope of research from armchair reading to the "thick description" method of fieldwork (Geertz 1973, 14), seeking a better understanding of experiences and expressions of unfamiliar others (Saliba 1974, 145; Moore and Reynolds 1984, 1-7). Frank E. Reynolds emphasizes the difference of an anthropological study of religion, which focuses more on the discussion of experience in the field, from analyses of historical accounts and traditional documents (Moore and Reynolds 1984, 2-3). Of particular relevance here is attention to the field context of people who have relocated to a immigrant context, which strongly affects the actual function of religious significances and activities. Immigrants' encounter with new experiences and demands for cultural assimilation to a new context inevitably produce a distance of practice from theory. New experiences lead to new meanings that are compatible with the new context, all of which ultimately change the footprint of religion in the new, immigrant context. In this regard, field studies offer an opportunity to observe changes in the experiences and expressions of religious routines of the immigrant community. Without actual field research, immigrants' religious practices under the impact of contextual change cannot be easily comprehended.

My study of Korean immigrant shamanism also benefited from the approach of the anthropological study of religion. Considering how few studies have been based on an ethnographic research method in the field of Korean shamanism, against the prolific research dealing with indigenous forms of Korean shamanism, this present study is modeled after the ethnographic study of my own teacher and mentor, Karen McCarthy Brown, who inspired me to explore the possibility of the present research and provided as well an example of ethnographic research through her own work. Brown's major study, *Mama Lola*, delineates both the macro- and micro-religious life of a Vodou priestess practicing in Brooklyn, New York, as well as in Haiti (Brown 1991). Brown delivered a "rich" and "thick" (Geertz 1973, 14) description of the individual and familial experiences of a priestess who survived immigrant routines and exigencies, fused with the cultural prescription of Haitian Vodou tradition. As Brown explained, "What the ethnographer studies is how people create meaning or significance in their lives, how they interpret objects and events" (Brown 1991, 14). Accordingly, my study seeks to apply an ethnographic method that involves a comparative look into the blend of the old and the new—for example, the diasporically individual and the ethnically collective cultural meanings in the practice of Korean shamanism.

One of the earliest ethnographies done by Youngsook Kim Harvey presents the biographical narratives of six female Korean shamans, through which Harvey elucidates the cultural roles and social standing of female shamans in the specific social structure and cultural location of Korea itself (Y. Harvey 1979). Her study serves as a turning point in the study of Korean shamanism, going beyond the traditional method of literary discussion and analysis so as to include participating in the everyday life of the shamans and their rituals, as she states:

> Even with these shamans who agreed to serve as informants, rapport was established slowly. They were most vexed that I was interested in them as individuals rather than as religious specialists who could give me information on various aspects of shamanism. (Y. Harvey 1979, 14)

Also, Chongho Kim's field study, *Korean Shamanism* (C. Kim 2003), has encouraged me to pay close attention to the context of Korean immigrant shamanism conducted in a location where Protestantism prevails in the U.S. As Kim addresses his central question, namely, the cultural paradox in the practice of Korean shamanism—inspired by Youngsook Kim Harvey (1979)[42]—his question also encouraged me to carefully investigate the particular contexts of my own research. Chapter 3 of this study discusses the incidents connected with particular Christian charismatic healing rituals that took place within the Korean immigrant community of the U.S. Upon a serious accident occurring in the course of the ritual and the news publication of this incident by the regional news media, the ambiguous title of "Korean exorcism" (Jackman 2009) raised instant misconceptions in the readers.[43] Granted, the ritual incident involved the issues of women, violence, and spirit possession. The extreme physical contact in the actual carrying out of the ritual, a context that caused physical damage or even death, was justified by the practitioner as being the action of the Holy Spirit. Korean cultural collectiveness widely shares an

42. As C. Kim raises the question of the paradoxical cultural attitude towards Korean shamanism in his field study, he cites Y. Harvey's inscription: "Still, I tried to read whatever I could find on shamanism to understand why it is so despised but at the same time so widely followed. . . . It's been with us from the beginning of our society, but none explained why the contradiction existed" (Y. Harvey 1979, 197).

43. A teenage girl named Rayoung Kim, eighteen years old girl, died after a deliverance ritual, a so-called Christian exorcism, in Fairfax County, Virginia, in July 2008.

animistic belief, regardless of the specific religious tradition of the healer. Perception reflects prejudice and blame on the part of the larger community who focus on shamanism when an unpleasant incident results from rituals, whatever the context. This prompt public misperception of the incident in question exemplifies the ambivalent cultural perceptions of the practice of shamanism in the Korean immigrant community.

Laurel Kendall, a Western white female scholar, is one of the most prolific writers on Korean shamanism. She began her field research in Korea in the 1970s, and her work has introduced readers to various sociocultural issues in the practice of Korean shamanism, especially dealing with the practice of female shamans in Korea (Kendall 1985). Kendall comments about what she judges to be a substandard ethnographic methodology utilized in the field of Korean shamanism:

> There exists a wealth of pure description. What is lacking is a systematic ethnographic appreciation of the who, why, what, where, and when of women's rituals, a gap that precludes generalization on the role of women and shamans in Korean religious life. (Kendall 1985, 38)

As I reiterate, concentrated fieldwork in the study of Korean shamanism in general and in Korean immigrant shamanism in particular is in its infancy. For my own part, I have concluded that the best model to effect field study comes from the ethnographic work of Karen McCarthy Brown and similar researchers such as the scholars aforementioned. In this present fieldwork, I pursue Geertz's description of ethnography in his short story in which he asks "what does the ethnographer do," and he answers, "observes, records, and analyzes—a kind of *veni, vidi, vici* conception of the matter" (Geertz 1973, 20).[44]

Korean Immigrant Shamanism and Hermeneutical Method

In keeping with acceptable analytic methods, the present ethnographic study employs some theoretical discussion while aiming at a balance

44. Clifford Geertz identifies the normal steps in answering the questions that are involved in fieldwork by describing the tasks of the field-worker. Geertz says: "He observes, he records, he analyzes—a kind of *veni, vidi, vici* conception of the matter—it may have more deep consequences than are at first apparent, not the least of which is that distinguishing these three phrases of knowledge-seeking may not, as a matter of fact, normally be possible; and, indeed, as autonomous 'operations' they may not in fact exist."

of practice and theory. My focus in this ethnographic study is on the dynamic tension and negotiation between the collective consciousness represented by the ancestral spirits in the practice and the individual charisma gifted to the shaman as a practitioner and intermediary between the protestantized Korean immigrant community and the tradition of Korean shamanism. My interest also includes, as previously mentioned, clarifying the role of women in the practice of Korean immigrant shamanism, a role that raises questions about the feminist advocacy for female power and autonomy, against the traditional role of woman in Korean society.

In light of this discussion, chapter 2 presents a theoretical portion of a brief history of Korean shamanism. The beginning of this chapter includes a discussion on the origin of Korean shamanism, especially indebted to the research of Hyung Il Pai, *Constructing "Korean" Origins* (Pai 2000). Pai's reconstruction of the origins and development of Korean shamanism in connection with the origin of the Korean nation is noteworthy as she stresses two important factors that are commonly noted in studies of the origins of shamanism globally: the southern Siberian Neolithic culture and the China Sea cultural origin (Pai 2000, 88–89; Sookjin Lee 2001).[45] Another analytic account involved in this chapter is a brief history of Korean shamanism, particularly focusing on the early *Joseon* era. The key purpose of this chapter is to provide a benchmark for the cultural construction of gender and class stratification that prevailed during the *Joseon* dynasty, a construction that has had a lasting impact on the contemporary moral ethos in Korean society as well as on the perception of the practice of shamanism. Concentrating on two particular issues,

45. In order to comprehend the individual characteristics that distinguish Korean shamanism from other shamanic traditions, Pai focuses initially on shared cultural aspects present throughout shamanism.

The Siberian Neolithic culture, which is called the northern system, *bukbang-gye*, provides traces of the hunter culture with a male predominant society as well as animal worship. The cultural influence of the *bukbang-gye* on the practice of Korean shamanism is illustrated by the sky and bear worship that are represented in the national creation myth of Korea.

The China Sea cultural origin, referred to as the southern system, *nambang-gye*, exhibits vestiges of agrarian culture, with its central role for women that has parallels in the shamanic ritual arena. This idea helps to understand the influence of the female gender, specifically in the tradition of Korean shamanism. Traces of prehistoric sun worship and an egg-modeled oviparous myth derived from the China Sea culture are also found in the egg myths of the births of national founders, particularly in the past southern kingdoms of Korea, such as Goguryeo, Silla, and Gaya.

chapter 2 addresses how the ideological interests of neo-Confucian literati historically constructed and took advantage of a strictly gendered and heavily stratified space from the beginning of the Joseon regime in 1392 CE. In this discussion, I draw heavily on the works of Boudewijn Walraven (1999; 2007) and Richard D. McBride II (2007), which help to explain how the new cultural construct formulated during the *Joseon* dynasty not only changed the footprint of Korean shamanism but also affected the cultural dualism of the period. Walraven notes:

> The refusal of the *yangban*[46] to participate in certain forms of worship was not merely a consequence of their philosophical convictions. It also depended on social factors, for example, taste, which as Pierre Bourdieu has reminded us, differs according to social class and serves to demarcate social distinctions. (Walraven 1999, 169)[47]

My discussion then takes up the cultural ambivalence between the collective consciousness that is called upon in shamanic rituals and the individual charisma that is gifted to the shaman in practice (Durkheim 1995, 280; Weber 1947, 358). Chapter 5 addresses how the element of ambivalence is inherently embedded in the ritual practice of shamans as intermediaries in the dynamic between the spirits and the shaman who acts on behalf of the client. Also, the rituals of the male shaman M. Doryeong, presented in chapter 4, are theoretically supported by Durkheim's discussion of the collective consciousness, in relation to the neo-Confucian moral ethos that is embodied in the command of ancestral spirits. A critical question as to the rituals conducted by M. Doryeong is, then: who is served in the ritual? Is it the collective consciousness associated with traditional morality with the consent of the spirits, or the whimsical ancestral spirits themselves?

Moral cohesion helps to sustain interrelational integrity in traditional culture, which is similarly found in the rituals that engage the spirits. Through shamanic rituals, the living kin are united with deities or ancestral spirits in lieu of moral servitude to the spirits (Durkheim 1995, 369). Considering that a remedy is effected for the client when the moral command of the deities or ancestral spirits is upheld in rituals, preserving

---

46. *Yangban* refers to the aristocrat status of the neo-Confucian literati and the upper-class military groups.

47. Bourdieu identifies *taste* as "a practical mastery of distributions which makes it possible to sense or intuit what is likely (or unlikely) to befall—and therefore to befit—an individual occupying a given position in social space" (Bourdieu 1979, 483).

moral cohesion in the practice of Korean shamanism is identified with serving the ancestral spirits. In other words, the sacred power served in the practice of Korean shamanism is not only the ancestral spirit but also the collective consciousness of the moral bond.

Max Weber describes charisma as a quality or gift granted to certain individuals chosen to become superhuman agents. Drawing on the vocabulary of early Christian history, Weber identifies a subjective quality as the foremost characteristic of charisma. Including as charismatic leaders those persons perceived as magicians, healers, prophets, or heroes, who can be differently named in distinctive cultural settings, Weber offers a notion of the shamanic quality of charisma (Weber 1947, 328; 1971, 229–30):

> Shamanist ecstasy is linked to constitutional epilepsy, the possession and the testing of which represents a charismatic qualification. Hence neither is "edifying" to our minds. They are just as little edifying to us as is the kind of revelation. (Weber 1946, 246)

The unusual leadership exercised by Korean shamans can be exemplary of "charisma given from above," vested with *shinbyeong*, the shamanic illness (Weber 1971, 229–30; Jung Y. Lee 1981, 12).

Two uncommon attributes are delineated in the tradition of shamanism regarding Weber's remark about "a break in the established normative order." One aspect is the woman-stream of leadership that represents a counter-gender phenomenon to the masculine hegemony in traditional Korean society, where the role of successful intercessor or impact-maker has ordinarily been a male privilege. The other feature as a break in the tradition of Korean shamanism is a spirit-given shamanic kinship with the master shaman that is inconsistent with the hereditary character of familial relationships.

The difference between the leadership of charismatic Korean shaman and Weber's charismatic leader may be in the shaman's inability to challenge the status quo of the Korean immigrant community.[48] However,

---

48. The communal nature of shamanic ritual was of critical importance in the ordinary life of the traditional village in Korea, such as is still found in rural areas of inland Korea. Shamanic ritual is rarely seen in public in the immigrant context of the U.S., because the rituals are performed in secluded places, at least in part to avoid coming to the attention of the dominant, oppositional Korean diasporic Protestant community. Similarly, the recent growth of shamanism in both Korea itself and apparently the immigrant context of the U.S. presses more towards the *gut*-less, i.e., the absence of

considering the facet of "routinization" as the anticipated ontology of charismatic initiative in Weber's analysis, the shamanic disengagement with protestantization acquiesces in the charismatic feature of the shaman taking the direction of being noncontroversial. Weber comments that charisma lasts unstable by shifting to be "either traditionalized or rationalized, or a combination of both" (Weber 1968, 54; Andreski 1984, 108). Similarly, the shamanic remedies begin with the objective of transforming ordinary conditions of life, but the shaman's ritual invocation turns time back to the traditional esprit de corps, the people's collective consciousness, en route to a moral bond with the deities or spirits (Grim 1984, 235; Covell 1983, 11). The individual presence of charismatic shamans—typically female—manifests a counteraction to the ordinary masculine culture. At the same time, the shaman's mediation actually facilitates reproducing the routine order of traditional Korean culture through the moral command of spirits. Charismatic gifts may therefore lead toward adjustments that enable shamans to fit in with or even strengthen the collective consciousness. This can lead to a kind of routinization of the moral bond.

Another subject theoretically explored in this ethnographic study is the issue of women, taken up in chapter 6. Some Christian feminist scholars advocate compassion and divinity of female shamans in an attempt to challenge and liberate the traditional role of Korean women against the ordinary image as an oppressed group overrun by the masculine power system. The image of female shamans is represented as the matriarchal character of sisterhood, the traditional matriarchal caregiver (H. Chung 1990, 66), female religious leaders (Sookjin Lee 2001), or even Korean goddesses (M. Choi, 1991b; Kwok 2000, 72–73). Identifying the role of female shaman with that of a superhuman maternal agency for the Korean *minjung* women, feminist scholars attempt to reshape the image of ordinary Korean women from *nai* to *oei*.[49]

There are some critical points lacking in the discourse of Christian feminist scholarship on this matter. The cultural system impersonated in shamanic rituals carries on a masculine ideology that demands the female shaman's compliance with the moral order of the spirits in order to conduct and satisfy her role. The majority of the deities encountered

---

formal rituals with brief performances for divination.

49. *Nai* in Korean symbolizes the interior, private, secondary, feminine, and inferior; whereas *oei* represents what is exterior, public, primary, masculine, and superior in traditional culture of Korean society.

in the tradition of Korean shamanism are masculine, whereas a few feminine deities are also identified as *samsin halmeoni* and elderly female spirits (Covell 1983, 11; Jung Y. Lee 1981, 108–10).[50] None of the feminine deities represents natural phenomena such as mountains or rivers. Conducting rituals for remedies by means of mediating between deities or spirits and the living kin is done in accord with the spirits' moral command that is exclusively linked to the tradition of masculine cultural hegemony. For the shaman who has been chosen and possessed by the spirits, the shamanic role, whether female or male, is not free from the command of the spirit. Only when the utmost moral virtue of filial piety and loyalty is physically observed by the shaman and the clients, so as to please the spirits in the ritual, can the objective of the ritual be achieved. In contrast to the feminist discourse, female shamans are always in servitude to the masculine moral ethos with no autonomy. In light of this discussion, the feminist discourses indicated above have failed to observe the actual mechanism by which the shamanic role is conditioned by the masculine moral order that the deities or spirits command in the actual practice of the female shaman called to serve it.

No theory is perfect. I bear in mind that in employing various theoretical approaches taken from the works of other academics, I alone am responsible for any unfortunate choices, misperceptions, and shortcomings of my study.

3. Fieldwork

Informants

For my ethnographic research, I have conducted intensive fieldwork with three main shaman informants and some fifteen clients of my informants from 2004 to 2011. The female shaman identified as Lee Bosal was in her early fifties in 2011 and has been practicing for some decades since her initiation at about age ten in Korea. Lee Bosal claims that she is one of the first Korean immigrant shamans to have registered as a nonprofit

50. This phenomenon seems to be reflective of the social system in Korea. Though women are accustomed to being disrespected as having only secondary status in traditional society in Korea, they gain standing when they become elders. Likewise, younger female spirits are predominately identified as dangerous spirits that have to be appeased through the rituals in Korean shamanism, whereas the representative "grandmother spirits," the *samsin halmeoni*, refer to three grandmother goddesses in charge of fertility and the successful birth of a child.

religious practitioner in the U.S. The second shaman informant has been the husband of Lee Bosal since 2010. He is identified as Kang monk shaman and was in his sixties. His shamanic spirit possession took place in his forties, following two decades of having been a celibate Zen Buddhist monk in Korea.[51] The spirit possession, however, interfered with his intent to pursue a scholarly career in the Buddhist order following his MA study in Seoul, Korea. His subsequent practice of shamanism is thoroughly fused with Buddhism and he chooses to identify himself as a Buddhist monk rather than a shaman, though he practices shamanic rituals regularly at his wife's shrine.[52] When he began serving as a Zen Buddhist monk, he committed to being celibate as long as he was serving the order. But before he married Lee Bosal, he switched his membership from the Jogye Zen Buddhist tradition to the Cheontae order, a Buddhist tradition allowing the monks to marry. The third informant is a male shaman identified as M. Doryeong, who was also in his sixties. He was initiated while in his twenties in Korea. In contrast to Lee Bosal and Kang monk shaman, his practice and life are tremendously affected by a personal sense of dishonor and lack of confidence. He lives and practices basically in a secluded fashion in a small urban apartment room, very aware of being disrespected within the male-dominant, protestantized Korean immigrant community in the U.S. This study also draws upon formal and informal interviews and observations of some fifteen clients whom I met in both shrines, though mostly at Lee Bosal's shrine.

In this study, my stay at Lee Bosal's shrine is used as the main background of my discussion as I incorporate the qualitative data that I accumulated from the beginning of my fieldwork. My stay at Lee Bosal's shrine produced richer data on account of close engagement in interviews of ritual attendees and careful observation of the interrelationships associated with various rituals. Also, more attention is given to the practice of Lee Bosal and Kang monk shaman than to M. Doryeong. The reason for this is that Lee Bosal has a much larger practice together with her husband than M. Doryeong. However, none of the shaman informants

51. The representative Zen Buddhist tradition in Korea is Jogye Buddhism. See the Jogye Order of Korean Buddhism online.

52. Kang monk shaman insists that he left home to enter the Buddhist vocation as a teenager and experienced being possessed by the shamanic spirit in his late thirties while still engaged in his Buddhist priesthood. His spirit possession led him to leave his reclusive Buddhist life in the mountains. Since the possession, he says, he went down to Seoul and started a practice of urban Buddhism from a location on the fourth floor of a modern commercial building.

were willing to disclose their ritual settings, residential environments, and/or clients to me as a sole professional observer, out of concern for their clients' privacy and confidentiality. Moreover, the residential environment of M. Doryeong, which was a tiny apartment room that includes his shrine, a place where he mostly stays alone during the day, restricted my opportunities for any extended interviews and observations of his practice.

As a single, straight, adult female ethnographer visiting the private household shrine of the male shaman by myself, I could not escape a sense of vulnerability due to my preconceptions of his explicit gender of maleness and the secluded location of his tiny apartment space. However, I decided to challenge myself to take the risk for my work. The sense of vulnerability was entirely my own agenda. M. Doryeong never evidenced any attempt to break the boundary between informant shaman and field researcher. My self-learning from the situation was to be aware of how an ethnographer's preconceptions based on feelings and attitudes shaped by prior experiences could screen reality, leading to mistaken and biased analyses in fieldwork. The danger inherent in the ethnographer's assumption can color the reality of the research subject and block the voices of informants from being heard, even before the thickness of meaning is uncovered.

M. Doryeong generally remained unwilling to allow me to observe his practice when he was with his clients, even after years of building up rapport. His protection of his clients' confidentiality restricted me to only one direct observation of his practice in the presence of his client in about seven years' communication with him. Another difficulty associated with the visits to M. Doryeong was that he was a chain-smoker. His dark and tiny apartment-cum-shrine was filled with smoke all the time. The windows were always closed, and that unpleasantness for me hampered my endeavor to have more time to converse with him during my visits.[53]

My visits to the shrine of Lee Bosal were not that much easier than those with M. Doryeong. Lee Bosal also required a significant period of time before she was willing to approve my presence in her shrine, together with observations and interviews. The process of building up the interactive relationship with Lee Bosal took about three years, though meetings

53. According to M. Doryeong, his chain-smoking habit was due to his body-governing deity, his *momju*, who controlled his personality and behavior. It was not his choice but was conditioned by his *momju* through spirit possession.

were irregular during that period. Gaining rapport eventually led to the first invitation to her shrine in an isolated, heavily forested location in the metropolitan area. The forest shrine is located a significant distance away from her local condo office in the Korean immigrant community.

Initially, all the shamans with whom I met were wary of my presence at their offices. They were curious about what I was doing, who I was, and what the objective of my visit was, as well as my personal background. They were also suspicious of the motives behind my field research, a suspiciousness that has also been mentioned by other researchers investigating shamanism (Sun 1991; C. Kim 2003). The shamans liked the topic of my fieldwork that focused on their practices, but they seemed to have difficulty grasping why I was doing this research. As Koreans generally are not hesitant to ask a lot of personal questions, those questions were addressed and responded to in ongoing routine conversations during the period of becoming interactive and of building up rapport. It was a process that served to narrow the gap between the informant and the ethnographer. Later, when Lee Bosal began to volunteer rather more about herself, she showed great humor, warmth, and concern as she came to acknowledge the appropriateness of my presence. She came to allow me to observe her practice after a certain period of time. She also explained to me various matters related to ritual practice, taking up associated topics one after another.

I first met Lee Bosal in the summer of 2004. She looked like an ordinary Korean woman in her late forties, in a formal black skirt suit, with her hair neatly held up with a pin on the back of her head. She looked rather serious and businesslike throughout our early conversations, rarely bearing a smile on her face. Overall, she seemed to lack any cheer and was not very chatty. I learned later that, during that first period of contact with her, she was undergoing a difficult divorce. By contrast, her recent manner is more outgoing, with big smiles on her face, a sense of humor, and a more relaxed and sociable manner.

Having visited the offices of other shamans prior to the visit with Lee Bosal, the luxurious furnishings of the office amazed me, particularly compared to the dingy apartment-shrine of M. Doryeong. I immediately wondered what had made her life condition much more successful financially, by comparison with the rather less pretentious offices and shrines of other shamans. Whereas other shamans barely provide basic needs for a tiny shrine, according to them, featuring a small portable altar decorated with inexpensive copies of shamanic paintings hung on the wall as a background for the altar, Lee Bosal seemed to have everything. She even subsequently established an elaborate residence-cum-shrine in the forest, where she could stage ritual performances at any time in serenity, with no outside interference.

Yet, when Kang monk shaman appeared to be her partner in practice in the early 2009, the rapport that I had established between Lee Bosal and myself seemed to disappear as it reverted back to the earlier, tentative stage of interaction. He routinely created complicated situations not only for me but also for others associated with Lee Bosal's shrine. As the ability of Lee Bosal herself to organize rituals and arrange ritual assistance was entirely subordinated to his control, my visits to Lee Bosal's shrine were also greatly affected by Kang monk shaman's interference in Lee Bosal's attempts to support my fieldwork. With Kang monk shaman compelling all others to follow his instructions in the shrine, any type of formal or informal observation, conversation, or interview could be initiated only with his explicit permission, regardless of Lee Bosal's willingness to assist my fieldwork. Even a brief conversation with Lee Bosal might be interrupted by him.

From my earlier visit, I had no idea about her relationship with Kang monk shaman. One day in May of 2009, when I called Lee Bosal, she surprised me with an invitation to visit her new condo office. She wanted me to meet someone whom she identified as a gifted Buddhist monk who was visiting her, and she said that it would be very interesting for me to meet him. I hurried over to her office and met Kang monk shaman for the first time. Wearing a neat grey traditional Buddhist monk garment that looked similar to the *kendo* uniform,[54] he seemed wary of me and rather controlling of the situation. We sat around the dining table in a corner of the kitchen and had a long talk about various subjects, especially shamanism, religion, immigrant life, and my fieldwork. He said that while completing an MA program in a Buddhist university in Korea, he had majored in Korean folk studies. As we shared a common interest in Korean folkore, he was enthusiastic about talking scholarly matters and my research topic, while seeking my agreement with his own perspectives. Since that meeting, every time I met with Lee Bosal, she was in the company of Kang monk shaman.

During these meetings, the issue of their possible marriage would be raised back and forth in their discussion, usually including either a

54. Kang monk shaman often wore a traditional, gray-colored, Korean Buddhist monk garment.

severe disagreement between them or their putting their heads together to discuss a detailed plan for their future together. Lee Bosal had first met Kang monk shaman in her thirties, and they had performed shamanic rituals together occasionally in Korea, according to her. Her intimacy with him apparently developed only following his move to the U.S. For Lee Bosal, considering her age and particularly her profession as a shaman, she said, Kang monk shaman seemed to be the last chance for a good marriage. However, Kang monk shaman, who had never married and who had an MA degree, clearly thought of himself as a major marital "catch," compared to Lee Bosal, who had been divorced three times and did not have even a BA degree.

The outcome of this situation was their wedding, finally agreed upon after a year's battle between them. A personal invitation was given to me to attend and to serve as a translator for their wedding ceremony, which was held on a hot summer afternoon in a municipal office near the Korean immigrant community in August 2010. Their marriage set in place for them a firmly vertical relationship of male supremacy, which required not only Lee Bosal but also any assistants at the shamanic shrine to be subservient to the orders of Kang monk shaman. No one, including Lee Bosal herself, could counter his directions. All of us could only try to anticipate his emotionally rocky or rattling notions and act accordingly.

My Fear of Spirit Possession

Some ethnographers adventurously engage in their fieldwork in a special way, employing the methodology of participant observation. Atkinson and Hammersley describe the character of participant observation as "observation carried out when the researcher is playing the established participant role in the scene studied" (Atkinson and Hammersley 1994, 248; see also Gold 1958; Junker 1960).[55] The discussion about the participant observation approach is still highly contentious as scholars seek to clarify the epistemological meaning implied with the typology of participation in ethnography in general (Atkinson and Hammersley, 1994, 248). However, as the methodology of participant observation may "thicken" experiences by a closer look at the subjects' practice through

55. The widely used fourfold typology that is employed to describe the methodology of field research falls into (1) complete observer, (2) observer as participant, (3) participant as observer, and (4) complete participant (Gold 1958).

active participation in the fieldwork, its tactical advantage is considered incontestable in comparison to other methodological approach, as for example, the work of my own original mentor, Karen McCarthy Brown.

I believe that field-workers often experience similar difficulty when entering into each distinct ethnographic setting. For instance, Brown details her own experience, particularly as an ethnographer at the shrine in Brooklyn (Brown 1991, 7–8). In her ethnographic study, *Mama Lola*, she describes how her methodological approach in participant observation, which was highlighted through her own initiation, may lead to an active partaking through serving the ritual, as she states:

> My change in status is a result of the initiation I underwent in the summer of 1981. . . . I am now one of the "little leaves" (ti-féy) on Alourdes' Vodou family tree, and she introduces me as her "daughter." (Brown, 1991, 8)

As a first-generation Korean immigrant ethnographer studying my own native cultural practice in the diaspora, I had some apparent advantages in regard to the ethnographic setting for the cultural and linguistic references. However, the issue of familiarity—as similarly indicated by Brown—also inevitably involves my own individual cultural ignorance, which stems from the limited experience even in the common cultural setting. So, there still remain difficulties for me to understand and fit in with the setting, just as would be the case for a non-native ethnographer who continues to struggle for better understanding of an unfamiliar other's cultural practice (Brown 1991, 7).

More than that, I was not myself adequately prepared for that particular methodology of participant observation with which I had to deal during the period of my stay at Lee Bosal's shrine in spite of my advantageous position as a native field researcher working with my own ethnic people within the framework of my own cultural practice and references. Perhaps I felt haunted by the fear of a potentially negative power coming from an unknown supernatural agency, a fear similarly noted by other field researchers (C. Kim 2003). The fear perhaps reflected my own hesitancy about the potentially unpleasant element presented by spirit possession, something not previously experienced, which would raise a concern about possible disorder happening in my life.

I also attempted to keep a certain distance from my informants and my own sense of cultural references in order not to take anything for granted from my own cultural familiarity as a native ethnographer. The distance also reflects the naive sense of insecurity that I felt in my depth as a Christian observer working at a folk religious shrine. The insecurity perhaps derives from my particular Protestant upbringing, in which I had been taught to regard non-Protestants, including even Catholics, as heretic. The approach that I had acquired in my experience of the Korean Evangelical Protestant church might still linger in my mind and imperceptibly led to fear for the potential actions of evil spirits. Intellectually, I understand that erroneous construction, but emotionally, my mind might still be wary of the unknown, possibly negative power that would be presented in the world of my folk religious research.

As I reflect on the distancing that resulted from my sense of insecurity as an ethnographer, that distancing may also paradoxically denote a certain arrogance as an observer of the informants encountered in the fieldwork. Paul Atkinson and Martyn Hammersley suggest a similarly paradoxical aspect. Just as the ethnographer in the field often cultivates the position of "marginal native" (Freilich 1970), so ethnographers collectively seek to distance themselves repeatedly from versions of "mainstream" orthodoxy (Atkinson and Hammersley 1994).

A Korean anthropologist also indicates an unequal benchmark between the field researcher and the research subject, "while always leaving 'other' by virtue of being the one who does the research" (S. K. Kim 1995, 6). Kim raised this issue from her own experience in a particular research context, in which she purposely misled others as to her identity and age in order to undertake a study as an undercover factory worker in a free-export zone in the southeast region of South Korea. The inherent intellectual distance constantly brought up a sense of insecurity for her as researcher in interaction with her informants in the field, a situation that required her to ceaselessly negotiate with herself (S. K. Kim 1995, 6). The distance in my particular research field provided a protective screen not only for my attempt not to take for granted any special familiarity with my own cultural setting but also to be able to deal with my fear of the unknown power of spirits. Overall, the distance might also be seen as a screen to camouflage my arrogance in setting myself apart from my informants as "the marginal native" or "the other."

The issue of negotiation enormously affected me in the fieldwork from the start. When I chose the research topic of Korean immigrant shamanism at the beginning of my doctoral program, I was an academic infant who had barely learned my own culture. My strict Protestant upbringing from my childhood onward had made me more of an onlooker regarding my own culture. Intellectually ignorant of my own cultural tradition and environment, and somewhat in the sense of an internal foreigner, I felt fundamentally challenged when I began recognizing who I was myself. Meanwhile, it was bittersweet to face the uncongenial atmosphere from both Korean and non-Korean colleagues at my school, as they responded to my choice of study topic, the practice of Korean immigrant shamanism being the focus of my doctoral research.

I still feel a similar sense of fear when I recollect the time taken in turning the pages of the immigrant Korean community business directory in search of local shamans in order to discover them and start conducting my fieldwork in 2004. As my own environment was secured by the Protestant community that had nurtured me not only with a Protestant worldview but also with disinterest in other religious or folk traditions, including my own, my disregard for my own Korean cultural assets and references seemed to be a kind of proof of my loyalty and fidelity to my own monotheistic faith. But my wholesome existence as a faithful Christian clashed in the encounter with my advisor, Professor Karen McCarthy Brown.

Developing My Research Subject
in Korean Immigrant Shamanism

My studies in Christianity began with the goal of seeking suitable answers for the personal questions of unknown destiny, unanticipated losses and sufferings, and unwelcomed deaths, all of which I had encountered early on and frequently in my life to that point. And even as a seminarian, I was still wandering about searching for answers to those questions, as well as looking for an area for continuing study, all while seeking a direction for myself to follow after graduation from my MDiv program at Drew University in 2004. In an attempt to sort out my own focus of study in an advanced degree program, I decided on the intermediate step of pursuing a post-MDiv master's degree, which led me to engage in the study of the anthropology and sociology of religion through the classes of Professor Karen McCarthy Brown. Her questions jumped out at me: "Why are you looking for someone else's world? Why don't you study your own?" Her brief question stayed in my mind, lingering along an extended trail of reflection. I was initially unclear about what "someone else" actually meant to me and what "my own" could supply. She asked me to write an autobiography as a course assignment, seeking to spur my reflections. I did not quite understand what my autobiography had to do with the course, "Introduction to Anthropology of Religion," but I knew I had to do it, because it was a course assignment that should be done as something interwoven with the course readings.

The assignment required me to look far back into my childhood and to reflect on all that had happened up to that time, to talk about my identity, gender, cultural location, family background, etc. It proved to be a bit painful time for me, as I realized later. While organizing my own autobiography, various bits that I remembered led me in turn to cry, scream, laugh, develop a sense of longing, feel saddened or hopeful, etc. Preparing the paper set me on a journey into the past to visit my family and acquaintances, who still lived vividly in my memory, though many of them were no longer living. It demanded self-reflection to reconstruct remote time and spaces that I recollected only dimly. Only much later did I come to really understand the purpose and value of Professor Brown's assignment, though she did not give me a detailed explanation at the time; the understanding had to emerge from myself as reorganizing the the significance of my life. In fact, the assignment was a practice of re-flexivity, through which I could locate the scope of the topic of my future studies. Having been assigned the paper at the beginning of the semester, I spent the entire semester thinking and writing about myself, something I had never done before. The highlight of reflection in my paper came as I spotted the traces of my struggle as a woman living in a male hegemonic family and social environment in Korea, and as a Korean immigrant woman in both the immigrant Korean community and U.S. society in general. I finally fully grasped the meaning of Professor Brown's brief remark about "someone else" and "my own" with which she challenged me. The reflective process led me to raise the topic of Korean shamanism, which involved the Korean collective worldview and cultural practice, a topic that was doubtlessly spurred by Professor Brown's own work on Haitian Vodou in the U.S. Alongside her encouragement in response to my autobiography, Professor Brown served as my advisor in my doctoral studies until an unfortunate illness led her to an early retirement from teaching and a full withdrawal from her scholarly work, all by the end of my comprehensive exams in 2009.

A final point is that the names of the informants or interviewees in this study are pseudonymous, in order to protect their privacy and con-fidentiality. Also, note that the Romanization of Korean language follows the most recent updated policy of the National Institute of the Korean Language.[56] For the convenience of non-native Korean readers, the Korean terms used in this dissertation are collected together in an appendix.

56. The currently updated policy started in July 2000. This organization is the national bureau to manage the system of Korean language in Korea. See their website for more information.

2

Cultural Mimesis in Public and Private

The Practice of Korean Shamans as Impacted
by the Neo-Confucian Cultural Negation of Religious
Others in the Early Joseon Society

KOREAN SHAMANISM IS AN unstructured folk belief tradition that has been gradually privatized and was often politically controlled and culturally disregarded in Korean history (Walraven 2007). Considering that the practice of shamans was markedly affected by the rise of neo-Confucian cultural politics in the early Joseon dynasty, it is not surprising that specific traces of neo-Confucian power relations and the moral precepts of the Joseon regime are not only vitally present to this day in the contemporary culture of Korean society but also noticeably replicated in the ritual mimesis of shamans in traditional practice.

Religion often politically undergirded the power regime in Korean history by providing moral support, as with Buddhism under the Goryeo society and with neo-Confucianism during the Joseon dynasty.[1] This observation fits well with the remark of Antonio Gramsci, as Gramsci asserts that religion functions critically on behalf of the socially dominant class, so as to morally sanction that class's cultural values and social interests and therein legitimize their power standing in society (Bullock and Trombley 1999, 387–88). Similarly, neo-Confucianism succeeded as

1. The Goryeo dynasty lasted from 918 CE to 1392 CE, followed by the Joseon dynasty. The official regime of the Joseon dynasty originated in 1392, in the time of King Seong-gye Yi, and lasted until the Japanese annexation in 1910.

a moral conduit for the ideological interests and hegemonic desires of the noble class, so as to sanction male hegemony in society. The prestigious *yangban* elite group took advantage of its morally segregated class stratum and its associated gendered social space, while being not only the main political performer but also the creator of cultural values in the society. In this light, certain questions are then reasonable to ask: (1) how were the ideological interests of the neo-Confucian rulers played out in terms of a strictly gendered and heavily stratified social space, and (2) how did the structure of gendered social space serve the preponderance of female-led shamanic practice in the private sector?

My discussion in this chapter focuses mainly on the multiple stratified and spatially gendered social context of the Joseon regime, so as to highlight the background of the neo-Confucian impact upon ritual mimesis as a cultural negotiation in the traditional practice of shamans.[2] In this regard, Homi Bhabha's notion of mimicry is noteworthy, as he insists:

> Mimicry reveals something in so far as it is distinct from what might be called an *itself* that is behind. The effect of mimicry is camouflage, in the strictly technical sense. It is not a question of harmonizing with the background but, against a mottled background, of being mottled exactly like the technique of camouflage practiced in human warfare. (Bhabha 1994, 120)

Similarly, the tradition of shamanism survived cultural persecution by masking the ritual through imitation of the power modality and authoritative characters of the Joseon period.

The counter-gender phenomenon in the shamanic arena, in respect to the preponderance of female demographics rather than male dominance, which is not associated with the legacy of gyneolatry (the worship of femininity or womanhood), also has been enhanced from the early Joseon period into the present. This was certainly advanced by the morally gendered social space in the private arena, while male supremacy of public life was promoted under the new cultural politics. Religious authority belonged predominantly to the masculine realm in traditional Korean culture whereas the lives of women could be justified when they were subjected to male authority as satisfying the stereotypes of gender roles. In like manner, the presence of the shaman as a folk religious leader

2. The term *yangban* includes the two basic top-ranking groups of governmental officers, such as the Confucian administrative-officials (*mungwan*) and the military-officials (*mugwan*). This term may also refer to the top rank of the male class structure in Joseon society. *Yangbam* literally means "two parties."

has also been frequently identified as a stigma by the culturally Confucian, male-dominant society of Korea.[3] In this regard, examining Korean shamanism prior to the early Joseon society may provide a better understanding of the neo-Confucian cultural impact on shamanic practice and Korean collectiveness.

This study of the particular context in early Joseon society seeks to enhance an understanding of the neo-Confucian footprint that is so firmly conveyed in the cultural characters and moral ethos in the practice of shamans, traces of which footprint are still ritualized in contemporary shamanic practice. Looking back into the locus of the shamanic cultural negotiation under the pressure of neo-Confucian cultural politics, this analysis also sheds light on understanding the practice of Korean immigrant shamans within the Protestant venue of the contemporary Korean immigrant community in the U.S. Accordingly, this chapter is composed of four main sections: a brief history of Korean shamanism; the practice of shamans in a new social strata; the practice of shamans in the interplay of gendered social space; and the mimetic practice of Korean shamans in a changed cultural venue.

1. A Brief History of Korean Shamanism

The shamanic folk belief system associated with the actions of spirits and with female gender-specific involvement in ritual tradition has very much attracted anthropological interests in how and what prevail within the sector of Korean shamanism. For more groundbreaking discussion of this specific gender-binary's impact upon the practice of Korean shamanism, more detailed investigation of Korean history and culture may be essential. Unfortunately, there are few core historical documents, records, or sanctioned canons that provide insight into the origin and history of Korean shamanism. Oral tradition is important, in this regard, to offer some information about regional varieties in Korean shamanism and some of the rituals (Pai 2000, 88; Ro 2012, 82–83).[4] The general

---

3. Though the constant waves of religious influx have shifted the religious footprint in the history of Korea, cultural hostility towards female leadership in public, particularly in the religious sectors, still runs deep in the Korean collective mind. I personally presume that such an unfriendly cultural demeanor towards the public female leadership is a consequence of the influence of the neo-Confucian cultural politics in Korean history. In fact, it is also reinforced by certain interpretations of Christianity.

4. A widely shared scholarly assumption regarding the origin of Korean

absence of primary documents leaves abundant room for surmising similarities and particularities in relation to other geographically diversified forms of shamanic traditions in Korea. Yee-heum Yoon, a Korean shamanic scholar, offers an answer to the question: "What is shamanism?" He simply responds by saying that shamanism depends upon "one's own point of view" (Y. Yoon 1996, 111). Yoon's response is perhaps adequate, considering that each topical research into shamanism forsakes homogeneous definition and makes integrated reference difficult. This difficulty seems to be particularly due to the fundamental difference in practice from one shaman to another, which is associated with the regionally diversified forms of shamanic tradition in Korea and the variations among the different body-governing spirits that possess the individual shamans. Yoon assures us, in this regard, that "confusion and controversies" are ordinary in the discussion of shamanism (Y. Yoon 1996, 190).

Korean shamanism is presumed to derive from two different cultural origins. The primary cultural influence is thought to be from the southern Siberian Neolithic culture, called the northern system, *bukbang-gye*; and the other influence is seen as coming from the China Sea culture, called the southern system, *nambang-gye* (Pai 2000, 88). The Siberian cultural origin is associated with a masculine hunter society that matches the mythological profile synonymously found in the traditional ritual of Korean shamanism. Meanwhile, the China Sea origin provides the female gender-specific agrarian cultural feature that provides a parallel to the predominantly female-led Korean shamanism (Pai 2000, 89).

The Turko-Mongols of Siberia used to worship the sky and the pan-Altaic sky god in the *tengri* cult, in which various animal figures came into play while representing different social roles in human society (Bonnefoy 2:1089).[5] The tiger that symbolized divinity in the Siberian ritual is the

---

shamanism is that it is a cultural blend originating from Siberia and Mongolia and/or South Asia. Meanwhile, the common Korean understanding coordinates Korean shamanism with the national creation myth, identifying *dan-gun*, the progenitor of the Korean national myth, as the prototypical shaman. This view has come under dispute and reconfiguration. Considering that this internal scholarly discourse began in the 1920s, a time of Japanese colonial control, it seems likely that the configuration of Korean shamanism as an archaic Korean religion, promoted as the emblem of Korean collectiveness, was at least partly an assertion of national identity against the occupying Japanese colonizer.

5. "*Tengri* was believed to watch over the cosmic, political, and social order. The many secondary powers—sometimes deities, spirits, or simply said the sacred—were

sole correspondent to the *sanshin*, the mountain deity, in the pantheon of Korean shamanism.[6] The bear is adored as "a man in disguise viewed as a father" in the bear ceremony, which continues among contemporary Siberians, particularly the Yakuts (Bonnefoy 2:1089).[7]

Animal worship in the Siberian shamanic tradition provides some background for understanding an important feature of the Korean national creation myth, the *dan-gun* myth. *Dan-gun wang geom*, the main character of the creation myth, reigns not only as the first shaman king but also as the founder of *Gojoseon*,[8] the first nation of Korea, in 2333 BCE. As the story continues, *dan-gun* was born to a bear woman who married *hwan-wung*, the heavenly son of *hwan-in*, the heavenly king (Ilyon 1972, 32–33). The heavenly son, *hwan-wung*, came from heaven wanting to become a human, supported by the heavenly king, *hwan-in*. When the heavenly king sent the son into the human world, along with the king's loyal servants, at the same time, a female bear and a tigress who resided in a cave were also praying to become humans. After twenty-one days of prayers, the female bear became human, whereas the tigress failed to do so. The bear woman and the heavenly son, *hwan-wung*, married and gave birth to the first shaman king, *dan-gun* (Ilyon 1972, 32–33).

This national creation myth provides a link between sky worship and the animal impersonation of human roles found in the Siberian *tengri* cult. Moreover, the term *dan-gun*, meaning a supreme figure, is considered to derive from the Mongolian *tengri*, the origin of which is the sky and animal worship (Sookjin Lee 2001). Thus, common components such as animals characterizing human society, the heavenly kingdom, and the epistemological origin of *dan-gun*, reflect possible shared cultural traits between the *dan-gun* national myth and the Siberian cult.[9]

---

almost always associated with *Tengri*" (Bonnefoy 2:1089).

6. The mountain deity in the tradition of Korean shamanism is illustrated as an elderly Confucian man in a long white robe, with a long white beard and a hair knot on the top of head.

7. The Yakuts are a Turkic people in northeastern Siberia.

8. *Gojoseon* is regarded as the origin of Korean nation.

9. The *dan-gun* national myth was first introduced in *Samguk Yusa* [The Memorabilia of Three Kingdoms], which was written by Ilyon, a Buddhist monk and writer of the late thirteenth century. Yet, key scholarly discussion and the following public awareness of *dan-gun* myth as the national foundation story occurred apparently in the postcolonial period, after Korea was released from the Japanese colonial annexation. Scholars appealed to the myth in advocating a new, reassuring foundation for a sense of national identity, after the experience of a loss of belonging,

Meanwhile, the origin of China Sea culture is identified in prehistoric sun worship and the oviparous myth, which are traced particularly through the Dong son bronze drums dating back to 800 BCE (Pai 2000, 89).[10] Similarly, egg or oviparous creation myths are also found in the nativity narratives of the national founders of the southern regions of historically Korean territory such as Goguryeo, Silla, and Gaya (Pai 2000, 88).[11] The implication of the distribution of this cultural trait may reflect the trace of an ethnic cultural migration occurring from the southern China Sea to the northern territory. Another important shared feature is the female gender specific environment found in both the agrarian southern China Sea culture and the tradition of Korean shamanism (Sookjin Lee 2001). The appearance of the bear woman in the *dan-gun* national myth, as well as the results of a few archaeological excavations, also corroboratively demonstrates the vestiges of female authority in the prehistoric religious tradition of Korea (Pai 2000, 81).[12] It is thus appropriate to examine closely the two distinctive cultural origins of the northern system (*bukbang-gye*) and the southern system (*nambang-gye*), in order to trace a better picture of the history and background of Korean shamanism.

Regarding the historical trace of Korean shamanism, the royal title of the second king, *chacha-ung*, in the Silla kingdom, located in the southeastern part of the Korean peninsula between 57 BCE to 935 CE, reflects a strong legacy of shamanism. The suffix *-ung* in the king's title signified a shaman king who served spirits in sacrificial ceremonies in a society where politics and religion were united (J. Seo 2003). Moreover, the *hwarang* system,[13] which operated in the Silla kingdom, is also be-

---

during the period of Japanese annexation, 1910 to 1945.

10. The Dong son bronze drums with the sun symbol at the round center are found exclusively in the southeast regions of Asia.

11. In regard to the egg nativity myth in the history of Korea, there are mythologies of national founders such as Silla's founder Hyeokgeose, Goguryeo's Jumong, and Gaya's King Suro.

12. Similarly, Jung Young Lee, a Korean shamanic scholar, concludes from his own research into Korean myths and folk religions that the particularity of female gender-specific leadership is well rooted in the tradition of Korean shamanism, despite the regionally varying forms of rituals (Jung Lee 1973, 147). Two archaeological finds in inland Korea, for example, are a goddess-like mask, symbolizing fertility and well-being, and a religious image of a female fertility goddess, both dating back to the Neolithic era.

13 The Silla government carefully selected brilliant youths for the *hwarang* system

lieved to have been an institution partially for the religious training of shamanic leadership. The "shamanic cult of sky" obtained in the *hwarang* system presents a ritual similitude with the Siberian *tengri* cult, which continued to be performed until the end of the Silla kingdom (S. Yoon 1964, 166; Cho 2004). A historical document notes that the ceremonies for royal inauguration were often incorporated with the shamanic initiation ritual during the kingdom of Goguryeo, which occupied mostly the northern part of the Korean peninsula from 37 BCE to 668 CE (J. Choi 2006, 10–11; Walraven 1999; Yi 1977). As shown by these sources, the role and status of the shaman were sanctioned by the political authorities and acknowledged as fully legitimate in the conducting of various public and private ritual ceremonies.

When the Goryeo dynasty arose between 918 CE and 1392 CE, following the Unified Silla kingdom, shamanism was still treated amicably in a society where Buddhism was promoted as the national religion, while Confucianism was employed as the bureaucratic ideology (Cho 2004). For example, the history of Goryeo records an account of the institutionally authorized shamanic rain ceremonies that were convened as often as twenty times a year by the king's order in the Goryeo dynasty (Yi 1977, 19; Walraven 1999). Two nationally monumental shamanic ceremonies, *Palgwanhoe* and *Yeondeunghoe*, also continued to be practiced throughout the Goryeo dynasty (Cho 2004; Y. C. Kim 1982, 23–24; Vermeersch 2007).[14] As national festivals, the two religious events maintained a blend of tri-religious components, with shamanic content, Confucian formulae, and Buddhist nomenclature (Cho 2004). Alongside the presence of religious diversity, which was still generously tolerated, a significant female presence might also have endured in these public religious performances during the Goryeo dynasty (McBride 2007, 236).

Yet, the rise of neo-Confucian politics in 1392 CE began publicly interfering with the welfare of the female-led shamanic tradition.[15] Sha-

---

that operated as a center for unifying the Three Kingdoms. The Unified Silla kingdom lasted from 618 to 935 CE.

14. "The *Palgwanhoe* was originated from the harvest festival held by the ancient farming communities as the special observance of Buddhist precepts, whereas the *Yeondeunghoe* was celebrated as the spring festival corresponding to the Lantern Festival, the lighting of lanterns in celebration of the Buddha's birthday" (Y. C. Kim 1982, 23–24).

15. Neo-Confucianism was promoted as the official policy by Taejo Yi Seong-gye, the founder and first king of the Joseon dynasty, thereby dismissing the practices of both Shamanism and Buddhism as debased belief systems.

mans and Buddhist nuns, as well as Buddhist monks, were newly classified as social outcasts under the new authorities. These outcasts were
publicly restricted, and their religious practices were severely deprecated
by the new order (J. Seo 2003; Kister 1997).[16] Shamans were not allowed
to reside in the urban capital area where the royal palace and the *yangban* class were mainly located (Walraven 1999). As a policy of elite male
supremacy was legitimated by the neo-Confucian moral politics in public affairs, religious participation of females was tolerated in private but
curtailed in public.

Nonetheless, some historical records show that shamanic rituals
continued to be performed in a covert manner under the hegemonic control of the neo-Confucian regime (Sookjin Lee 2001). While both the shamanic tradition and the Buddhist tradition managed to survive the loss
in status brought by the political suppression of religious others in Joseon
society, the shared oppression served to encourage some blending of the
two traditions. As Buddhist temples and shamanic shrines were forced to
relocate to the outskirts of society, Buddhists and shamans found common ground. Forests or mountains were sought out for the dwellings of
Buddhism, and shamans found Buddhist temples and mountains to be
suitable locations for prayers and shamanic rituals (Sookjin Lee 2001).

2. The Practice of Shamans in a New Social Strata

Upon the advent of the new cultural politics of the Joseon society, class
standing determined social mobility and legal rights, whereas the public arena was inflexibly subdivided in terms of gender. Social space was
clearly dichotomized into public and domestic arenas, as the neo-Confucian moral order helped to secure the power of the small ruling class who
constituted the *yangban* group (S. M. Lee 1994). Lower-class standings
and women were disadvantaged by the strict class system of the highly
stratified society, the social character of which could be comparable, in
general, to the traditional caste system of India or to any other society
that was dominated by traditional male supremacy (S. M. Lee 1994; Berreman 1972).[17] Relegated for subjugation and obedience, the socially

16 New outcast groups were classified by the neo-Confucian regime. Those who
were physical laborers tended to be belittled and placed in the lowest class standing,
with prostitutes, butchers, clowns, monks, shamans, and slaves.

17. The class strata in the early Joseon society were primarily divided into two
groups, *yangin* and *cheonin*. The *yangin* class itself had a three-level hierarchy:

powerless had limited capacity to act, other than loyally observing the established moral order and responding with filial piety toward their elders, superiors, and males, in general. In this regard, it is certainly proper to say that the strict neo-Confucian class politics constituted a de facto self-beatifying power mechanism and thereby supported the ideology of male supremacy in early Joseon society.

In the practicality of neo-Confucian cultural politics, the practice of shamans was put in a difficult position. Shamans were subjected to negative perception, while suspicion grew about their engagement in the public arena under the changes that accompanied the rise of the Joseon regime. A better understanding of the ongoing practice of shamans may be glimpsed by examining two emblematic issues, class stratification and gendered social space, in the given condition of political segregation under the neo-Confucian regime.

At the end of the Goryeo dynasty, when the Buddhist regime had become a markedly corrupt and incompetently administered society, the *yangban* group took the lead in shifting to the succeeding regime with a new moral politics, with what became the Joseon dynasty (Y. C. Kim 1982, 22–23).[18] They were a twofold ruling group, with Confucian literati and military personnel ranking at the top of the class strata, both in Goryeo and early Joseon societies (S. M. Lee 1994; Yun 1996; J. Hwang 1995; K. B. Lee 1984, 58).[19] The revolutionary spirit settled in as supportive of

yangban as the high-ranking group, *jungin* as the middle-ranking, and *sang-min* as the low-ranking group. The lower status *cheonin* group belonged to government, while being in charge of all kinds of grunt work, with little autonomy. Both the high-ranking elites and military commanders belonged to the *yangban* class who constituted the ruling class, protected by the law and politics of the early Joseon society, and who could have landholdings and slaves. The middle class *jungin* group was in charge of regional administration and skilled work, while the low-level *sangmin* class included farmers, local traders, and handicrafters who did not have any opportunity for formal education. The established social class structure of the early Joseon society was dominated by the top-ranking royal class who obtained legal rights to essentially enslave the lower-ranking classes, while treating them harshly.

18. Buddhism became the established ideology as the national religion during the Goryeo dynasty (918 CE–1392 CE).

19. A precise date for the entry of Confucianism into the Korean peninsula from China cannot be stated, but it was in place in Korea by at least 2200 years ago. Confucian teaching and practice expanded its influence upon the moral ethos in Korean society from that time on, helped by the fact that its philosophical prescripts were not judged to be hostile to other religious traditions such as Taoism, Buddhism, and even Shamanism. Simply put, prototypical Confucianism was at ease with the pluralistic and syncretistic religious perspectives in Korea until the rise of a stricter

the neo-Confucian ideology that became the backbone of morality, so as to control and unify society. Religious others were officially out of step from the new monolithic Confucian moral politics, with its authoritarian atmosphere. In practice, the welfare of the common people and society was subordinated to the vehement desires of the neo-Confucian leaders who concentrated on the sustainability of power by means of the new religiopolitical configuration.

Buttressed by the new politics, the social status of each distinctive class standing was justified by reference to mandated moral practices in social relations, not only to the superior classes but also to their own internal levels. For example, the virtue of *hyo* (filial piety) could be interpreted as appropriate servitude by younger people to the elderly and by children to parents, whereas that of *choong* (loyalty) could be applied to a lower class to serve those of higher class or superior position. So, the socially stratified system served the *yangban* group in securing benefits to control the public arena as its own locus for social and legal power. Violation or disobedience of the mandated neo-Confucian moral order was often labeled as political treason and led to harsh condemnation and punishment. This system was particularly costly and disadvantageous for the lower classes and the socially powerless. In striving to ensure *yangban* loyalty both within and beyond the circle of *yangban* and thereby their neo-Confucian identity, the ruling class sought to maintain their self-serving neo-Confucian norms (Ministry of Culture 1996, 60). The prestigious *yangban* status itself could have been at stake when their religious engagement in other than Confucianism was recognized by their *yangban* colleagues (Walraven 1999).[20]

Meanwhile, the sudden fall of shamans shifted the shamans' cultural venue to the fringes of society, as then belonging to the "margin of mess," where their anti-structural life and deviant cultural practices nonetheless managed to continue (Babcock 1978, 28). The "margin of mess" is a locus of cultural paradox in which cultural biases and social contempt prevail, although cultural deviance itself emerges as a social threat (Babcock 1978, 28). In order to affirm the critique of the mainstream cultural politics, the Joseon regime advanced a strategy of labeling any types of cultural deviance as social stigma by penalizing them to be marked as socially illegitimate and immoral. This dualistic moral paradigm ultimately

---

neo-Confucianism in the Joseon dynasty.

20. Song Siyeol was one of the most famous Confucianists in the second half of the Joseon period.

helped to provoke public obedience in naïve collectiveness, in accord with the mainstream order, from fear of social condemnation or segregation. In other words, categorizing the "margin of mess" in the cultural politics of Joseon served to sanction the mainstream order's ideological values and institutional power in society and therein benefited its political sustainability.

In respect to the interplay between cultural anomaly and status quo in the social process of the present post-structural era, Cornel West comments:

> There can be no artistic breakthrough or social progress without some form of crisis in civilization—a crisis usually generated by organizations or collectivities that convince ordinary people to put their bodies and lives on the line . . . but there is a guarantee that the status quo will remain or regress if no pressure is applied at all. (West 1994, 66)

Here, the paradox is the mechanism between the "margin of mess" and the mainstream power that they mutually rely on each other regardless of either upheaval or the status quo. That is, the dynamic between the mainstream culture and the "margin of mess" never ends with cultural separation but ultimately and mutually reincorporates in new forms. Society progresses in the encounter through engaging various forms of turning points in history that could cause various forms of crisis and thus create pain for the common people who frequently suffer further in the aftermath. However, turning points and historical breakthroughs ultimately replicate the more-or-less status quo of a society in the course of a social process that, in the absence of immediate pressure, reverts to ordinariness, as noted by West.

Globally, numerous non-Western others used to be compelled to assimilate to the master culture, virtually forced to surrender their own cultural values and practices in the history of "religious" expansion. It was a historical disjunction on the part of the natives, yet native cultural particularities in the non-Western hemisphere have not been annihilated in their culturally constituted collective consciousness, as practiced in their ordinariness. This somewhat explains the tendency of cultural "routinization" in human society despite either internal or external power interferences.

Similarly, when the traditionally routine practice of shamans faced a crisis of eradication under the new power politics of the neo-Confucian regime, shamans were not alone. Buddhism, which had been nationally esteemed during the Goryeo regime that preceded the Joseon dynasty, was also reproved in the public arena. Nonetheless, both traditions survived, in continuation of cultural practice, by keeping themselves in the "margin of mess," notwithstanding the abrasive political shift that sought to create a uniform society by eliminating the former rationale of culturally accepting shamanic or Buddhist practices.

Labeled as *umsa* under neo-Confucian politics, which implies secretive or licentious sacrifices, according to the references in the Chinese characters, the shamanic practice was institutionally banned for public engagement unless there were specific administrative approval (Walraven 1999). Shamanic ownership of private land was ruled out to be illegitimate (Walraven 1999). This was an entire dismissal from the formerly prestigious role and status of shamans.

In contrast to the cultural negation during the Joseon regime, the practice of shamans had previously been incorporated into various ritual ceremonies and divinatory consultations concerning communal, national, and religious affairs. Some ritual vestiges are still found in contemporary community-based shamanic rituals in Korean life. For example, rituals for a big catch of fish are still performed in oceanside fishing communities, while rituals for a good harvest are also still presented in traditional farming communities. Prior to the Joseon regime, female shamans were not deprecated but venerated as public figures. Frequently serving as counselors and/or superhuman agents in cases of national or royal affairs, shamans had a power and authority that were nationally recognized as aiding the wellness of the nation and the local community, at least until the rise of Joseon regime.

A historical record indicates the female *seon-guan* as an officially entitled shamanic intermediary and therein granted authority to officiate at state-sponsored religious ceremonies during the Goryeo dynasty,[21] particularly for the two previously mentioned nationally monumental ceremonies, the *Palgwanhoe* and *Yeondeunghoe* (Ilyon 1972, 52; Cho 2004; Y. C. Kim 1982, 23–24; Vermeersch 2007). The same document also provides an account of the royal order of King UiJong, issued in the third month of the twenty-second year of his reign during the Goryeo dynasty (Y. Kim 1992). According to the royal order in the document,

21. Ilyon (1206–1289) was a Buddhist monk under the *Goryeo* dynasty when Buddhism buttressed the political regime. The original document comprises five parts in two books.

one of the first things the king commanded on a trip to the capital city, Pyeongyang,[22] was to take a selection of *seon-guan* (Y. Kim 1992). Informed by the given role and status of the shaman, these illustrations derived from historical documents suggest positive and unbigoted social reactions to shamanic practice, distributive religious diversity, and secured female ritual authority until the Joseon dynasty. Particularly, the record of the female *seon-guan* as the governmental shamanic intermediary states that the social standing of *seon-guan* was as an older sibling of a high-ranking governmental official linked to the royal family (Ilyon 1972, 52). The aforementioned illustrations from a time prior to the Joseon dynasty suggest that the shamanic tradition was closely associated with the ordinary lives of the common people, regardless of class status and gender difference. Shamans themselves held a socially prestigious position in the traditional society that preceded the Joseon dynasty. However, the new cultural politics no longer sanctioned shamans as superhuman agents but reduced them to subhuman trivia (J. Seo 2003; Kister 1997).

3. The Practice of Shamans in the Interplay of Gendered Social Space

As the prestigious public status and amicable social reaction previously granted to the practice of shaman were dismissed by the inauguration of the neo-Confucian regime of the Joseon dynasty, the earlier cultural routine of gender inclusiveness and tolerant class diversity was no longer the atmosphere encountered in the tradition of shamanic practice under the new order of male supremacy and strict social stratification. The collective solidarity of the traditional community was challenged by a new climate that fostered tension through stressing nascent dichotomies, such as new and old, neo-Confucian and the rest, the upper-class *yangban* and the lower-class *cheonmin*. The community fell apart in a cultural break between the neo-Confucian public and the folkloristic private, and the male public arena and the female private underground. Cultural activities and social behaviors were mandated to conform to the new Confucian moral ideology of Joseon regime.

People experience an "intellectual and moral schizophrenia" when their autonomy to access spiritual powers is interfered with by the

22. Pyeongyang was one of the capital cities in early Korean history, a site presently located in North Korea.

institutional order, as noted by Sidney Mead, an American historian, in reference to major contextual changes (Mead 1975, 125). So to speak, the mental and ideological lives of communities experience a fictional world when their freedom is restricted, so as to fit in with an imposed cultural uniformity, and when they are therein institutionally limited from seeking their accustomed spiritual power (Mead 1975, 125). Although the locus of Mead's discussion is particularly situated in the American immigrant context, his discourse is nonetheless illuminating for any discussion of the experiences and associated expressions caused by spiritual anomie when confronted with contextual impediment. Indeed, any structural distress may produce cultural undergrounds created as an anti-structure, remote from public attention, so as to serve as the locus of deviant spiritual practices. The undergrounds thus serve to preserve miscellaneous cultures as a "margin of mess" on the fringes of society (Babcock 1978, 28). One of these affected practices was shamanism when faced with the oppressive cultural pressure in the Joseon regime.

The female crowned with religious authority in the shamanic tradition was previously revered but then belittled under male supremacy, as the practice of shamans was officially deprecated as a sordid custom. Within the mainstream hostility, immersed in widespread negation of religious others, the practice of shamans was displaced into the underground and preserved in private, largely reliant upon individual callings with a rather minimal role in public and communal affairs (Walraven 1999). That is, the tradition of Korean shamanism began settling in more as a modest subculture in survival mode, due to mainstream negation. It was thereby more internalized as part of the cultural ethos in the Korean collective consciousness than externally celebrated as explicitly active in society.

The de facto cultural politics of the Joseon regime created a prototype of moral dualism, so as to establish a fixed order to control society, a structural dichotomy that not only separated but also gendered the social space between the public arena and the private sector. The social space was morally ramified into two arenas; a male public arena, *oe*, meaning "outside," to be communal; and a female private arena, designated as *nae*, implying "inside," to be individual. Gender roles were socially determined in accordance with the masculine moral distinction of class stratum and the locus of spatial belonging. What was thereby morally postulated was not only gender disparity but also social immobility, associated with spatial stratification for male and female, and for the public and the private.

When dismissed from communal affairs in the public arena, the lives of women became entrenched in only domestic roles. Lowborn women were doubly disfavored by not only their female gender but also their lower social standing, in which the female shaman, *mudang*, took part. An intriguing question in this matter is how the practice of shamans was negotiated to engage in the strictly gendered space.

When the social space is stratified to be gendered and thereby re-served for men, the division itself quintessentially advances a taken-for-granted social environment for men, so as to uncomplicatedly control public affairs and affirm the legitimacy of male supremacy, while imped-ing the social mobility of females. Therefore, demarcating the private sector as a feminine space for domestic roles renders women socially powerless, those not to be heard or seen in public. Rather, women are to be circumscribed within a locus of vulnerability, easily marked for blame, shame, and guilt (H. Seo 1991). In this regard, the location of the shamanic practice was more in the cultural *nae*, the domestic or private arena, under the cultural politics of the Joseon era.

The calling for the shaman continued in part due to a culturally pos-tulated nostalgia under situations of urgent and unresolved personal and familial mishaps as well as ordinary needs to be met. A selected few sha-mans were still called upon to serve in the royal quarters for particular ceremonies related to natural disasters, country-wide traumas, or royal familial affairs (Walraven 1999). In this light, the practice of shamans was located in the mixed atmosphere between public disregard and private want, generally branded as "low culture," in contrast to the seemingly prosperous neo-Confucianism (Walraven 1999).

The cultural admixture was already impending as the earlier Go-ryeo dynasty drew near to its end (A. Kim 1996, 20).[23] A poem composed by one of the anti-shamanist literati at the end of the Goryeo dynasty foreshadowed what was lying ahead in the sense of antipathy, by means of a pungent satire of the female shaman,

> In *Goryeo* these customs have not yet been swept away,
> Females are witches and males are wizards.
> They say of themselves "Spirits descend into my body."
> And yet, I hear this, smile, and sigh. . . .

23. The Goryeo dynasty immediately preceded the Joseon dynasty, at which time the *mudang*, the female shaman, was classified as belonging to the *cheonmin* class, the lowest social class standing. Seven more categories were included in the *cheonmin* class in Joseon society.

My intent is to get rid of [these shamans] completely
And wash clean the shelters of the people. (McBride 2007,
241–42; Walraven 1999).[24]

An aura of distaste and contempt in the portrayal of the shaman runs through this poem.[25] Yet, considering that both this poem and the royal document were produced during the very same period, the sense of aversion imparted in this poem looks quite remote from the mainstream cultural tolerance toward the practice of shamans, granted particularly to the female *seon-guan*, the governmentally assigned shamanic intermediary. Presumably, the cultural atmosphere in that society at the end of Goryeo dynasty could have contributed to the belittlement of shamanism (Ilyon 1972, 52). That is, an antipathetic climate for public persecution of shamans and their practices was already imminent by the end of the Goryeo dynasty, although society during this earlier period was more tolerant of shamanic practice than during the Joseon dynasty.

A stern rejection of shamanism in the Joseon dynasty decreed that the pantheon of many shamanic deities be officially removed from the public scene. A narrative from the *Sejong Silok*, the chronicles of King Sejong as a historical document from the beginning of the Joseon dynasty, briefly illustrates the altered climate and thereby maltreatment of shamans, particularly female shamans, while shifting from the earlier cultural leniency to an institutional negation under the new regime:

> The king said, "There was an evil *mudang*, the female shaman, during the King Taejong regime. She was expelled out of the capital city, Gyungseong, and not allowed to mingle with people."[26]

24. The poem is entitled "Nomu p'yeon" [Lay of the Old Shaman] and was composed by Yi Gyubo at the end of the Goryeo dynasty. Yi described shamanism as a degenerative form of religion of Buddhist origin.

25. The poem particularly details the description of a female shaman: "Her face is rough, the hair on her temples is separated; she is fifty years of age . . . she fills her belly with sour and sweet, tasteless wine; jumping and dancing, raising her body, her head touches the ridgepole."

26. *Sejong Silok* [Sejong Chronicles] consists of 163 sections in 153 books. It was recorded during the regime of King Sejong (1418 to 1450 CE) of the Joseon dynasty. The document is currently located at *Gyujanggak Hangukhak yeonguso* [Gyujanggak Korean Research Institution] in Seoul, Korea. It was classified as a national treasure in 1973 and added to the UNESCO World Heritage List in 1997. The specific section quoted in this discussion is from part 72, written in May 12, *Jeongchuk* Day (day of the ox), 1436.

No additional explanation is provided in this record as to what aspect of the *mudang*'s demeanor was considered to be evil, why she was required to remove herself, or what physical restrictions were imposed upon her social connections. However, this brief illustration still provides a glimpse of the neo-Confucian royal administration's cultural and physical mistreatment of shamanic practitioners, who were mostly female. Not only had shamans fallen socially into the lowest of the low class, but also they were institutionally written off as immoral (Jeon 1994). The *mudang*, the female shaman, suffered the critical loss of ritual freedom that was requisite for the ordinary activities of the shamanic practitioner. Shamans were jettisoned from society, suffering dismissal from the community that was supposed to be the main ritual stage of the shamanic profession (Jeon 1994).

As to the sense that desperate punishments must have desperate rewards, the option of heavy taxation left a door open to public opportunities for shamanic practice. The limited opportunities for public ritual opportunities were unbarred in favor of the hefty amounts of taxes paid. This policy was challenged by the cultural politics among the *yangban* administrators who were ultimately divided into two contrasting parties: the assenters' party, in support of shamans, with more interest in the economic profit from the tax revenue acquired from shamanic practices; and the dissenters' party, who were more desirous of the neo-Confucian cultural uniformity of the community, so as to sanction the contemporary political regime (Y. C. Kim 1982, 130–31; Walraven 1999).[27] The tax revenue conformists of the *yangban* party ultimately prevailed and therein selectively loosened the suppression of shamanic practice in the public arena, giving way to the cultural continuance of shamanic practice despite the limited extent of support (Walraven 1999).

Shamans who desperately desired rewards by seeking opportunities to practice publicly chose to register their names with the governmental administration, notwithstanding the heavy taxes that were federally levied on their practices. Given the rather limited scale of openings for public practice, two groups of shamans emerged, settling on their own shamanic community at the margins of society: some shamans registered with the government, whereas others served privately (N. Lee and Seo 2008, 204; P. Lee 1993). Referred to as superhuman counselors and/or healers, some shamans acquired public sponsorship in order to perform

27. For a discussion of shamanic taxation, see citations from *Sejong Sillok* [Joseon dynasty chronicles] in bibliography.

ceremonial rituals at the royal courts, such as those for rain or the healing of the sick (Y. Kim 1982, 31).[28] Only a select few shamans gained the
privileged status of becoming a royal shaman, *gungmu*, or a governmental shaman, *gwanmu* (Y. Kim 1982, 31; A. Kim 1996, 21). Some of them
also served poor patients by becoming official shamanic healers at public
health centers such as the East and West Medical Center, *Dongseohwalinseo*, during the Joseon dynasty (A. Kim 1996, 21).[29]

Yet, unforeseen shamanic activity was nurtured in the private sector,
which was segregated from the masculine, public arena. The private sector ultimately served the preponderance of the female population, while
assisting women to have easy access to private shamanic rituals. Female
shamans also had easier access to female clients in the private sector.
Concerned about familial welfare, the success of male households, the
health and peace of their lives, etc., women of the *yangban* class, the social upper class, actively resorted to shamanic consultation in the private
sector (Y. C. Kim 1982, 131).

The irony therein was the indulgent demeanor of the neo-Confucian
literati toward these private shamanic ceremonies, the men being well
aware of the reasons for their wives' engaging in shamanic rituals, particularly in seeking for public success and well-being for their husbands,
as well as for familial welfare. That is, the *yangban* households were willing to overlook the official illegitimacy of the private shamanic ritual in
which the wives and female households were involved (Y. C. Kim 1982,
131). The harshness of public policy was set aside when male supremacy
was promoted behind the public arena, therein encouraging the private
sector to be a more cultural periphery. The de facto cultural politics subdivided the social space to masculinize the society of the Joseon dynasty,
but the private sector was subversively allowed to flourish in the growth
of the shamanic practices (Walraven 2007).

Domestic private space was also morally gendered in a dichotomy
in a similar manner. The women's quarter, named *anche* as the inside sector, was more privatized from the men's quarter, *bakkatche*, as the outside
sector. Particularly in the dwelling of the noble class, the women's quarter
was protected from random intrusion by outsiders or males who were

28. The Joseon government controlled the number of appointments of registered
shamans whose service was focused on the concerns of the royal class or the shamanic
healing of the sick, particularly at the public health center.

29. *Dongseohwalinseo* was the public health service center operated particularly
for those lower-class people who could not afford to pay for medical treatments.

morally prohibited, except under special circumstances. In this regard, the private sector—again, gendered between *an*, the women's quarter, and *bak*, the men's quarter—further contributed to an increase in women's engagement and in the female shaman's activities that were shielded from encounters with *yangban* males as well as from public attention (Walraven 2007).

Shamans survived the disconcerting cultural politics of the controversial male/female, inside/outside duality of the Joseon regime. While shamanism was disregarded as profane by the *yangban* administration, shamans were welcomed as superhuman intermediaries by women in the private sector. As the *yangban* group, the ruling class, governed the public arena while sustaining the top rank of the class strata in society, upper-class wives and women also contrastingly controlled the private realm, with privilege in the same manner. The vertical power practice of the *yangban*-class women in their private sector was disrupted by aspects of competition and jealousy within the circle of the many wives and concubines of the polygamous family structure in traditional Joseon society. Given these circumstances, the female shaman, *mudang*, could have been a great companion to those upper-class women who were unheard in public but were tempted to consult and hear from superhuman agents more safely and privately. In other words, it was easier for female shamans to serve clients in the private sector, thus avoiding official and public contempt. This particular environment also enabled female shamans to take advantage of privileges associated with working with the upper-class *yangban* women who enhanced the shamans' sense of worth and compensation while surviving as the socially untouchable, *cheonmin*.

Interestingly, the very shamans who suffered immensely from the neo-Confucian *yangban* male power system mimetically operated similar power relations among themselves. It is still unclear if a certain power mechanism already existed in the pre-Joseon shamanic tradition. Yet, a clear status distinction prevailed between the governmental and the private shaman, as well as between the initiated and the novice shaman, a stratification that resembled the power relations of the Joseon regime and therein led to an operative power structure among shamans themselves (Y. C. Kim 1982, 130–31). The shamans sponsored by the royal and upper-class women benefitted more from their professional opportunities and upper-class connections. These conditions then led them to imitate the power practice of upper-class prerogative against the underprivileged shaman (Y. C. Kim 1982, 130–31). Likewise, the experienced senior shamans harshly dominated and exploited assistant or neophyte sha-mans. This mimicry of the upper-class power practice can be interpreted as an ambivalent "sign of resistance" to the dominant power and/or as expressing desires to be empowered like the master. This atmosphere ultimately produced a form of ambiguous hybridity within the shamanic tradition (Bhabha 1994, 121).[30] Continued to this day, this vertical power mechanism is particularly visible in the locus of traditional shamanic apprenticeship.

Meanwhile, suspicion grew from the clientele, when the outcomes from ritual or divination did not satisfy the costly shamanic fees, as sha-mans sought to increase economic profit for survival under the political pressure against them (Y. C. Kim 1982, 130–31). Given all these cultural impacts, the aspect of ambivalence continued to affect the cultural aware-ness within and beyond the shamanic tradition, in regard to social re-sponse from the class and gender strata, including the conflict between private calling and public deprecation, and between superhuman power and mere superstition.

4. The Mimetic Practice of Korean Shamans in a Changed Cultural Venue

Specific traces of power relations and moral precepts of the Joseon regime are markedly reproduced by cultural mimesis in the practice of shamans, as the indelible impact of the neo-Confucian cultural politics continues into contemporary Korean society. The survival of the shamanic prac-tice involves using the camouflage of mimetic performance of the power modality and authoritative character of the *yangban* class in the Joseon regime. Clearly marked in contemporary ritual, traces are still visible in the images and personae of the *Janggun shin*, the military general deity in military costume, and the *Daegam shin*, the prerogative foreman deity (Jung Lee 1981, 31–34).[31] The masquerade ritual performance of shamans

30. Bhabha indicates that mimicry represents a form of defensive mechanism for resistance, while creating a form of hybridity, as he states: "To the extent to which discourse is a form of defensive warfare, mimicry marks those moments of civil dis-obedience within the discipline of civility."

31. The world of shamanic deities is mostly masculine, with only a couple of deities being feminine such as *Bari Gongju* and *Samsin* grandmother (J. Kim 1996). These deities are impersonated by means of shamanic possession in each act over the course of the twelve episodic segments, *gori*, in the shamanic ritual, *gut*. The *gori* refers to "the

is acted out as a defensive mechanism in the shamanic ritual, implementing military equipment reflective of the weaponry of the Joseon regime, such as moon-shape swords, tridents, and flags. These forms of military weaponry are still employed as important ritual props in contemporary shamanic performances (Haeoe Gongbo-Gwan 1996, 65; Jung Lee 1981, 32; J. Kim 1996).

Above all, central among the neo-Confucian elements, is a moral ethos that is also thoroughly embodied in the shamanic practice. This moral ethos includes male supremacy as a core cultural element, which is manifested by the neo-Confucian moral values of loyalty and filial piety in social relations, as well as the related moral virtue of *mubyeong jangsu* (good health and longevity) as a key aspect of individual life.[32] Although the item of *mubyeong jangsu* itself is not considered as directly representing a neo-Confucian moral virtue, its importance in the moral ethos cannot be disregarded in connection with a premature death or illness that prevents fulfillment of the essential moral obligation of filial piety. These moral values are materially represented in both religious traditions, as manifested in the shamanic ritual, *gut*, and in the neo-Confucian tradition of ancestor worship. The difference between the two rituals in respect to the moral ethos is that the ancestral spirits are experienced as actively responsive in the shamanic ritual but not in the Confucian ancestor worship. Thus, it is proper to say that ritually addressing the moral violation for remedies or good fortune is the shamanic construct, though the moral ethos deriving from the influence of neo-Confucianism.

Cultural negotiation through mimesis played a prominent role in the survival of shamanic practice in the face of neo-Confucian cultural disparagement, which ultimately promoted a form of religious hybrid, with neo-Confucian cultural characters in the shamanic ritual. The physical evidence of political suppression upon the rise of Joseon dynasty in 1392 CE is strongly engrafted, particularly in the cultural images and personae of deities or spirits. The social figures who ascended to the throne of

---

sequences of acts" that are composed of a stream of entertainment, such as with music, dance, chanting, narratives, oracles, emotions, etc. (Ch'oe 1989).

32. In traditional Korean culture, there are ten natural objects, *sipjangsang*, that symbolically represent *jangsu* (longevity). The ten longevity symbols include the sun, mountains, water, clouds, rocks, pine trees, elixirs, tortoises, cranes, and deer. The oldest historical record that identifies these ten symbols is the work of Yi Saek, *Mokeunjip* [Mokeun Collection]. Saek was a neo-Confucian scholar who lived at the end of the Goryeo dynasty. The ten recognized symbols became culturally popular in various arenas during the Joseon dynasty (H. J. Lee and Lee 2010, 133; K. P. Kim 2011, 361).

deities in the shamanic ritual represent images in the power structure of the early Joseon dynasty, such as a military general, authoritative upper-class male personae, military instruments, and uniforms. These images are still visible in the contemporary practice of shamanism. The restive context of neo-Confucian politics no longer exists, but the forms of cultural mimesis and the associated ritual hybridity have become significant components in the shamanic tradition. These mimetic features provide a good means to trace how the oppressors of the past have been ritually consecrated by the cultural mimesis of shamans, notwithstanding the loss of the original reference.

During the reign of King Sunjo (1800–1834 CE), the number of registered female shamanic practitioners was 1,519, which constituted two-thirds of the entire shamanic registration, as noted in Joseon financial and military documents (Y. Seo 1972).[33] Nonetheless, the entire number of shamanic practitioners, including unregistered shamans, private shamans, and shamanic assistants, has been estimated to have been about 45,000 during the same period (Y. C. Kim 1982, 133). Later, the Japanese census conducted in 1930 under the Japanese annexation of Korea recorded 12,380 as the total numbers of shamans. Of this number, again, two-thirds were female shamans (Governor-General 1932, 10–12). Recently, the population of the active shamanic profession has been estimated as about 500,000 in contemporary South Korea (*Chosun Ilbo* 2022; Song 2020).[34] The statistical data points to shamanic rituals, wisdom, and fortune-telling as having a long and active history in Korean society, while functioning as a culturally therapeutic mechanism, although various developments, such as the growth of Protestantism, modern science, and medical technology, over the last century have encouraged cultural hostility toward and moral contempt for the practice of shamanism.

---

33. This data was found in *Chaeyong Pyeon* (a finance chapter) and *Musejo* (an article on taxation for shamans) in *Man'gi Yoram*. *Man'gi Yoram* is a document from the financial and military records of the later Joseon dynasty. The document was compiled by Youngbo Seo, Sanggyu Shim, and other governmental scholars by the order of King Sunjo in 1808, Sunjo's eighth year of kingship. The finance section consists of 6 parts and 62 articles in 6 books, while the military section consists of 5 parts and 23 articles in 5 books. *Man'gi Yoram* was originally handwritten, but it was copied as a typed record at Jung Chuwon of Joseon Chongdokbu in 1938. The most recent publication was edited in modernized Korean by Minjok Moonhwa Yeongooso of Goryeo University in 1972.

34. The current shamanic professionals are mostly shamanic fortune-tellers, as there is rather less interest in traditional rituals.

The traditional practice of Korean shamans has been blamed and therein labeled as superstitious or false, time and time again, by the power of political hegemonies. These bigotries have fostered cultural biases in regard to the practice of Korean shamanism. Meanwhile, pro-shamanic voices have continued to be raised for shamanic rituals and academic attention, together with many scholarly publications. One of the most globally acclaimed Korean shamans, Keum-hwa Kim, states in a recent interview that she finds the practice of Korean shamanism to be of great interest to the current public (J. Park 2012). Kwang-yeong Shin, a sociology professor at Chung-Ang University, Seoul, is quoted in the same article, commenting on the present cultural role of shamanism in Korea. According to Shin, shamanism in Korea serves to assist people who face the pressures of modern Korean life, with that life's uncertainty and insecurity, and to ameliorate the unsatisfactory religious life in mainstream institutions that do not provide "tailored" answers to individual needs or demands (J. Park 2012). Also to the point is the comment of a shaman dancing about in the colorful dress of a former time, which might seem outdated in terms of the techno-savvy culture in present-day Korea, a comment that changes the focus: "We are like a hospital . . . . We do surgery on people's bad luck" (Choe 2007).

Summing up the situation, in seeking to understand the comparative components that have altered the practice of Korean shamanism, this account of the brief history and cultural role of Korean shamanism significantly assists the examination of the shamanic practice in a specific time and space in a new cultural context, engaging a Christianized Korean community. In like manner, as the practice of shamanism was fashioned with the image and moral ethos of a neo-Confucian regime, the pantheon of the Korean immigrant shamanic practice of the U.S. is already marked with the U.S. national flag and the regional mountain deity on the altar. Cultural belittlement in the perception of shamanism may be more abrasive in the protestantized Korean immigrant community in the U.S. than in the Korean homeland. However, a culturally attributed therapeutic mechanism persists in private calls, mostly of the first-generation Korean diaspora who support a culturally postulated nostalgia in the practice of shamans.

3

Korean Exorcism

Charismatic Christian Exorcism or Shamanic Exorcism?
Driving Out Demons or Women?

IN THE NINETEENTH CENTURY, the arrival of Western Evangelical Protestantism in the land of morning calm, Korea, severely disrupted the native culture with its insistence on converting the people to Western Christianity and serving to fragment the coalition of traditional Korean collectiveness, communal solidarity, and pride of cultural assets. This endeavor, as an outreach of the dominant Euro-American world, had some initial success. Consequently, the diverse religious traditions and folk cultural practices that had long been observed in Korea suddenly faced a major challenge and became, in part, something to discard as a subject of repentance and even as even an object of exorcism.

Meanwhile, the growth of the immigrant Protestant church has played a central role in the life of Korean immigrant community since the first group of immigrants, providing a center for bonding ethnic solidarity and for supporting the immigrant adjustment in U.S. mainstream society. This community's progress has also fostered the growth of an uncharitable wall of segregation against non-Protestant others who are often rigorously denounced by their own community that thrives on a kind of ethical monotheism. Culturally, the legacy of gender disparity, which is defensively buttressed by Protestant institutionalism, also persists in the Korean diaspora.

The fears and worries about survival that play a vital and immediate role in the life of the diaspora community often lead to odd incidents that then bring an aggregation of cultural particularities to public attention. Included in this mix, with Evangelical Protestant beliefs, are the peculiarities of Korean shamanic religiosity, culturally emphasizing belief in spirits, institutionally appropriating belief in the inferiority of women, and correspondingly religiously encouraging subordination of women, which frequently is accompanied by violence.

This chapter examines some peculiar aspects of cultural presentation in the life of the Korean immigrant community, focused on a form of charismatic Christian ritual called *anchal-gido* (O'Neill 1997).[1] This form of Christian prayer includes physical contact, often forceful, and can lead to injuries, ranging from minor bruises to broken bones and even to the death of the ritual recipient. I am personally intrigued by this form of ritual, for it seems to involve multifarious aspects underpinned by collective cultural perceptions on the subjects of women, mental illness, male dominance, spirit possession, etc. Above all, note that this form of prayer, which is occasionally very violent, provokes some public bias particularly related to shamanic practice, which is prompted partially by the culturally shared belief in spirits within both the shamanic and the conservative Christian traditions. This type of ritual, associated with incidents that have been highly publicized, may offer a window into the cultural location of Korean shamanism by illustrating the culturally constituted public reactions in the immigrant society in the U.S. Furthermore, such ritual incidents may also provide an insight that closes the gap between shamanic practice within Korean itself and the transnational shamanic practice in a preponderantly Christianized Korean immigrant context. In pursuing this connection, this chapter seeks to understand the cultural atmosphere of the immigrant shamans and the characteristics of their shamanic practice.

Additional questions that will be raised in this chapter are: (1) How does the collective cultural sharing of the traditional Korean folk belief in spirits bring about confusion between two different religious traditions,

---

1. The *anchal-gido*, a prayer with laying on of hands, is the title of a Christian charismatic healing ritual performed so as to drive out demons from mentally ill persons, in the belief that demons dwell in the body of the mentally ill person, causing affliction. The form of *anchal-gido* potentially involves physical contact, seeking to force evil spirits to depart. When the form of *anchal-gido* develops into violent beating, punching, and/or choking, it can cause serious physical injuries to the person, even death, in extreme cases. This ritual is performed mostly in the Christian charismatic Protestant sector, and therein "the ritual process includes loud prayers, singing hymns, laying on hands, speaking in tongues in the invocation of the name of Holy Spirit" (O'Neill 1997).

namely Korean shamanic practice and the charismatic Christian healing ritual, the *anchal-gido*? (2) What was the preexisting condition that encouraged the erroneous presumption that shamanic ritual involved instances of violence, when the ritual involved was actually from a particular Christian group? (3) Why is it that Korean women frequently become "willing victims" in the religious worlds of both shamanism and the charismatic Protestant community?

The discussion in this chapter, responding to these questions, is organized into four sections: (1) being marked as a perpetual stigma: Korean immigrant shamanism in the dawn of Korean Protestantism in the U.S.; (2) Korean exorcism: "bare-knuckle style"; (3) the Korean collective consciousness in the belief in spirits; and (4) Korean women religiously portrayed as perpetual wretches.

1. Being Marked as a Perpetual Stigma

Korean Immigrant Shamanism in the Dawn of Korean Protestantism in the U.S.

Alongside the neo-Confucian cultural politics that fundamentally shaped the Joseon society and continued in their cultural impact even afterwards, Korean society underwent an additional major religio-cultural influence with the arrival of Protestant Christianity in the inland Korean peninsula in the early nineteenth century.[2] From the very beginning of its presence,

---

2. In fact, Catholicism had already been introduced into the Joseon society prior to the coming of Protestant Christianity, and had faced physical persecutions for about one hundred years, followed by a period of considerable religiopolitical resistance to any Western cultural influx. During the Japanese invasion of Korean territory in 1594, there were two Catholic priests—the Spanish Jesuit priest Gregorio de Céspedes and the Japanese friar Foucan Eion—who came to the Korean peninsula so as to provide sacraments for the Japanese soldiers. Moreover, about seven thousand Korean war captives in Japan converted to Catholicism during the same period of invasion. From 1784, when an early Joseon Catholic, Seung-Hoon Lee, presided over the baptism of two adult Koreans, the small Catholic populace began to be subjected to long-term political persecution that lasted for about one hundred years. The first Protestant Christian missionary arrived in Korea in 1832, a German named Karl Friedrich August Gützlaff. He initiated a Western Evangelical expansionism into Korea. In 1884, the first Methodist missionary, R. S. Maclay, and the first Presbyterian missionary, G. W. Knox, came from Japan to open up Christian missions in Korea. Shortly thereafter, in 1885, three additional Protestant missionaries arrived and significantly expanded the process of protestantization, namely, the Methodist H. G. Appenzeller, who mainly led an educational mission, and the Presbyterians W. T. and Mary Scranton, who focused on

the Western Protestant cultural credo was deemed too foreign to be accommodated within the traditional Korean community, and it provoked immediate resistance and mainstream hostility. That is, Korean society faced a tremendous challenge from the encounter with the new and radically different cultural perspectives, producing anxiety and fear. Western culture came along with Protestant Christianity, and the combination fundamentally changed the contours of Korean culture. In particular, the Protestant Christian populace has grown ever since.

Ordinary people were suffering from both internal and external social adversity in Korean society at the close of the nineteenth century. Internally, they were exploited by the entrenched bureaucratic feudal system, and externally, they were devastated by the Sino-Japanese war of 1894 (Y. C. Kim 1982, 190).[3] The entry of Protestant missionaries, bringing a package of welfare benefits for the poverty-stricken Korean society, aroused much interest and also provided fascinating opportunities, particularly to women and those of low-class standing who had been barely able to survive under the grim socioeconomic conditions that prevailed. Advantages such as medical benefits, social welfare, and even educational opportunities were welcomed, particularly by the socially underprivileged population who were being encouraged to seek access to opportunities that could reverse their social inaccessibility. Yet, anyone who was attracted to those advantages had to first accept dogmatic subservience to Protestantism and therewith to disregard their own traditional culture in order to experience any given benefits (Y. C. Kim 1982, 198–210).

Less than a hundred years after the onset of Protestant missions in the Korean peninsula, the first group of Korean immigrants embarked in 1903 to immigrate as agricultural laborers in the sugarcane plantations of Hawaii (Guillermo 1991, 40; H. Kim and Patterson 1974, 2; Institute of Korean Church History Studies 1989, 57).[4] They brought with them their early missionary Protestantism even before the Western

---

a medical mission. Note the discussion in the publication of the Institute of Korean Church History Studies (1989).

3. There was a form of national insurgence that was led by the oppressed supporters of Eastern religious groups against Western Catholicism and the internally dominant feudal class, known as *Donghak*, in 1894.

4. The first ship to the U.S. territory was loaded with 102 Koreans, including "56 men, 21 women, and 25 children to arrive in Hawaii" (Y. C. Kim 1982, 190). The number is counted differently in the record shown in the book *Churches Aflame*. According to the book, the number of those Korean immigrants aboard the first ship was 71 adults and 30 children.

Protestant tradition was well settled in Korea itself. Some members from the Naeri Methodist Church (Task Force 2000, 21),[5] a church founded by the Methodist missionary Henry G. Appenzeller, were on board among these first immigrants and took a leading role in laying the cornerstone of a long-standing history of protestantization in the Korean immigrant community in the U.S. (H. Kim and Patterson 1974, 57–58). Although the working conditions were excruciatingly exploitive on the sugarcane plantations, and the living situations were at poverty level (Guillermo 1991, 51),[6] the very first thing that the Korean diaspora accomplished as a group in Hawaii was to organize a Christian church by the following year in 1904 (Task Force, 2000, 21).[7] This church, the Korean Methodist Church, was the first immigrant church operating not only as a faith-based religious community but also as a multifunctional ethnic resource center for the Korean immigrants. This church laid the groundwork for the extensive and continuing spread of Korean immigrant Protestant churches throughout the U.S. ever since (Guillermo 1991, 50).

Becoming a Christian in the immigrant context of the U.S. connotes an important and necessary rite of passage for Korean immigrants, initially focusing on survival in the presence of otherness. Obtaining church membership is an important step in succeeding in the immigrant life, so as to effectively engage the ethnic network and to gain resources, the foremost requisites for the immigrants' survival (Ministry of Culture 1996, 133; Min 1996, 41–42). Essential resources for immigrants are offered by way of the intra- and interchurch networking, which is vital for job opportunities, housing and school information, cultural learning, and social activities, in general. The immigrant church community also becomes a fundamental support for dealing with the routine experiences

5. The Naeri Methodist church, the first Methodist church in Korea, was founded in Incheon, South Korea, in 1885.

6. The first Korean diaspora workers normally toiled six days a week in the sugar plantation, but during the harvest season, they worked even seven days from 6:00 a.m. to 10:00 p.m., with only a thirty-minute lunch break. Their earnings ranged from sixteen to eighteen dollars per month, and they were not even allowed to use their personal names as identification but, instead, had ID numbers and cards. Moreover, the residential condition was wretched, entailing emotional suffering, physical sickness, and even fatalities, particularly from tuberculosis.

7. The first Korean diasporic Methodists purchased a new building, drawing upon three hundred dollars of fundraising among Korean immigrants and a one-thousand-dollar donation from American supporters. This church was the first Korean American Protestant Church in the U.S. territory and is still known as the Christ United Methodist Church of Honolulu.

of cultural shock and the associated language barriers that contribute to the sense of vulnerability and risk in the immigrant context. Regardless of their religious affiliations prior to immigration, therefore, Korean immigrants are eager to stay in connection with the Protestant church in the U.S. Associated with this specific environment, the thrust of Protestant evangelism seems to be an unavoidable medium for creating a collective Korean solidarity both within and beyond the church community, an environmental condition in which existential needs for survival are interlocked with a dogmatic demand for conversion and vice versa. In fact, the Korean Protestant immigrant church and the general community concur in evangelical outreach as their most pivotal mission to be achieved.

In a context where a Protestant ethos is dominant, shamanic practices are immediately ruled out as not just inappropriate and unacceptable but as intolerable. Shamans are seen as more or less demonic and accursed. Labeled as idolatry, thus, shamanic practices are officially tabooed within the Protestant environment (Guillermo 1991, 50). This Protestant ethos has a kind of mesmerizing effect on the Korean immigrant community, given the ethnic monoculture with its emphasis on personal conversion, repentance, and salvation. By contrast, Korean shamanic tradition does not foster any form of organized community as a group that could serve as an ethnic community for encouraging resourceful networking, developing a sense of belonging, and providing a cultural ground for self-identity, which are the needs met mostly by the Protestant religious community in the immigrant context.

Prema Kurien presented in her study that Asian immigrants, in general, become more religiously associated in the immigrant context than they were in their home country (Kurien 1988). Raymond Brady Williams provides a similar emphasis upon the role of religion, particularly with its function for networking, among the south Asian immigrant community (Williams 2004, 178). Williams emphasizes that religion functions as a means to serve "cultural ethnization," especially as a channel to conserve particular ethnic cultural traditions within each immigrant religious community in the U.S. (Williams 2004, 34).[8] Meanwhile, the phenomenon of "becoming more religious" in the immigrant context represents urgent needs of spiritual support in the process of an immigrant's cultural assimilation into a nontraditional society. In the uneasy process

---

8. Williams refers to "traditioning" as it relates to "cultural ethnization," which he views as "the essential social act" that reflects "the way we have always done things or thought about them in our family or group."

of Americanization, the immigrant religious community effectively provides the advantages of both religiously reassured belonging and culturally shared identity by means of the more unique "Asianness" of the immigrants (Kurien 1998).[9] In other words, each immigrant religious community may function to assist the ethnic immigrants in securing their social status, even if minor, and in establishing a sense of cultural community—a critical issue in the context of the transnational migration of the immigrants (Kurien 2002).

Asian immigrants in the U.S. are labeled as the "model minority" (Võ and Bonus 2002, 5), being widely regarded as a group who work hard in pursuit of a successful life. Each Asian immigrant community is viewed as encouraging, morally and/or culturally, a conservative style that is more traditional and foundational than that of the parallel ethnic community in their homeland. In so doing, each particular Asian ethnic community fashions its own distinctive cultural outlook as well, while preserving each group's otherness in the diversity of the U.S. immigrant society. According to Rudolph and Rudolph, this particular social condition can be referred to as the "modernity of tradition" (Rudolph and Rudolph 1967, 14), promoting a familiar context for the diaspora in the process of the "Americanization of Asianness" (Yang and Ebaugh 2001). Differently expressed, the Asian ethnic diaspora attempts to maintain access to each of their own distinct moral and cultural meanings as still relevant to their immigrant situation in the U.S. The communities translate their traditional, accepted rationales into a new context, producing an ethnized religiosity. In this light, the major religious community of each ethnic group plays a significant role in accommodating and assisting the cultural continuity of Asian immigrants in the U.S.

The Korean immigrant community also presents a different configuration that distinguishes its cultural representation from that of other Asian immigrant communities in the U.S. In establishing itself as an ethnic religious community, the cultural impact of its particular combination of a traditional neo-Confucian moral ethos and shamanic religiosity shapes its own ethnic otherness; the otherness combines in a specific collective common sense and a distinctive style of cultural

---

9. Kurien insists that assimilation by becoming "more like whites" resembles identity reconstruction for ethnic groups. However, the more ethnic groups try to be like the white European establishment, the more their identity crisis increases, according to her. Thus, the only resolution that emerges from accepting one's ethnic heritage and its associated identity in terms of "integration" leads Asian Americans into "more being religious," which helps them to sustain their own culturally unique "Asianness."

behavior.[10] Furthermore, a strong Christian environment, a characteristic grown from the very beginning of the immigrant history, has added its cultural influence in assisting Korean immigrants as a group to feel "at home" in the U.S.

It is thus not hard to understand why Korean immigrant shamanism faces such isolation and stigmatization in the given U.S. immigrant environment. Along with the absence of any organized and shared community as a group that can assist with urgent resources for survival, Korean immigrant shamanic practices are unable to meet the expectations of a *Gemeinschaft*, a value community, while being confined to a complementary, peripheral role for Korean immigrants in the U.S. As a folk belief system, shamanic tradition was communally supported by and formally celebrated within Korean societies of the past, notwithstanding the absence of a structured community, historical canons, or records that could have been resourceful for sustaining the shamanic practitioner or audience. Yet, the practice of shamanism endures, becoming increasingly privatized over time and now more popularized as an entertaining folk tradition in Korea.

The immigrant practice of shamanism primarily serves a temporary incoming clientele in search of instant redress by means of therapeutic rituals or divinations for individuals or families. As traditional rituals that involve assembling the community seem to be more and more infrequent and downsized in Korea, the emphasis is on private, abbreviated rituals for "survival" in the contemporary immigrant practice of Korean shamanism in the U.S. None of the once common communal activities or gatherings for "doing together" as a group exist in the absence of a shared community in Korean shamanism in the U.S. Once a ritual is convened for a certain particular ritual purpose, the temporary gathering of immigrant shamans, shamanic assistants, and client audience is dismissed from the ritual setting as soon as the divination or main ritual performance is completed. Unless there are further immediate promises to reassemble or some specific instruction for an additional ritual sequence, it is similar to when the curtain rolls down after the play on the stage has ended.

Surviving as non-Protestants, with no clear sense of community in the immigrant context, Korean shamanic practitioners are vulnerable to condemnation, and their clients, if publicly known, are at risk of

10. Needless to say, the influence of all other non-Protestant religious traditions gives rise to otherness within the same community of Korean immigrants.

denunciation by the protestantized Korean immigrant community. Also, for the shaman as a cultural agent, routine encounters with challenges and cultural segregation create a difficult working environment in the given context in which she/he works or resides, at a location geographically accessible to, if not within, the immigrant Korean community. Many of the Protestant churches across the Korean immigrant community actively attempt to drive out shamanic practitioners, which forces shamanic practice to become more private and secluded while attempting to remain connected with their ethnic immigrant clients. Avoiding public negation in the protestantized community, in which immigrant shamans engage a private clientele, contributes ambivalence to the cultural location of shamanic practice. Unless willing to render themselves to repentance by radical conversion to Protestantism, Korean immigrant shamans dwell as ever otherness in their own Korean immigrant community, labeled as demonic agents and yet secretly sought out by many.[11] Becoming doubly othered, the Korean immigrant shaman survives as an unacceptable other not only in the protestantized Korean immigrant community but also in the mainstream immigrant society in the U.S. in general, based on my observation.

2. Korean Exorcism: "Bare-Knuckle Style"

Back in October 22, 2009, the death of a Korean American teenage girl was reported in the news under the title "Korean Exorcism." This report immediately prompted accusations against Korean immigrant shamanism, which quickly led to a heated public debate (Jackman 2009). The initial news article concerned the death of a Korean American teenage girl, Rayoung Kim, which was described as the consequence of a grim religious ritual. The eighteen-year-old high school girl was repeatedly and forcefully beaten, then died as the result of a ritual attempt to cast out demons from the apparently mentally ill teenager. Kim had not received any appropriate treatment by a health care or mental illness professional. Instead, her mental condition was treated by charismatic Christian healing practitioners[12] who regarded her condition as a case of demonic possession. Their ritual treatment(s) led to her eventual death, which had

11. One of the ethnographic researches that represents the central function of Evangelical Christianity in the life of the Asian diaspora is Guest's (2003).

12. I personally use the term *charismatic* rather than *Pentecostal* in order to situate an emphasis on culturally shared features in both traditions.

occurred in Fairfax County, Virginia, in July 2008, the year before the news report, according to the police affidavit.

When the *Washington Post* released an account to the general public with the specific title, "Teen May Have Died in Korean Exorcism," this report of a fatal ritual consequence produced mixed reactions from area reporters, Korean immigrant communities nationwide, and various scholars of religion (Jackman 2009). Within days of the release of the news report, some individuals allusively assigned the tragedy to Korean shamanic involvement, presuming that the incident was taken to be the consequence of a culturally "primitive" or "barbaric" ritual, in which they did not hesitate to accuse Korean shamanic ritual as the main culprit. But others responded in a culturally neutral manner, based on their general knowledge of diverse religious practices. The news subject, Korean exorcism, and the comment of Fairfax police in the article, that they thought "a spiritual shaman and family members [tried] to force evil spirits to leave a possessed person" (Jackman 2009), nonetheless sufficed to create enough ambiguity for readers to add to public bias in the circumstances of the teenager's death.

The same article included some comments about the girl's death from three specific sources. The first source was an individual from the local Korean immigrant community association in Fairfax County who stated that he had no knowledge of any Korean shamanic ritual exorcism being performed within his resident community. The second source was a Korean immigrant religious scholar, Peter Cha in Illinois, who spoke in a nonjudgmental but informative manner about the character of Korean shamanism in relation to the incident. Cha highlighted in his comment two critical features of Korean shamanic tradition: that it is a polytheistic religious tradition in a predominantly female-populated environment, which uses therapeutic, problem-solving rituals for clients. Rather more detailed, the third comment came from Prof. John Goulde, director of an Asian Studies department near the locus of the incident in Virginia. He described Korean shamanic practice as including rituals that were somewhat physically and materially involving in character (Jackman 2009).

Among the voices of interviewees who gave immediate comments about Korean shamanism as the context for the ritual incident, supporting quick condemnation of the practice of Korean shamanism (Kendall 2013), the most antipathetic remarks came particularly from the side of Christian institutions within the Korean immigrant community. Yet, the reports and comments provided no clear evidence but an unproven assumption of Korean shamanic involvement in the incident (Jackman 2009).[13] Meanwhile, although the official police findings had not been announced, I found that some people, including the already cited faculty member from a local private college, remained convinced that the incident might have been related to a charismatic Christian healing ritual rather than to any Korean shamanic exorcism.[14]

Fortunately, I was able to interview some people who were able to offer significant comments concerning the incident. The incident indeed had drawn my attention from the beginning, as the news made its way to the general public, because at that time I was struggling to answer my own research questions concerning Korean immigrant shamanic practice within the predominantly Christianized Korean immigrant community. Thus, as soon as the news was published by the media in 2009, it provoked me to react by making a phone call to the faculty member in the department of Asian Studies, having seen his name in the newspaper article. I was very interested to learn particularly his perception of the incident. He remarked that the fatal incident was possibly associated with "a Pentecostal or charismatic Christian church that is a highly emotion-packed form of religion" rather than with a Korean shamanic exorcism. He emphasized, slightly deviating from other responders, that the incident seemed focused more on physical contact than on religious ritual, and in that regard, it seemed much more closely related to a charismatic ritual prayer.

A even more interesting conversation that I had was with an immigrant Korean newspaper reporter who at the time worked for the

13. In respect to the evidence, the same article included a statement of Kim's teenage brother to the effect that "his mother and two other people were performing a religious ritual on the victim prior to her becoming unresponsive." The newspaper article also reported a comment made by the Fairfax County police: "Fairfax police think the fatal injuries occurred . . . during a Korean exorcism, in which a spiritual shaman and family members try to force evil spirits to leave a possessed person." However, I soon realized that the reference to a "spiritual shaman" was erroneous, though it unleashed a widespread misrepresentation of the incident. Subsequently, I was informed by *Korea Times* journalist, Mr. Lee, whom I interviewed, that the fatal incident was the result of a Pentecostal healing ritual.

14. The most antipathetic comment of which I was aware in response to the incident was given by a party identified as Peter Kim: "Korean Protestantism has almost been reduced to a Christianized *mudang* religion. . . . Korean Christianity has become almost completely shamanized" (see comment from Oct. 30, 2009, 7:15 a.m., below Badger, "Shamanism and Korean Protestantism").

Korea Times, Washington, DC.[15] The reporter was apparently the first Korean commentator who publicly described the incident as involving the charismatic Christian *anchal-gido,* a prayer that involves the laying on of hands. On that point, I considered that the reporter for the Korean immigrant newspaper seemed to be the perfect individual with whom to talk, especially in that he might have been the main source for all the information relevant to the incident coming from the immigrant Korean community, even from the police department. Thus, I decided to have a direct, personal interview with the reporter, Mr. Lee,[16] following a few phone conversations with him. Lee graciously agreed to meet with me that May, now 2010, at his office in Fairfax County, Virginia.

A formal interview began after brief mutual introductions. I was eager to ask my initial question as to what made him so sure that the incident might well be the result of a charismatic Christian healing ritual, not of a Korean shamanic exorcism. Lee answered in Korean:

> It was known that she [the victim] was affiliated with a church, first of all. Also, by word of mouth, it was also known to people that she had suffered with a certain mental illness. So for me it was easy to think that the ritual might be a Christian healing ritual, the *anchal-gido,* for the mentally sick that led to her tragic death. I figured that she died of fatal injuries from a charismatic ritual performance. My generational people mostly know what *anchal-gido* looks like, if they grew up in Korea. If you went to *gidowon,*[17] the *anchal-gido* would be routinely performed as a form of healing ritual for the mentally ill so as to drive out demons. Korean people tend to identify mental illness as the result of demon possession. I remember that I had often seen healing ritual scenes in my childhood. This ritual is often seen in the Christian environment in the Korean community that resorts to poking and beating the mentally ill patient. So, summing up the entire story of the incident from a reporter's perspective, I could well imagine that a teenage girl died of a poor practice of the healing ritual named the *anchal-gido.*

15. After his brief comment, Professor J. Goulde suggested that I contact a Korean diasporic professor for an extensive conversation, Y. C. Ro, chair of the Religious Studies department at George Mason University and the newspaper reporter.

16. The full name was not used, in order to protect the identity of the informant. Lee was not only a news reporter for the *Korea Times* but also an assistant minister in a small local congregation of the Korean diasporic Baptist church.

17. *Gidowon* literally means in Korean "the prayer garden," a common Christian phenomenon found in connection with Christian churches in Korea.

Lee seemed to be certain that Korean shamanic exorcism had nothing to do with the incident, but rather, it was a case of the *anchal-gido*. He regarded the charismatic healing ritual to be an ordinary cultural practice in the fundamentalist, charismatic, evangelical Christian sector associated with the specific culture of *gidowon* in Korean Christianity.

The *gidowon*, a form of center, is frequently visited by Korean Christians for prayers, revival meetings, and/or church retreats. Its function is purportedly to escalate belief in actions of the Holy Spirit among Protestant Christians in general, particularly among the charismatic Christian churches in Korea. They are mostly located in remote areas, away from residential areas, such as in the mountains, at the seaside, along rivers or creeks, or in the general countryside.[18] The *gidowon* often function as a facility for accommodating the physically disabled, the mentally troubled, the homeless, even abandoned elders, thereby frequently neglecting basic human rights. They often involve abuse and perpetuate violence upon needy people. The actual situations inside the *gidowon* are associated with religious activities and are not fully visible or open to the public. Although there may be good reasons for this lack of visibility, appropriate public supervision or review of the activities at the *gidowon* is at best rare. A news article published in the *Segye Ilbo*, one of the official Korean newspapers, in June 5, 2005, specifically reported on improper, illegitimate activity taking place in some *gidowon*, such as forms of incarceration, sexual harassment, laborer exploitation, and/or profits extortion (K. E. Lee 2005). Also, one of the national broadcasters, *SBS News*, released an on-air report that informed the public about routine wrongful practices prevailing in a local *gidowon* that was located in the city of Paju in the Gyeong-gi province of south Korea (Jonghun Lee 2010).

It should be clear, then, why the *anchal-gido* matters. What is it that makes the form of *anchal-gido* so easily confused in the public mind with shamanic rituals, so as to magnify negative perceptions of Korean shamanism? The initial link between the two forms of practices is a spiritual dualism in the belief in spirits, both good and evil, that affect human life. This belief is, in general, culturally shared in both folk religious tradition and Korean Christianity. Demonic possession is taken seriously in the Korean Christian Gospel tradition, particularly in the charismatic Korean churches. It is often dealt with by physical application of hard blows,

18. Some Korean diasporic *gidowon* are also found in busy urban areas or within a commutable distance, so as to be accessible for Korean immigrants.

such as are involved in the so-called *anchal-gido*.[19] The use of physical force in the *anchal-gido* is thought to defeat—to drive out—the demons that are believed to possess persons who, in the views of the practitioners, thereby became mentally disordered, disobedient, broken, and failed. In this regard, mental disorders and failure are commonly considered to be the result of afflictions by negative spirits that need to be cleansed in ritual exorcism, by means of the power of the Holy Spirit in Christian ritual or through engaging the superhuman power of the deities in shamanic ritual. In keeping with the power of the Holy Spirit, routine piety is often assisted by intensive fasting and aggressive prayers, and also by avoiding the secular environment so as to purify and recover good spirits, thereby minimizing the threat of demonic possession. Korean Christians thus make frequent trips to a *gidowon* in some isolated location in order to fulfill this purpose. The intensity of healing prayers for cleansing demonic spirits in the Christian sector also often accompanies intense physical contact, in the belief that physical assaults intimidate and assist to expel demons. Thus, the healing ritual may well become so fierce as to involve physical striking, beating, poking, or choking of the "possessed" individual, though each action is viewed by the "healers" as attacking the demon, not the person. This form of ritual performance sometimes results in various types of physical injuries, ranging from minor bruises to broken bones and even to death, leaving visible and painful outcomes for the troubled person.

The cases of *anchal-gido* that are reported in the news media frequently include descriptions that would normally be regarded as illegitimate physical assaults but are claimed as "sincere" actions by the practitioners. The practitioners falsely perceive physical assault as harming only demonic spirits, not persons. In my own research into recently published news articles, I found at least four similar ritual incident cases that took place in the Korean immigrant community in the U.S. and one instance that occurred in New Zealand by the year 2013 (Jackman 2009; Kavan 2007; O'Neill 1997; Salopek 1996; H. K. Lee 1995). For example, one of the *anchal-gido* practitioners in an incident was quite clear about what he was doing: "I wasn't striking Mrs. Yeom, but the devil. I still feel quite righteous about it," according to Detective Lawrence Oliver who investigated one of the *anchal-gido* incidents that took place in the Korean immigrant community in Chicago in 1996 (Salopek 1996). Jean Park, a

19. This ritual process includes loud prayers, singing hymns, laying on of hands, and speaking tongues in the invocation of the name of Holy Spirit (O'Neill 1997).

Korean immigrant and "the self-claimed female reverend at a sect calling itself the Jesus-Amen ministries," provided a similar claim about another tragic incident of the *anchal-gido* that led to twenty-five-year-old Korean immigrant woman's death after ritual violence (H. K. Lee 1995). Park attested to the police at the death of the young Korean woman, Kyung-A Ha: "I laid hands on Ha . . . but the damage to Ha was done by demons. . . . I was practicing in the name of Jesus Christ" (H. K. Lee 1995).

All five victims were women, and four met tragic deaths as the consequence of the *anchal-gido*. There was one survivor, as noted, of a ritual that took place in Chicago in 1996. All of the articles citing these cases are similarly titled with a reference to "Korean exorcism," with similar phrases in the comments, including "cultural norm," "cultural defense," or "Korean culture."[20] In other words, the titles and comments retained in the news articles encourage readers to draw rather negative conceptions about Korean culture and practices, with no clarification as to the actual ethnic cultural particularities reflected in the incidents. On this point, Lee, the reporter for the *Korea Times* mentioned above, offered his own experience, differentiating himself from other voices:

> My grandmother held lots of the shamanic ritual, *gut*, in her life time. She even adopted a *baksu*, a male shaman, as her son. Even in my poor neighborhood in Korea, there existed multiple shamanic shrines which served many different deities and spirits. Nonetheless, I had never seen any occasions when the shaman physically abused or was violent to the clients. My childhood experiences taught me that this incident did not involve shamanic practice.

Lee again vigorously insisted that Korean shamanic rituals were unrelated to the incident of the teenage girl's tragic death.

In fact, Lee's comment was significant, particularly in that he spoke from the "in-between" context of his considerable experience of shamanism in childhood and his current position as a part-time assistant minister at a local immigrant Korean Baptist church that purportedly sustains an evangelically inimical relationship with Korean shamanism. Oddly enough, hearing his unambiguous understanding of native Korean shamanism, I wondered about his personal perception and/or impression of Korean immigrant shamanism in the U.S. and how he might speak of this with his Korean immigrant congregation and neighbors. He replied:

20. "Cultural norm" is cited by O'Neill; "cultural defense" by Salopek; and "Korean culture" by Jackman.

"I think that shamanism is part of the Korean consciousness, the depth of our tradition and the way of our life. But I have chosen the Christian faith to be my way of life now." His comment was very concise, but it profoundly shook my mind. Lee's brief answer seems to reflect an example of how the traditional Korean shamanic ethos has become subjugated or internalized to the new cultural layer in the life of diaspora. Traditional Korean shamanic ethos is deeply rooted as the cultural grassroots that has now settled in as a subculture within the mainstream Protestant Christianity in the Korean immigrant community in the U.S. Traditional Korean shamanic consciousness functions as a cultural insider, motivating the collective common sense in the life of the protestantized Korean diaspora in the U.S. In this mixture, the shared cultural particularity in the dualistic belief in spirits, good and evil, leads to some confusion and ambivalence in the eyes of the general public. This atmospheric condition reminds me of a remark of Robert N. Bellah, to the effect that "both the historical past and the social milieu are causal factors in sociological explanation" (Nisbet 1965, 157). Simply stated, the cultural compound formed by the sharing of belief in spirits, between the Korean shamanic tradition and charismatic Christianity in the Korean immigrant community in the U.S., reflects how the culture of the past continues to function as a cultural insider in the collective common sense, to affect the new cultural references of the present. Notwithstanding the shared belief in spirits, and how many discuss the ways that Korean Pentecostalism has absorbed shamanic influences, the two religious cultures fundamentally run into conflict, presenting an unresolved antinomy between Christian monotheism and a traditional polytheistic practice.

3. The Korean Collective Consciousness in the Belief in Spirits

Korean shamanic tradition is associated with an animistic belief that is responsive to issues of life and death in the natural world, fostering a dualistic perception. Natural objects are believed to retain the form of spirits, having supernatural power, that can affect the human world both positively and negatively.[21] Moreover, deceased ancestors and general

---

21. As an example, the mountain deity is portrayed as an elderly Confucian man with a long grey beard and a mustache, a tied knot on the top of his head, and a long white robe. The deity is pictured as dignified and calm, detached, and neat. A tiger with threatening eyes always accompanies the mountain deity.

heroic figures of the past are believed to be active as spirit forms that have needs and desires similar to those of the living. People's present life conditions come to be the critical resource for determining whether the spirits are beneficial or harmful. In the encounter with life's mishaps, in which people experience problems of failure, brokenness, illness, or death, an affliction may be understood as caused by the action of negative or evil spirits. These spirit forces can be contacted and influenced through shamanic rituals, in response to such occasions. By means of offering food, money, clothes, kowtows, etc., the spirits are appeased or even exorcized in the ritual for achieving effective remedies and good fortune in this earthy life.

As to the belief in spirits, the shared conviction between the Korean shamanic tradition and the charismatic Christian *anchal-gido* is the activity of negative spirits in possession, which is believed to disturb the lives of the living. Yet, the two distinct traditions have differences in their ritual responses, differently naming or identifying the spirit possession. For example, the spirits in the shamanic tradition are dealt with in terms of multiple, varying forms and therein are classified as either good or ill, in a form of shamanic dualism. Even the very same shamanic spirit can be determined differently, either as good or as evil, according to the specific context that the living clients experience, the context that is perceived as influenced by the spirits' desires that are either satisfied or unfulfilled. In contrast the perception of the Holy Spirit as a unified force for goodness or purity, the Korean shamanic spirits tend to be perceived as profane or secular, as stamped with earthly cravings. Thus, these spirits are often subjected to exorcism. As noted, both the *anchal-gido* and the shamanic religious tradition are commonly centered on access to the power of spirits as well as on exorcism, and are associated with human existential realities. Thus, a superficial understanding of the culturally shared belief in spirits in both traditions can result in ambiguity for those who have no clear knowledge of these two different ritual traditions.

Note also that the group of Korean shamanic deities or spirits features gender and character differentiation. Various cultural representations characterized by these spirits are very reminiscent of a definition of religion that is put forward by Melford E. Spiro. Spiro crystallized his definition of religion based on his fieldwork, particularly concerning the Burmese Buddhist tradition; according to Spiro, religion is "a culturally constituted defense mechanism" represented by "the culturally postulated superhuman agents" (Spiro 1987, 159; see also McCauley and Lawson

2002, 8).[22] Spiro asserted that religion was culturally produced by representing certain behavioral patterns that were socially constructed and collectively shared in common experiences (Spiro 1987). The religious practice in a particular setting encloses culturally encrypted references that are collectively shared within a specific society, differentiating the character of one religious tradition from another.

Similarly, culturally postulated features are incontestably noticed in the characteristics of deities and ancestral spirits in the tradition of Korean shamanism. Most of all, aspects such as a culturally demanded gender disparity and a strict relational hierarchy, which are the central features of traditional culture in Korea, mark the shamanic practice as a culturally constituted mechanism. The spirits are also represented particularly by the personae that are often vividly performed by the shaman in a state of spirit possession during the ritual. Each spirit is identified by its given title, and the persona of each spirit is recognized in the ritual behavior of the shaman under the condition of spirit possession.

Shamanic deities and spirits are categorized generally into three groups, typically nature deities, ancestral spirits, and miscellaneous spirits or *japshin* (Haeoe Gongbo-Gwan 1997, 127; T. Kim 1996a, 236). Ancestral spirits, who are named after deceased historic figures or familial ancestors, are believed to have superhuman power so as to remedy misfortune and protect the lives of the living. Meanwhile, these spirits are also believed to have the power to afflict the lives of the living, should the spirits be upset or displeased by inattention or neglect from the living. The category of *japshin* represents the motley group of spirits known to always bring about undesirable and unpleasant life situations for the living, and thus this group of spirits is typically the object of ritual exorcism.

The characters of deities and spirits are differently personified in each ritual segment by the performance of shaman. Twelve episodic segments formally compose a complete formal, traditional charismatic shamanic ritual, naming each enactment as *gut gori* (Haeoe Gongbo-Gwan 1997, 128; Huhm 1980, 11; T. Kim and Chang 1998, 20; Yoon 1996, 190; Yu and Phillips 1983, 146; C. Kim 2003, 38). Referring to the archetypal shamanic ritual that is still performed in contemporary Korean society, the *gut* mediates between nature and human, between the living

22. Related to the definition of Spiro, the work of McCauley and Lawson may be interesting to help further an understanding of the cultural representations performed, particularly in religious rituals associated with the cognitive senses that are collectively shared.

descendants and the deceased ancestors, and between life and death. The *gut* is a shaman-centered, materially represented, multifariously enacted, and culturally attributed remedial mechanism in traditional shamanism. The critical moment in *gut* occurs through the shamanic possession by various spirits, during which the shaman performs the distinct characters of the deities or spirits of the deceased ancestors or the deceased heroic figures. In this regard, the shamanic state of spirit possession or even the trance state, namely the condition of ego-exchange between the shaman and the spirits, marks not only the "expressive" (Lewis 1986, 24) but also the ecstatic, particularly in traditional Korean shamanism.[23] The deities' or spirits' wants or unfulfilled desires, identified as the cause of the living kin's mishaps, are mostly related to relational loyalty and filial piety, as the grassroots morality in the neo-Confucian society. Throughout the mediation of the shaman, material presentation as part of the physical manifestation of moral piety, such as with food, monetary offering, and physical kowtows, is the quintessential medium not only for negotiating with the deities or spirits but also for achieving the desired remedy or material success of the living kin. In spite of undergoing historically repeated sociopolitical oppression, such as from neo-Confucian cultural politics, Christian institutionalism, and military dictatorship, the Korean shamanic tradition is still located not only externally in contemporary practice but also internally in the Korean collective consciousness.

Meanwhile, the various shamanic costumes and ritual tools that are worn and carried during the ritual differentiate the character of each personified spirit in terms of social standings and roles.[24] Representing demeanors of dictation, cynicism, and even humor, the shamanic enactment of the deities or spirits brings back to life a former long-enduring social system and its moral ethos for the sake of the contemporary life of the living. This embodies and reconsecrates the male hegemony of the deceased, while demanding subordination from the living. The question is, then, who is identified with or by the deities and spirits that are engaged. Do they represent society of the past that is reinvented in the present, or men of the past who are manifested in the spirits, or both at the same time? My informant shamans briefly replied by saying: "I am serving the deities."

23. I. M. Lewis employs the term *expressive* to explain general scholarly interest in the subject of spirit possession.

24. The ritual props and costumes that the shaman uses in contemporary ritual resemble or even replicate materials of the early Joseon society. See ch. 2.

The conventional moral ethos rooted in neo-Confucian ideology such as filial piety and loyalty plays a central role in ascertaining whether shamanic deities or spirits are either satisfied or dissatisfied, either good or evil (Yun 1996). In this grassroots morality, those who are born as males and grow to become elders are thereby validated as persons to obtain honor and privilege, whereas females and children, in general, live always in a vulnerable position (H. Yoon 2007; Janelli and Janelli 1982, 167). Women in particular, according to traditional culture, were demanded to provide lifelong servitude to males, *samjong-jideok*, "obedience to father; obedience to husband; obedience to son" (A. Kim 1996, 7).[25] The traditional moral values that were culturally embedded in the former Joseon society featured a strong male hierarchy, which continues to be honored and enacted in the present, even after the death of the specific individual. Furthermore, keeping in step with the moral demands of the deceased is regarded as fundamental in enhancing the welfare of the living (C. Kim 2003, 61; Janelli and Janelli 1982, 164).[26] This represents, borrowing the remark of Melford E. Spiro, "the return of the culturally repressed": reinventing the neo-Confucian moral ethos of the past by means of the present enactment within the shamanic consciousness and sharing it in the common sense of the Korean collective consciousness (Spiro 1967, 141; Spiro 1987, 159).

Unfortunate life situations such as illness, accidents, insanity, brokenness, or any forms of downfall are interpreted in traditional Korean shamanism as the consequence of actions by resentful spirits, particularly by ancestral spirits (Janelli and Janelli 1982, 156–60). Laurel Kendall offers a relevant but symbolic description of this occasional condition that comes from the narrative of a woman: "The hand of the dead is a hand of nettles" (Kendall 1984, 217). Thus, unanticipated misfortunes that befall the living kin should be considered as a reminder of the living's neglect of duty and failure to filially and loyally serve the deities or ancestral spirits. A rich materialistic presentation is to be dedicated, in this regard, in order to please the deities or spirits and thereby to obtain a negotiation for either a remedy of troublesome life situations or good fortune.

25. Derived from the social principle *namjon yeobi*, "men are superior to women."

26. For example, in the fieldwork of Chongho Kim, a woman, Oki's mother, achieved gratification from the spirit of her deceased grandfather after offering a ritual to him, which was translated as good fortune to her (C. Kim 2003, 61).

Certainly, changes in family structure and in the moral values of the current younger generation in the immigrant context have altered the cultural perception of the powers of the deities and ancestral spirits. However, whenever fears and worries come to terrify those in the Korean diaspora, particularly the first generation, they often attempt to access more traditional cultural meanings, such as a sense of resentment on the part of the ancestral spirits and/or their own sense of guilt for abandoning the dutiful service offered to the ancestral spirits. The goal in drawing upon more traditional meaning by resorting to shamanic rituals is to solve the problems in their life realities as they strive for survival. In this regard, Korean disaporic shamanism, as a culturally supplied therapeutic mechanism, becomes an alternative means in support of Korean immigrant life. The ritual allows demonstration of traditional moral values that are reassured in the collective consciousness and addressed by rituals for the deities and ancestral spirits. As an alternative cultural practice to the Protestant faith, members of the Korean diaspora may seek relief from general malaises and various dilemmas through consultations with shamans who can offer evocative ritual enactments, so as to resolve their fears and worries.

4. Korean Women Religiously Portrayed as Perpetual Wretches

When I first encountered the news about the Korean teenager's death (Jackman 2009), the thought that powerfully struck me was, why a female again? I had already realized, through my research, that males were only rarely the victims of this particular type of ritual incident in the Korean immigrant community. All of the ritual recipients in the publicized tragic incidents of the *anchal-gido* were women. Of the many women who were considered to be demon-possessed and subjected to this type of healing, the *anchal-gido*, and whose severe injuries prompted public reports, only one female who lived in the Chicago Korean immigrant community survived the charismatic ritual exorcism. Yeong Yeom was rescued because she had been able to secretly call 911 after the traumatic healing ritual (Salopek 1996). At the beginning of the ritual, she had agreed to be the subject of an *anchal-gido* so as to please her husband and the purportedly masculine God. But later, after undergoing the very severe physical contact in the ritual, Yeong Yeom testified: "I was beaten so badly that my entire chest and abdomen were covered with a single purplish bruise. . . . [I] was believed to be possessed by the spirits of suicide . . . 10 or 11 devils were in me" (Salopek 1996).

Two things are noteworthy about the ritual involving the charismatic Christian exorcism and the alleged Korean female demoniac. First of all, in the publicly known instances, the charismatic Christian *anchal-gido* is disproportionately gendered, being strongly biased to the female gender. That is, Korean immigrant women are prone to be judged as demon-possessed, as manifested through behaviors and ideas that deviate from the cultural stereotype. These women are easily shamed and subjected to a "purifying" or "healing" ritual such as the *anchal-gido*, a ritual that is often violent and that occasionally leads to a tragic death. And, even in death, these women are still posthumously shamed, because the death was the consequence of a ritual that was purportedly associated with the condition of demon-possession and the following exorcism. Related to the gender bias represented by this particular ritual, the second emphasis is the shared traditional cultural belief in possessing spirits that has already been discussed in this chapter.

Heather Kavan, an anthropologist, identifies the particular cognitive states of the charismatic Christian practitioner as a "hyper-aroused religious altered state of empowerment" (Kavan 2007, 57). This reference by Kavan is reminiscent of the unique condition of "shamanic ecstasy," a quintessential characteristic of shamanism as observed by Mircea Eliade (Eliade 1964, 19), and the altered state of consciousness engaged in a possession trance, to cite the phrase used by Ericka Bourguignon (Bourguignon 1973a, 42). Moreover, Kavan, as a Western scholar, identifies rather strong traits of Korean culture in the practice of the *anchal-gido*, based on her own study of a similar case that took place in New Zealand (Kavan 2007).[27] The animistic beliefs that are part of the Korean collective consciousness culturally motivate special attention to the matter of exorcism. In this regard, the cognitive state of the charismatic Christian healers is rather parallel to that of the shaman in the state of spirit possession and trance, the state of which contributes to the charismatic "bare-knuckle" style in the practice of *anchal-gido* (Salopek 1996).

---

27. Dr. Heather Kavan researches cults, extreme religion, and altered states as a lecturer in the department of Communication and Journalism at Massey University, New Zealand.

Many of the strongly gendered cultural traditions nurture a sense of guilt and associated shame in the consciousness of women by demanding normative thought and behavior, so as to reinforce their compliance with the male-dominant system. Women in this condition of cultural consciousness become compulsorily prone to vulnerability for the sake of enhancing masculine supremacy. Perhaps, this cultural demand may provide an understanding for why Korean women are more responsive to the pursuit of religious piety than are men, particularly to the *anchal-gido*. Religious experience offers them a sense of compensation for their subservient roles in the patrilineal family and power system, an experience of sublimation that is religiously aware in practice as uplifting the respect of their subordination, even with a sense of willing sacrifice, rather than being merely ordinary victims. Therein, the masculine supremacy of religious institutionalism is left undisturbed as a power mechanism, whereas the religious reaction of women allows them to be happily trapped in awe of the masculine-imaged divinity. In this regard, Korean immigrant women are directed to willingly allow themselves to become preyed upon in rituals such as the *anchal-gido*, in seeking purification, even bruised or beaten to death, for the sake of demonstrating their loyal faith in the power of the Holy Spirit. Being nurtured to be culturally receptive to their role for subordination, Korean immigrant women tend to take for granted their sense of guilt and shame and their position of subaltern within the male-dominated household and religious institutions. The more they identify themselves as seeking the approval of the masculine world and the masculine divinity in the power mechanism, the more they are susceptible to shame and condemnation.

"How much I have loved Jesus and complained that demons are killing me," said Joanna Lee, who died after a grim ritual *anchal-gido* in New Zealand in 2000 (Kavan 2007, 54). Kyung-Ja Chung in Los Angeles said that she "agreed to the exorcism because demons were making her arrogant and disobedient to her husband" (O'Neill 1997). Given as testimonies by the Korean immigrant female victims, these statements show how dedication to their Christian faith prompts the victims to fit in with the male-dominant family structure and abusive religious institutionalism. The Korean immigrant women are culturally blocked but viewed as virtuous, and thus they are forced to be willing to submit themselves to ritual exorcism, in order to prove their sincerity and loyalty, in servitude to the masculine divine and institution.

Women in the former neo-Confucian society were rarely respected
. The female body was depreciated as filthy, unsuitable for any type of
religious leadership or public role, a perception that still more or less
continues in contemporary Korean society. Note the denigration of female leadership and religious authority in the contemporary protestantized Korean immigrant community. Male leaders in the religious sector
are more respected than female, while the divine is identified with the
masculine. Women are expected to remain quietly subservient to male
authority. This tendency is not only encouraged and desired by male
leaders but is also endorsed by female members in Protestant Korean
immigrant congregations. As a reaction, female leaders often attempt to
mimic the authoritative style of male dominance over women. One extreme instance is presented in the case of a twenty-five-year-old Korean
immigrant woman's death in San Francisco Bay in 1995 (H. K. Lee 1995).
Kyung-A Ha died during a charismatic Christian exorcism, following
severe physical contact performed by five female charismatic Christian
practitioners, including Russian female immigrants (H. K. Lee 1995).

It looks somewhat progressive when Korean society takes note of
women's abilities and capacities and offers them opportunities to obtain
various leadership roles in social and religious arenas. However, the
culturally constituted image of Korean women as secondary and under
male supremacy is still dominant in the Korean immigrant community
that judges the proper position of women to be as inferiors, appropriately
patronized by male authority. This culturally imposed image of female
inferiority is especially active and prevalent in the religious arena that
continues projecting the morally virtuous, traditional image of women
for the sake of the masculine institution. Korean immigrant women are
therefore directed to take this self-image for granted and apply it in their
lives. To become good wives, mothers, and servants, Korean immigrant
women willingly submit themselves to being "good," not only in regard
to their male household but also to the masculine-imaged divine. The
anchal-gido survivor in Chicago, Mrs. Yeom, testified that she was willing
to surrender herself to the anchal-gido so as to "satisfy" her husband, who
was a strong evangelical Christian (Salopek 1996). Similarly, the lives of
Korean immigrant women are caught up by a sinner's mentality, with
a persistent sense of shame and guilt as they try to fit into a stereotype.
In this regard, they have been easily judged as wretched or as demon-
possessed and, as such, to be subjected to the ritual exorcism that men are
much more unlikely to experience.

Shamanic practice formerly contributed in a major way to the bonding of the community by providing a publicly accessible space for rituals and food shared within the traditional society. Often performed in the public space, the shamanic rituals attracted communal attention to the bodily representation of shamanic entertainment, involving the process of negotiating, even bargaining, with the deities or spirits for the well-being of individuals and/or community. The shaman, usually female, was fully subjected to compliance with the commands of masculine deities and traditional morality that conditioned and controlled the shaman's state of consciousness. The shamans dance, sing, and feed the masculine deities in the aesthetic entertainments and dialogic narratives in the immigrant ritual, in order to achieve remedies and good fortune for the Korean diaspora. It is the culturally condemned body of the female and the shaman—usually both combined—that enacts and expresses, by means of spirit possession, the commands of the deities or spirits. In doing so, the status quo of traditional masculine moral ethos is reinvented and applied to contemporary immigrant life in the U.S.

The self-awareness of Korean immigrant women still under the control of a male power system leads them to accept the judgment that they are disobedient and insincere, which labels them as shamed and often even demon-possessed. The system of male authority and masculine divinity in the charismatic Christian institution directs Korean immigrant women to willingly yield themselves to the ritual treatment of *anchalgido* as offering the promise of spiritual well-being, physical health, and relational welfare in the power of the Holy Spirit. The tragedy is that this form of ritual exorcism often, to the contrary, leads Korean immigrant women to irrevocable damage, rather than to a beneficial outcome. To the extent that the traditional masculine moral ethos is reasserted in the belief and enactments in spirits, the lives of Korean immigrant women remain too easily the willing prey of violence under control of the biased male patriarchal institutions.

4

Serving the Spirits or the Culturally Constituted Social Facts

The Practice of a Korean Diasporic Male Shaman

M. Doryeong, a male Korean shaman I interviewed,[1] sighed disapprovingly while shaking his head, as he displayed a sense of pathos in his struggle to survive as a shamanic practitioner in the immigrant context of the U.S.:

> I am unrelated to any shamanic group and isolated from the Korean community here. My Korean neighbors go to church that I don't belong to. They dislike me. They even vandalize my property, and so I often find that my business sign, which I hang outside my apartment, is broken or trashed, put into the dumpster. At such a time I feel insulted. People from the Korean church randomly stop at my apartment door and harass me as they call me a demon or Satan. Other times, they attempt to evangelize me with threats, saying, "Repent, are you not afraid of God's punishment?" Following that, they unreservedly curse me when they realize that their evangelism is not effective with me, saying, "Go to hell." Honestly speaking, Korean people here treat me much worse than non-Korean neighbors. Non-Korean

1. My initial meeting with M. Doryeong took place in April 2005. From the first meeting, our conversations continued until August 2010. This chapter is based on the qualitative data of a total of twenty meetings with M. Doryeong. The length of the sessions varied, often ending after about forty minutes, but at times lasting two or three hours. This case study is particularly based on the meeting in which his divination ritual took place on April 11, 2009. His professional shamanic title *Doryeong* refers to "bachelor" in Korean.

> neighbors at least leave me alone, but Korean Christian neighbors don't.

Looking very frustrated, he blew cigarette smoke into the air as he continued speaking:

> What can I do? Unless I quit this shamanic practice, I have to live with this hostility and discomfort. I am part of Korean shamanism; I am not a gypsy or a Western psychic. I have to deal with this unfortunate condition, because I am called to be a Korean shaman. It is likely to be the *eop*, karma, to me that I have to pay for being a shaman, and it is unavoidable.

1. Prelude

This case study of a Korean immigrant male shaman who has been active in the practice of Korean shamanism for over two decades in the Korean immigrant community, particularly in a metropolitan area, explores M. Doryeong's use of the diagnostic role of the introductory divination ritual, which is always preliminary to determine the direction of the main ritual, *gut*, as well as intermediating time to time during the ritual. Korean shamanism is renowned for its main ritual, *gut*. Performed by the shaman, the *gut* utilizes a variety of ritual forms and objectives, as it takes aim at providing remedies for life mishaps and calling forth good fortune. Each different ritual purpose is associated with a specific ritual formula and conjoined with particular ritual components in each *gut*, making up the characteristic Korean shamanic ritual. Yet, what has not been very widely recognized is that the divination ritual typically precedes the main *gut* as a diagnostic procedure, so as to identify the proper cause and effect of the unfortunate life condition that is addressed by the main ritual. This is analogous to a medical procedure that first seeks a proper diagnosis, so as to lead to effective treatment of the patient. Likewise, the diagnostic divination is performed initially in order to determine the causes of the life troubles and so to be able to select the correct therapeutic direction for the Korean shamanic ritual, *gut*. Yet, the matter of diagnostic divination has not been much discussed, as the scholarly attention has centered on the main shamanic ritual in the study of Korean shamanism.

The unusual feature in the practice of M. Doryeong is the importance of the specific gender of the shaman performing the divination. Korean shamanism is well known for the marked preponderance of female shamans, in keeping with the dominance of women among the clientele. Thus, the presence of male shamans is exceptional in the traditional practice, as well as in the immigrant practice of Korean shamanism. In this respect, the diagnostic divination that was performed by this immigrant male shaman for a female client was noteworthy.

Scholarly understandings vary in interpretation of the traditional prevalence of females in the realm of Korean shamanism. Jung Young Lee, as well as some other scholars of Korean shamanism, identifies the female preponderance in the tradition of Korean shamanism as a degenerated form, departing from an originally male-dominant shamanic tradition (Jung Y. Lee 1981, 13). Lee and some other scholars simply adopted the perspective of Mircea Eliade in this regard, although that is unverifiable (Eliade 1964, 461–62; Jung Y. Lee 1981, 13; Ch'oe 1984).[2] The preponderance of women in traditional Korean shamanism might also be regarded as a counter-gender sectarian phenomenon, a stereotypical response to male dominance in contemporary society. Differently put, the shamanic domain is considered to be part of the private sector, in contrast to the mainstream male public domain in Korean traditional society (Pai 2000, 88–89). As such, it may be viewed as an attempt to separate gender roles and the associated cultural space—men for outdoor activities and women for inside, domestic chores.

In accordance with some sociological discourses (Bourguignon 1973b, 23; Boddy 1989, 141; Lambek 1981, 60), women's preponderant involvement in the shamanic domain might be understood from a functional perspective as a compensatory apparatus for womanhood within a society of male supremacy. In other words, women living in a socially disregarded condition are more susceptible to religious and ritual experiences of their own womanhood and therein experience spiritual empowerment more within their own context. This discourse can be an explanation for the phenomenon of female preponderance in the traditional realm of Korean shamanism.

While partaking in traditional Korean shamanism, M. Doryeong, though a male shaman, is subjected to the traditional female shamanic order in practice. This factor counters his position as a man in the ordinary masculine system of the traditional Korean society. His belonging to shamanism postulates a form of inter-gender subjectivity,

2. "The present predominance of shamanesses in Korea may be the result either of a deterioration in traditional shamanism or of influences from south" (Eliade 1964, 461–62).

as his shamanic role engages in an interchange between the female shamanic religious order and the masculine social order. Due to his cross-gender spirit possession by the *momju*, the bodily governing deity or spirit (Y. Harvey 1979, 291; Jung Y. Lee 1981, 171),[3] his maleness has to cope with a doubled condition of inter-gender subjectivity between the male body and female spirit. In this regard, the existence of M. Doryeong as a shamanic practitioner also reflects an unusual dual liaison with the moral demands of traditional heterosexuality in Korean culture and his deviation from those demands. So, this raises the question of whether or not the cross-gender dialogical condition of M. Doryeong differentiates his practice from that of female shamans in general and the impersonation of the personae of the spirits in particular. Simply put, the question is whether or not the unique inter-gender subjective condition of the male shaman leads to differences in ritual forms and performances. Moreover, if there are actual differences, it would also be interesting to note in what respect a traditionally female-gender normative analysis in the study of Korean shamanism is different from that of the description of male shamans.

In light of these questions, M. Doryeong's divination performance, through which he gave a diagnosis of the unfortunate life experience of a female client, may illustrate these issues. Yet, it should be clear that this particular case study cannot be taken to represent the full spectrum of the male shamanic practice, although it is hoped that it provides resources for such a discussion. Ritual formulas and proceedings in traditional Korean shamanism, in general, vary from one regional tradition to another. Each individual shamanic performance is also differentiated from all others, in its reliance upon each distinct gift in the representation of various deities or spirits in the spirit possession (Mintz 1992, 62–63). To this end, comprehension in depth of these variables of the ritual components in Korean shamanic tradition can come only from further discussions that are more focused on the specific subject of shamanic ritual studies.

The overall discussion in this chapter is a conglomerate of the data accumulated from my many visits, interviews, and routine conversations in fieldwork conducted at the shrine of M. Doryeong in a metropolitan area from 2004 to 2011. In this particular divination setting taking place in April 2009, M. Doryeong was conducting a ritual for a female client in

3. Once the novice shaman is possessed by the specific *momju* spirit, she or he is subjected to the particular deity or spirit for the lifetime of her or his practice as a shaman.

her early forties who had questions about the reasons for her unfortunate life impasse and the possibility for her to have good fortune in the near future. Despite having permission to sit in the studio shrine and observe the divination performance, I was nonetheless strictly prohibited from taking pictures or making a tape recording, so as not to disrupt the proceedings of the ritual, in which M. Doryeong was interacting with the spirits and his client. I was advised in advance that these restrictions were necessary in order to protect the privacy and confidentiality of the client whose personal information and whose very visit to the shamanic practitioner should not be made known to anyone outside the shrine. Such a protective attentiveness was unspoken but was a fundamental promise between shaman and client, a contextual requirement given the predominantly protestantized public environment of the Korean immigrant community (Chen 2002). The possibility of this delineated ritual observation was offered to me when M. Doryeong became interested in my academic project after over twelve or so meetings that followed my initial meeting with him in 2004. Having been given permission to sit and observe his performance of a divination, my only role was to be exclusively silent, as becoming to a "subaltern," as if I were not present at his ritual practice (Ashcroft et al. 1998, 215–19). The primary purpose of his demand was to protect his ritual from any outside participation or interference, so silence would be a typical modality for the field-worker. This particular situation thus led me to a brief but paradoxical reflection on a remark of Gayatri Chakravorty Spivak: "*Subaltern* is not just a classy word for the oppressed, for [the] Other, for somebody who's not getting a piece of the pie" (quoted in Kock 1992, 63). This state of subalternity externally marks the particular cultural location of the one in charge, M. Doryeong, as a Korean immigrant male folk religious practitioner in a predominantly Protestant immigrant context in the U.S.

Sharing the common space where the divination ritual occurred, I was not to be heard or noticed. However, M. Doryeong's shrine was too small for me not to be noticed. So, on my part, the tension in my nervous system was continually mounting, as I was cautious not to create any minor noises during the ninety-minute divination. Sitting in a designated corner of the tiny shrine, I was active only in my silent note-taking, striving not to miss any segment of his performance while concentrating on observation and remembrance.

I was particularly attentive to his divination performance, along with the associated inquires as to how he accessed meaning for his

Korean female client who survived in cross-cultural adversity and how he validated the invocation of the deities or spirits for the client's life in a nontraditional immigrant context. Above all, as noted at the beginning of this chapter, the aspect of his male gender specificity could be an additionally unique characteristic in being attentive to this shamanic practice of M. Doryeong.

2. M. Doryeong: A Korean Male Immigrant Shaman

M. Doryeong was in his early sixties at the time of my fieldwork, with over thirty years' experience of Korean shamanic practice following his own initiation in the early 1970s. He had been in and out of shamanic practice in the U.S. since the date of his immigration in 1991, which reflects an ongoing struggle to support himself by his profession as a shamanic practitioner in an immigrant context. He tried but failed in his attempt to run away from his calling to the shamanic profession, according to him. His intent to shift immediately led to mishaps and troubles for his family, particularly for his children. So, in the long run, he had to surrender himself to his call, creating a professional title for his own practice as M. Doryeong at the end of 1998. He then practiced Korean immigrant shamanism in a small room on the second floor of a small house in a residential area close to the city, where, for economic reasons, he shared the rental unit with a male Caucasian housemate. It was actually the third location for his work site, since I first met him when he was also practicing in a small studio apartment at the edge of the Korean immigrant community. The tiny room in which he had recently set up his shamanic altar was dark and musty. The windows were fully closed and entirely covered with a big nylon square of the Korean national flag. He seemed more relaxed in his current residence than in previous residences where I had visited him, though his anxiety seemed still somewhat remaining, in spite of several relocations of his reclusive immigrant shamanic practice.

M. Doryeong survived with a twofold otherness, not only being a blasphemous presence within the protestantized Korean immigrant community but also being an alien in regard to his non-Korean neighbors (Chen 2002). Being aware of the consequences of becoming a shaman in an immigrant context, his life looked very isolated, even from his own community. He suffered from the loss of belonging, lacking a sense of collective solidarity. Thus, his identity as a shaman prevented him from being able to connect with the "peopling and sharing networks" widely offered, particularly within the Korean immigrant church (R. Kim 2006, 40). Alongside his call to be a shamanic practitioner and the inevitable loss of any sense of coexistence with his own ethnic community, the cultural and language barriers that he encountered in his routine also made it difficult for him to communicate with his non-Korean neighbors in the nontraditional environment. All this directly affected his survival, particularly his finances. He once shared with me his thoughts relative to his economic condition, as someone who was isolated from routine interaction within his own immigrant community:

> I don't suffer that much from economic difficulties. But I am not wealthy either. As a shaman, I help to bring good fortunes and to solve problems. Therefore, as far as I do help people to improve their life situations, I should not be greedy for money. My *momju* does not allow me to earn big money. Whenever I make more money, it is somehow destined to be wasted.

In reality, the visible condition of M. Doryeong's residence did not suggest to me anything other than economic hardship. However, he had little difficulty in speaking about his financial needs at the meeting in March 2010. In asking me to be courteous to the deities on the altar by means of a monetary offering before continuing our conversation, he indicated a sense of urgency about his financial situation.[4] He explained:

> My adopted son recently had twin boys with his girlfriend. I need to help them because they don't have enough income due to my son's current unemployment. I also got divorced from my wife. So, now I am working at a Korean-owned nail salon three days a week and stay at my shrine for the rest of the week. I need to make more money. I am also waiting for the Social Security housing help, because I have had trouble paying the rent.

The drastically changed family situation of M. Doryeong seemed to add his financial difficulties. I heard nothing about the financial control of his *momju* at this time in regard to his urgent needs. Instead, he emphasized his own material needs in this earthly life. M. Doryeong was not only a shamanic practitioner but also a parent who deeply cared about his children, just like other Korean parents. However, the pursuit of his

---

4. M. Doryeong customarily asked me to make a contribution of some monetary offerings to the deities on the altar as a courtesy, which, he said, would please his deities during our conversation.

shamanic practice meant that he had an unusual relationship with his wife and children, in that he mostly stayed alone at his shrine, in isolation from his family residence in the city.[5] His wife had, in fact, endured the unusual lifestyle of her shamanic practitioner husband, handling by herself most of the family chores, while he was physically apart from her and their children. So, although she had a so-called husband, she lived mostly like a single mother, taking care of all kinds of family affairs and her children's routines by herself. This perhaps led to the divorce.

Following his divorce in his early sixties, M. Doryeong's life prospects seemed to be failing in manifold ways. He was a poor, single, socially powerless man, living in a diaspora. Moreover, as a shamanic practitioner, he was an outsider in his own community. In explaining his situation, he seemed to curiously rationalize his current life condition, but in fact, he spoke in terms of keeping with his *momju* spirit at this time:

> I am not wealthy because I am not greedy. My *momju* makes me distant from money and a wife. That's what my *momju* wants me to do, and thus I have to comply with what my *momju* commands me to do.

He interpreted the condition of his poverty-stricken life and his divorce as dictated by the wishes of his bodily governing deity, the *momju*. In other words, he felt his indigent life condition was his destiny, a necessary part of his world as a shamanic practitioner. In his shrine, cigarette smoke filled the tiny studio space, making it murky and polluted during our conversations. The stifling air soured my throat and nostrils. I wanted him to stop his chain-smoking, at least for a few minutes. For M. Doryeong, though, his chain-smoking was not under his control. It was not his personal behavior but an aspect of the physical personification of his *momju*. As he stated:

> My *momju* is a heavy smoker. She keeps making me have a cigarette in my mouth. My body complies with what my *momju* desires. But, smoking does not physically hurt my lung or liver because it is my *momju* who is smoking, not me.

---

5. His deity, *momju*, did not like him to stay with his wife, according to him. His *momju* was very jealous of his relationship with other women, including his wife. So, he attempted to spend his extra time mostly with men, playing card games or drinking, instead of going back home, even during his marriage.

He continued, accentuating that his annual physical checkups had never indicated anything unusual or negative in his lungs and liver; his lungs and liver actually seemed clean and healthy. His insistence that his chain-smoking did not hurt or harm his internal organs was puzzling, since medical studies indicate that heavy smoking harms the human respiratory system and leads to the risk of lung cancer. He took the absence of such harm as an indicator that his *momju* was protecting him.

His remark, indeed, reminded me of the somewhat similar argument by one of the Korean immigrant Christian charismatic healers who testified that "I wasn't striking Mrs. Yeom but the devil inside her," after beating and hitting Mrs. Yeom to the extent that she was severely bruised and injured as a result of the performance of the *anchal-gido*, the charismatic Christian exorcism that literally applies laying on of hands (Salopek 1996).[6] The charismatic Christian practitioner was convinced that he beat demons, evil spirits; but it was Mrs. Yeom's person herself who was abused and wounded in the incident. Similarly, M. Doryeong was confident that his chain-smoking did not harm his physical organs, as it was his possessing spirit that was smoking. So, what was puzzling in this regard was how M. Doryeong's chain-smoking apparently did not damage him physically, quite unusual from the statistical norm. M. Doryeong's chain-smoking certainly bothered me when I was forced to breathe the murky air in his tiny shrine. As a nonsmoker myself, I was constantly coughing and my eyes were tearing, when sitting in his shrine. In this regard, one might also be curious why Mrs. Yeom was suffering with severe wounds bruised at the ritual exorcism when the charismatic Christian healer struck only demons inside her body. These two contradictory occasions could make one also wonder about the mystery of spirit possession, as it remains unfathomable in fully understanding the way in which spirit possession may lead the practitioner on and how the practitioner's perception may be affected.

The possessing *momju* of M. Doryeong was an elderly female spirit, a grandmother spirit. In other words, M. Doryeong manifested a feminine persona in compliance with his female *momju*, frequently displaying cross-gender behaviors such as with feminine vocalization, gestures, and even his outfits. He grew his hair long, well over his shoulders, and often gathered it up with a clip pin with flowery ornaments, such as are similarly used by ordinary Korean women. The feminine baggy pants

6. See ch. 2 for questions about the Christian charismatic exorcism.

he often put on also gave a glimpse of a cross-gender style. Although I did not ask, he once explained the reason he grew his hair lengthy was that haircuts were too expensive. But he seemed to enjoy his lengthy hair, often softly running his fingers through his loosened hair or combing his hair from the top all the way down towards his shoulders during our conversation. His effeminate, soft, kindly, and tranquilizing vocalization also sounded far removed from that of the typical first-generation Korean immigrant male. His physical motions were unusually reserved and cautious. He looked rather more feminine than masculine, in terms of a Korean cultural perspective.

The condition of spirit possession is, in general, referred to as an ego-switch between the shaman and the spirit, presenting a change of persona and behavioral pattern of the shaman such as is associated with an "altered state of consciousness," or ASC, as Erika Bourguignon describes it (Bourguignon 1979, 233; Chilson and Knecht 2003, 9). This typical condition of ego-exchange (Brown 1991, 353)[7] on the part of the shaman can be referred to from the psychoanalytic perspective as amnestic, according to John Curtis Gowan (Gowan 1975). So to speak, the shaman attains an unconscious state in the condition of spirit possession, which involves the ego occupancy of the spirit upon the ego absence of the shaman. Jung Young Lee labels this condition in Korean shamans simply as a "psychic turnover" (Jung Y. Lee 1981, 12)[8] in the representation of the deities or spirits, which thereby conveys the messages of the spirits with remedies and/or good fortune. The terms most frequently used to describe spirit possession are turnover, switch, or exchange between the ego of the practitioner and the ego of the spirit.

7. See Karen McCarthy Brown for a description of ego-exchange in spirit possession among the *Iwa* in traditional Vodou practice, in the African-based Haitian religion.

8. Becoming a shaman is signaled by a spirit possession that causes an individual experience of physical and mental ordeal or suffering. Jung Young Lee designates such shamanic symptoms metaphorically as "psychic turnover." In other words, the *shinbyeong*, shamanic illness, represents a battle between the shamanic candidate's consciousness with the power of the spirit that attempts to inhabit the shaman as her or his bodily governing deity or spirit. Therefore, the *shinbyeong* provokes a "radical change in personality and behavior" in the condition of spirit possession of the individual. Once a shamanic novice is possessed by a specific bodily governing deity, she or he is expected to serve that spirit for life throughout her or his shamanic profession following the performance of the initiation *gut*, the shamanic ritual. Likewise, neither the *shinbyeong* nor the *momju* is chosen by the shamanic candidate but, instead, represent gifts given to her or him as a chosen one.

In traditional Korean shamanism, spirit possession is identified as the shamanic illness, *shinbyeong*, as a primary sign of a spirit calling upon a given individual to becoming a shaman. In this initial stage, the shamanic novice undergoes varied anomalies such as of physical, psychological, and/or social breakdowns under the impact of the spirit possession. After an initiation, the condition of spirit possession is taken advantage of by the shaman as the means of communication with the spirits, for receiving divinatory messages that are prescriptive for remedies or good fortune. Simply, after the shaman convalesces, the initial illness is converted to spiritual mediumship, by means of acceptance of the spirits by the shaman.

The active shamanic turnover takes place in ritual, mostly between the resentful spirits of deceased ancestors and shamans as the social minors—predominantly women, in Korean shamanic practice. Not limited by certain gender-specific representation in spirit possession, the once ill but then convalescent shaman undergoes an ego-switch with the *han*-ridden spirits (U. Kim and Choi 1995; Ch'oe 1984, 231; T. Kim 1996b, 46),[9] crying from resentment of "unfortunate" life experiences that are perceived as the countervalue to the traditional moral virtue of the good life. John Curtis Gowan explains the condition of spirit possession cognitively as a "sandwiching effect," which highlights "the escalation of the action of both the id and the super-ego derived from the shaman's ego-excursion" (Gowan 1975, 51). According to him, this condition of spirit possession is generated by an odd concert between "the id's archaic impulse and the super-ego's moral verdict" (Gowan 1975, 51). The cries of spirits brought up by the Korean shaman in the state of ego-switch are a complaint of forgetfulness of their *han*, as they cast blame on the living. Related to Gowan's discussion, in this regard, the shamanic remedy is associated with the "return" of conventional morality with which to treat the displeased spirits, such as with filial piety and loyalty, so as to ritually appease them, ideally accompanied by generous material presentations. In traditional Korean shamanism, seeking the remedy or good fortune is achieved by treating or comforting the spirits' resentfulness of the unfortunate existential realities represented in the condition of the shamanic spirit possession. In this regard, the occasions of spirit possession in traditional Korean shamanism may not be properly explained in terms of either an "epidemiological" or an "incidental" conception (Lewis

9. *Han* denotes a distressed emotional condition that is culturally shared as the common sense, referred to as the collective psyche, of Koreans.

1986, 25).[10] It is but the quintessential mediumship in the shamanic ritual that explicitly reproduces the traditional collective consciousness in the cross-contextual union between the *han*-ridden shamanic body and the possessing spirit, while the spirit is morally sublimated and materially served in the ritual performance of relational morality and ultimately sought for remedy or good fortune of the living.

The life of M. Doryeong, impoverished and disregarded in the immigrant context, might survive in the experience of spiritual compensation. The experience of spirit possession might provide him a sense of his own spiritual remedy from his real-life struggles for survival at the margin of the immigrant society. Identifying himself with the deities or spirits in the state of ego-exchange in the experience of spirit possession, M. Doryeong might be empowered to overcome his life in the physical world of deficiency (Brown 1991, 353; Gowan 1975, 53; Bourguignon 1973a, 23). This may sound like an experience of a certain fantasy, a paradox combining material poverty with spiritual wealth, the physically unreal with the spiritually real, a masculine body with a feminine spiritual being, etc. In this regard, he lives simultaneously in two different worlds, body and spirit, as a male shamanic practitioner not limited by time, space, gender, etc. His profession as a shamanic practitioner provides his own empirical remedy in the experience of psychic turnover and thereby able to help call forth good fortunes and therapeutic resolutions for the Korean diaspora in the U.S.

3. Symbols

The current shrine of M. Doryeong was hidden in the midst of serenity, being located on the shady outskirts of a Korean immigrant community. The building with M. Doryeong's rental unit was only a few blocks away from a local highway. The nearby roads were teeming and abuzz with heavy traffic, but his building was sitting on a secluded corner. Surrounded by private housing, his rental unit was located near the

10. The "epidemiological implication" refers to the sociological discussion of spirit possession that is related to a particular social context and the correspondent susceptibility to spirit possession in each practice. Regarding the "incidental implication" of spirit possession, I. M. Lewis agrees with the discussion of Eliade, indicating that "all this is bound up with the cult of a supreme celestial being. Thus the spirit-possession is not for Eliade an essential or intrinsic element but one that is incidental to the shaman's ecstatic mystical flights and his communion with supreme celestial beings."

long-standing array of rectangular apartment buildings that made up the residential complex. The adjacent three-row townhouses were homes for mainly three different ethnic immigrant groups: Koreans, Hispanics, and European—mostly Italians. They were huddled together, neighboring one another.

In providing residences for a busy working-class neighborhood, the lives of the ethnic immigrant groups gush with a daily flow of cultural pluralism, routinely presenting a variety of cultural particularities. The Korean diaspora is predominantly affiliated with the Evangelical Protestant Christian church. The routine life of the Korean immigrant community draws heavily on the strong networks of church members, elders, and pastors whose religious manner exudes a strong barrier against religious others in their neighborhood. This environment, for certain, challenges the survival of the practice of the Korean immigrant shaman who has to frequently face Protestant Christian hostility. As such, this setting can be described as fostering a cultural crusade against particularly the shamanic practitioner and more generally against non-Protestant Koreans. M. Doryeong was often targeted for judgmental messages from Protestant Evangelicals who showed up from time to time at his residence. Therein, he was menaced and humiliated when they disparaged his profession as idolatry. M. Doryeong voiced his sense of injury, stating:

> They upset me when they randomly show up at my entrance door, often breaking my business sign and throwing it into the dumpster. That they abuse my signboard is humiliating not only for me but also for my *momju*. My commercial signboard is not simply a piece of wood but something that represents me as a shaman and my *momju* as my deity.

The life condition of M. Doryeong appeared to have reached an impasse, being held in disregard by the mainstream Protestant Korean immigrant community, although that community also supplied most of his clients, whom he served as a "culturally postulated" therapeutic agent, directed by his *momju*, not himself (Geertz 1973, 92; 2002).[11]

---

11. I cite Geertz here in order to provide the emphasis on cultural adherence to the shared collective consciousness of Korean diasporic community: "As the order of bases in a strand of DNA forms a coded program, a set of instructions, or a recipe, for the synthesis of the structurally complex proteins which shape organic functioning, so culture patterns provide such programs for the institution of the social and psychological processes which shape public behavior."

My visit to M. Doryeong on this particular occasion took place on a rainy and misty spring day. The area where he was located seemed to emanate a spooky air, aided by the murky weather. The road by his residence was a long street made narrow by the cars parked on both sides of the street. Quiet and empty, the residential section was serene. A few people emerged here and there on the dark, foggy sidewalk. As I approached the narrow, towering three-story building where M. Doryeong privately engaged in his shamanic practice, my eyes were seized by a huge square of the Korean national flag hung so as to cover an entire window on the second floor of the building. I immediately assumed that it might be the shrine of M. Doryeong.

The Korean flag itself not only symbolized M. Doryeong's ethnic identity as Korean but also marked the space as representing a shamanic practitioner. The display of the Korean flag was reminiscent particularly of the time of the Japanese colonization of Korea from 1910 to 1945. It symbolized the Korean people's collective desire for freedom and independence from Japanese annexation, particularly during that period. Similarly, the Korean national flag posted in the window of M. Doryeong's shrine appeared to reflect a certain symbolism in regard to his life situation as a male shamanic practitioner. Surrounded by a mainstream Protestant society, it seemed to reflect his yearning for freedom as a shamanic practitioner from segregation and his insistence on the propriety of his work as belonging to the Korean collectiveness. Fixed in its exhibition space, the flag did not flutter in the air. In a sense, it seemed trapped from inside in its function as a curtain that marked off the secluded life of M. Doryeong behind the window, thereby separating the interior space from the hostility of the outside world. The symbolic meaning of the Korean flag was "multivocal" (V. Turner 1967, 50) in the insistence that the shamanic practitioner survived in a kind of protest against the routinely antagonistic separation from his own ethnic, immigrant community.

The wooden frame of the entrance door to M. Doryeong's building was worn out, and the white paint was peeling off. A badly rusted round iron bell was dangling at the shoulder-height center of the entrance door, with a thin black wire protruding from the small round body. Momentarily, I worried about it working well enough to alert M. Doryeong, so that he could open the door for me. So, I decided to press the bell as forcibly as I could, hoping that the noise would be loud enough for M. Doryeong to hear up on the second floor. Yet, I soon realized that my presumption was wrong and that the buzzer worked reasonably well. As

I pressed the bell once, the door immediately opened, making a whizzing noise. Stepping into a small square space behind the entrance door and glancing up, I felt woozy all of a sudden, seeing the long, dark, and tilted wooden stairway leading up to the second floor. The steps were at quite a slant, making them look about ready to collapse. Carefully climbing the steps, one by one, while firmly holding on to the wooden railing by the wall, I tried to ignore the creaking noises, all of which added to my sense of the visit as a difficult pilgrimage, like going up a long set of steps on one's knees to visit a shrine. I had images in my mind of religious ascetics who sought out physical afflictions for self-denial and austerity to be able to approach the divine. Thinking of clients cautiously climbing up and down the tilting stairway so as to reach the shamanic altar seeking remedies or good fortune, I wondered if M. Doryeong dedicated each step as an act of devotion to his deities and sacred altar.

At the top of the flight of stairs was M. Doryeong's rental unit with the tiny shrine that also served as his bedroom. The apartment was modest, another indication of the difficult situation of M. Doryeong. He shared the two bedrooms and one bath with a housemate. M. Doryeong cynically stated: "Having a roommate means saving money."

The entrance of the shrine was on the right of the landing. It was a rather tiny room that was very dimly lit inside. In the shadows behind the Korean flag that covered an entire window, the space was basically shut off from any sunlight. A lamp with a low-wattage bulb at the corner of the shrine provided very little light, and at first glimpse, the room seemed quite bare. As my vision adjusted to the dim light in the room, a space with murky air and reeking of smoke, I had trouble seeing the furnishings of the shrine.

The altar was set up at the center of the wall on the right-hand side of the door of the room. Facing to the front, towards the right side of the altar, a black wooden shelf held a pile of CDs and cassette tapes. Three sets of small chairs were placed on the left side, under a shelf on which several framed pictures were displayed, with a pile of plates set on the narrow wooden rail attached beneath the window.

The altar was decorated in a rectangular showcase, the interior of which had a three-tiered shelf. The first bottom shelf of the altar was about three times wider than the other two shelves and was filled with miscellaneous items, including sugar and salt containers, bottles, tissue boxes, rice bags, etc. Two candles were burning on a pair of long bronze stands at the center of this first tiered shelf. A table between the candle stands held two pieces of paper with inscribed names for prayer. In front of the candle stands, some tangerines and bananas were placed on a small table. To the left of the table, there was another little, wooden, legged table that held M. Doryeong's shamanic instruments for divination, such as charms, a folding fan, coins, and a rice bowl. On the second tiered shelf, three wine cups were placed at regular intervals, with an incense burner at the center. The top shelf was arrayed with several bouquets of fake flowers, as if they were offered to the deities. The shamanic deities were represented in paintings hung on the wall as the background of the altar. The top and both corners of the altar stage were shrouded with curtains.

Interestingly, three small American flags were pinned, along with two little Korean flags, under the drawn curtain at the fringe of the bare right side of the second level of the altar. The American flags on the altar represented an act of veneration for the American deities and spirits, according to M. Doryeong. In this regard, the American flags were an addition to the Korean immigrant shamanic altar, signifying the new context and the partaking of unknown American spirits in the circle of deities for the practice of Korean immigrant shamanism in the U.S. This unusual addition to a traditional shamanic altar was important for identifying changes of ritual reference in the globally relocated practice of Korean shamanism and would merit further discussion.

Various paintings of shamanic deities covered the center wall, providing a proper background for the altar. The painting of the *chilseong* deities was hung at the center of the wall above the top level of the altar, the deities as a group representing "the deity of the seven stars of the Big Dipper" (Pai 2000, 13; Covell 1983, 63). The characters of the seven star deities in the painting wore long robes, each in a different color, shown sitting tightly together as a group. These deities serve for "easier childbirth, healthier babyhood, and also wealth, prosperity, long life and virility" (Covell 1986, 80). To the left of the painting of the seven star deities, there was a picture of a seated female deity holding a shamanic folding fan in her right hand and charms in her left hand. The female deity wore traditional feminine clothes, such as a yellow feminine jacket, *jeogori*, and a long red skirt, *chima*, over which a pair of long red strips hung down. Her hair was neatly combed back and tied up with a traditional ornamental hairpin, *binyeo*, such as was worn by married women in traditional Korean culture. The painting of the mountain deity was placed to the right of the painting of the *chilseong* deities, showing an elderly man with a lengthy gray beard, wearing a long white robe and holding a black triangular hat on his head. A dignified-looking tiger was resting its head on the lap of the mountain deity who was sitting cross-legged in the painting. To the left of the female deity was a painting of the *jeseog* Buddha, also called the *samsin* or *sambul*, as the guardian of fertility (Covell 1986, 83). Three figures in the painting looked like hearty mothers, with their benign faces and warm smiles, wearing white three-cornered pyramidal hats and lengthy white robes (Jung Y. Lee 1981, 196). Also, a figure in the painting to the left of the *jeseog* Buddha had a long wooden rosary around his neck, made of small dark-brown wooden beads. A rosary with larger wooden beads was also shown around his wrists, joined together as if praying a Buddhist prayer, with hands held together.

Prayer beads or rosaries—also found in other religious traditions such as Hinduism, Islam, and Catholicism—are purported to be one of the Buddhist ritual props for devotion. In one's rubbing and fingering the prayer beads one after another, the circling rosary symbolizes, in Buddhist meditation, that human suffering and karma are relieved. Particularly, the deity in the shamanic painting with the Buddhist rosaries implies becoming a Bodhisattva, the title that has been applied to a devoted Buddhist layperson. Bodhisattva implies a "light-being" in Sanskrit (Canda 1995, 35). Such a person, as envisaged by Koreans, is "an ideal individual who pursues or has attained a lofty state of liberation but participates in and takes cares of worldly matters for others' sake" (B. Chung 1996, 44). So, the Buddhist rosary represented in the shamanic painting reflects a bit of a religious syncretism between Shamanism and the Buddhist tradition in Korean history. Interestingly, however, M. Doryeong objected to the suggestion of a cultural blend with Buddhism in traditional Korean shamanism. He stated:

> I am a *hanyang gut* practitioner.[12] My *gut* tradition belongs to the fully genuine origin of Korean shamanism, never compounded with any other religious tradition.

12. The practice of shamanism varies regionally in Korea. The tradition of *hanyang gut* regionally originated in Hanyang, the ancient capital city of Korea, reflecting the northern style of shamanic ritual tradition. As a representatively charismatic shamanic practice in Korea, the tradition of *hanyang gut* is performed in colorful costumes and diverse ritual formulas. Meanwhile, the regional shamanic traditions in the southwestern province and on Jeju Island involve hereditary shamans with rituals and costumes that differ from those of the northeast (K. O. Kim 1992).

His assertion sounded unshakably firm, so as to proudly articulate his own shamanic affiliation. He continued by assuring me that: "My *hanyang gut* teacher is still alive in Korea. Everyone nationally would acknowledge her popular name if I gave her name to people." M. Doryeong seemed to be fully confident, with reference to his well-known shamanic teacher, that his regional affiliation derived from the strictly genuine origin of Korean shamanism. So, he was rather displeased by the question of a possible cultural mixture between shamanism and Buddhism, when we discussed the representation of a Buddhist rosary in a shamanic painting hung on the wall by his altar. More paintings of shamanic deities were hung at the edges above the altar, next to other shamanic paintings, but they were hardly recognizable, due to the curtains that were drawn over the paintings, obscuring the upper portions.

The altar looked like a rectangular stage when viewed from its front that was shrouded by dark purplish polyester curtains at the top, embracing both side edges of the altar. The interior of the altar stage with a three-level structure in a hierarchical sequence from the floor up displayed the uniqueness of M. Doryeong's particular arrangement.[13] It seemed unusual that a pile of cigarette boxes was placed alongside children's dolls, toys, miniature toy cars, and even Legos set on the altar. M. Doryeong explained:

> My *momju* is a grandmother deity. She is a heavy smoker who loves children, as the usual grandmothers love their grandchildren. So, she prefers to be served with the materials that she likes.

Giving his best to his *momju*, a grandmother spirit, might be the most important element in obtaining her favor for his service, that she might move smoothly in calling for remedies or good fortune for his clients.

It would have been interesting to learn how M. Doryeong was able to serve a feminine spirit in the performance for a cross-gender persona, through his male body.[14] Yet, he surprisingly and simply responded to my curiosity by stating: "I do not worry about how and what to enact because I am not *performing* ritual, but I myself am *performed* by the spirits, no

13. The altar arrangements vary from shaman to shaman, as each shaman seeks to serve each distinctly individual spirit, including all other deities.

14. The gender specificity of deities in the Korean shamanic pantheon is predominantly masculine, with only a few feminine deities that are "classified even as grandmother spirits" (Covell 1983, 11). A few feminine deities are also fully rooted in the patrilineal structure and social hierarchy, such as the elderly female spirit.

matter how my *momju* plays with me." He continued asserting that his performance was beyond his control but entirely under the control of his *momju*. He acted only in compliance with what and how his female spirit desired. That is, he let himself be led by his *momju* or other spirits, whenever the spirits occupied his body and altered his consciousness. M. Doryeong again concisely expressed the condition of his possession, saying: "I am driven by the spirits."

At about 1:30 p.m. that same April day, he gave me a brief orientation before the arrival of his client. He detailed his instructions for me, making it very clear that I was not to interrupt or interfere in any fashion with his conversation with his client and divination proceeding. He stated:

> You should know that this has rarely happened in my practice history, particularly here in the U.S., to give permission so as to observe my practice. You have to know that my clients may feel insecure when someone else sits in here during their visits. They are very cautious about visits to me. They repeatedly ask on the phone, before making appointments, if there will be other people present. They worry about their visits becoming known to other people. The other thing that I am concerned about is that observing my practice can pollute, *bujeong tanda*, my ritual.[15] Should my ritual be polluted, my *momju* becomes upset and hostile at the unwanted *bujeong*. Since you have told me that my practice helps your academic research, I attempt to help you. So, you should do nothing but observe. Again, just stay silent as if you are not here. Unless you follow the rules, my ritual will be interrupted and messed up. No tape-recording, no pictures allowed!

M. Doryeong's tone was resolute, making it clear that I was to be absolutely silent and noninvasive while observing his performance. So, I, of course, gave my full consent to his requests. After the brief but intensive orientation for me, he began preparing himself for the meeting with his client, arranging the ritual materials and the food on his altar. In the silence of the preparation time, his chain-smoking continued.

Then, suddenly, a clamorous bell rang, breaking the silence. He stood up hurriedly to press the button on the wall, so as to open the entrance door for his client. As soon as M. Doryeong pressed the button, a

---

15. *Bujeong-tanda* means "touched by the unclean spirits" or simply "polluted" (Jung Y. Lee 1981, 41).

squeaking sound was heard as the door opened, followed by the noise of the client's footsteps on the stairs, one step after another. Slow and steady, the footsteps came closer to my ear while the client ascended the steep, sagging stairs up to the tiny area of the shrine. Meanwhile, M. Doryeong stood on the landing outside his shrine, waiting to welcome his client as he watched her climb up the last of the tilted stairs. When his client stepped securely onto the second-floor landing, M. Doryeong greeted her at the door: "Welcome! Come in."[16]

In response, a female voice was heard: "How do you do?"

During the dialogue, the female client walked into the room and sat down in front of the altar. Then, she looked alarmed as she noticed me sitting in a corner of the room. M. Doryeong immediately introduced me to his client with a smile, being aware of her frightened face: "This is my *shinttal*, my spiritual daughter, my disciple" (see J. Kim 1996). What a surprise! It was never my expectation or his prior indication that I would be introduced to his client as his *shinttal*. His client seemed to relax instantly, being alleviated of anxiety. Following his quick introduction, she actually acknowledged me, gazing at me with a smile. M. Doryeong then attempted to quickly move on, to change the subject by getting her attention: "How did you find me?"

The client replied: "I saw your phone number in the Korean business directory."

M. Doryeong asked, nodding his head: "What made you come to see me?"

While the question was awaiting an answer, M. Doryeong kept moving about, taking out his shamanic implements, one after another, from the altar and arranging them on a small, round, wooden table, so as to be prepared for a divination. A packet of a fan, charms, coins, and a rice bowl was set on the round table that was put between his client and himself. This was, then, the signal for the start of a divination performance. As soon as the table was ready, his client finally began her story, leading to her request for a divination: "M. Doryeong *nim*![17] I am here to ask you if I have good fortune this year."

M. Doryeong responded by asking: "Are you married?"

---

16. The conversations between M. Doryeong and his female client were conducted originally in Korean. Here, as elsewhere, I have transcribed the conversation into English for convenience of readers.

17. *Nim* is a respectful term in Korean.

She softly answered: "No, but yes. I am single now! I have been married twice before, but they seemed not to be my men." She continued her story:

> I first married when I was twenty years old in Korea. Since we met in high school, we were blindly in love . . . But I was beaten and hurt almost every day since my marriage. He often broke furniture, turned over the dinner table, or broke the window glass and some kitchenware . . . I was dragged around by him like an animal in front of bystanders even in the street . . . In the midst of all these happenings, I had a baby boy. I expected that having a baby would change the situation. But, I was wrong. He even hit my baby boy [crying]. One day, I decided to run away from him with my son . . . [sobbing] I married again after two years and came to the U.S. in 1995. My second husband was an alcoholic . . . He did not beat me as my first husband had done, but he was drunk most of the time . . . Two daughters were born between us. I tried to help send him to a rehab facility, but it never worked out. He drank and slept with other women . . . [shaking her head] I tried hard to make it work, because I did not want to fail again. But tragedy ran toward me from a different direction. He was struck and badly injured by a hit-and-run driver while walking drunk in the pedestrian crossroad. Since then, with two jobs day and night, working at restaurants and nail salons one after another, I felt burnt out to support not only my three children but also my penniless disabled husband. We separated three years ago. Now I don't even know if he is dead or still alive . . . [tearing up]

She often paused while speaking and sobbed throughout her story.

While staring at her, M. Doryeong suddenly began shivering, as if he were already entering into a spirit possession. He then asked her: "How old are you?"

She answered, wiping away her tears: "Forty-three."

Nodding his head, M. Doryeong asked in continuation: "You have already met a new man, haven't you?"

She answered: "Yes . . ." Her voice sounded a little changed as she talked about her new boyfriend:

> He is an American, a white man working at an auto shop. He is not rich but seems like a good man. Yet, I feel afraid. I have undergone enough pain because of men. I think I don't have a good fortune for men. I feel like I am nobody. Why am I unable

to live like anyone else? [tearing up] I want to live a normal life, just marrying, having children, and growing older together with my husband in a loving family. I just want a loving family. Is it too greedy? Why is it so hard for me but looks easy for others? I feel like my life is cursed . . . M. Doryeong *nim*, would you divine a good fortune for me?

M. Doryeong replied emphathetically: "Let's see." He was pulling the small, round table closer to him, a brown mahogany table with the finish peeled off and the edges cracked but still showing an inlaid floral design with mother-of-pearl at the center. The table seemed to suggest many years of history in his practice. M. Doryeong then began rearranging the ritual implements that he had previously set on the table. A small round bowl was moved to the far left from the right. The bowl was made out of bronze, such as was used particularly for religious ceremonies or formerly as a kitchen utensil in traditional Korean culture. Such bronze kitchenware is still often used in traditional religious practices but is no longer commonly used as daily tableware in contemporary Korean life. Two sets of Buddhist rosary beads were placed inside the bronze bowl. One was a long rosary with one hundred eight tiny beads, and the other, with large wooden beads, was much shorter and normally used as a wristlet (W. Kim 1994, 363).[18]

Ritual symbols represent cultural emblems that exhibit features of cultural particularities and unique historical references, which are distinctively constructed in the social process in a specific time and cultural location. Ritual materials necessarily emit "meta-lingual significances" in the projection of multiple meanings through the various symbols involved in ritual (V. Turner and Bruner 1986, 163; V. Turner 2004).[19] In turn, a ritual symbol may designate "social facts"

---

18. In the Buddhist tradition, praying with the rosary is an ordinary activity within and beyond the formal ritual setting. Prayer with a rosary accompanies contemplations, chant, and/or bows to Buddha. The rosary is often worn around the neck and/or wrist. It may also be fingered, turning beads one by one by using the thumb of the right hand. Particularly, in the Buddhist tradition, praying while fingering the rosary with one-hundred-eight beads is to eliminate existent cravings and agonies of humankind. Yet, it is unclear how the Buddhist rosary came to be part of Korean shamanic practice. It raises the question as to where or not there are other particularly shamanic references symbolized by the prayer with the rosary that are distinct from the Buddhist tradition.

19. Victor Turner refers to the feature of condensation (condensing) as the core property of ritual symbols.

by representing the "collective consciousness" of a particular cultural group, while enclosing traits of the sociocultural particularities of a community (Durkheim 1982, 35). Similarly, the Buddhist rosary as a ritual symbol in Korean shamanism functions as a medium to call forth "moral and sensory *significata*" (V. Turner 2004)[20] to life here and now, by embodying an aspect of the cultural sharing of the past through the symbol. Whether or not the symbolic meaning of the Buddhist rosary is differently acknowledged, particularly in the shamanic performance of divination, it is surely clear that the Buddhist prayer beads, as imperative *significata* (V. Turner, 1967b), are used to partake in an invocation of superhuman power upon the shamanic performance.

A folding fan was set next to the bronze bowl. It was made out of a combination of bamboo for its frame and *hanji*, a traditional Korean paper, for its skin. Provided with a long strip of red strips tied to the bamboo frame, the unfurled paper folding fan was covered with an image of a female deity wearing a traditional Korean feminine costume, specifically a yellow *jeogori*, a short jacket, and a red *chima*, a lengthy skirt. M. Doryeong later indicated that the fan was one of the traditional shamanic ritual props that he used for his own practice, particularly because it included a female image that was analogous to that of his *momju*. He also told me that he often wore a ritual costume identical with that of the female deity represented on the fan. In this regard, the fan partook in a role for "summoning the spirits and sweeping up blessings" in his ritual, while it was repeatedly furled and unfurled during the ritual (Covell 1986, 150).

To the right of the fan, there was a brass gong with the handle attached by means of a tightly braided yellow strap. It would be used to call forth beneficent spirits, whereas it would drive out the evil spirits when clanged loudly (Jung Y. Lee 1981, 89; 212). M. Doryeong had previously advised me that metallic sounds were used in most of the traditional rituals for calling out the spirits.

The last item on M. Doryeong's divination table was a Chinese *Iching* book set under a little wood bowl (Jung Y. Lee 1994, 17).[21] The *Iching*,

---

20. A sensory pole, according to Turner, comprises physiological and natural representations that are stimulated for people's desires and feelings.

21. The combination of the Chinese letters *Iching* contains two syllabic characters, *I* as "change" and *ching* as "book." The *Iching* is also known as Zhou I or the Zhou Book of Change, since it is believed to have been written by the founder of the Zhou dynasty (1122 BCE–256 BCE) in ancient China. The main text consists of sixty-four

known as the Book of Changes, has been widely used in many different forms of fortune-telling in the cultural tradition of Korea, particularly in the shamanic tradition. When the shaman entirely relies upon the spirit(s), primarily her or his *momju*, while in possession for divination, this is called the *shin-jeom* in Korean shamanism. Korean shamans also frequently use the discipline of *Iching* in divination (Jung Y. Lee 1994, 17). M. Doryeong kept the book as one of his ritual implements for his shamanic practice, although he did not actually use it on this occasion. He put it in his ritual setting because it belonged to the ancestral spirits, according to him. In a sense, it reminded me of Janice Boddy's reference to a "reflexive" discourse in her discussion of the Hofriyati women's *zar* possession in northern Sudan, which "provides a context in which contemporary experience can be actively mediated by past mythic models, and vice versa" (Boddy 1989, 399). Likewise, the philosophical reference to ancient China suffices to provide a context for meaning in the practice of divination in contemporary Korean immigrant life. An interesting point in this regard is that the ancient wisdom of otherness, rooted in the Chinese tradition, is accessed in order to grasp a life meaning for the context, here, the cross-cultural contextuality of the Korean diaspora (Boddy 2002, 413).[22]

The fact that shamanism is the oldest form of folk religion in Korea suggests that shamanic awareness is deeply rooted in the Korean collective consciousness, as referred to in the title of the book by Ronald L. Grimes, *Deeply into the Bone* (2002). Thus, it can be surmised that the shamanic worldview in the recognition of spirits has greatly influenced the construction of cognitive and behavioral patterns in Korean cultural particularities. The impact of the shamanic ethos cannot be overlooked, even in contemporary Korean life. It is observable in the collective awareness and reactions in the process of mainstream culture, such as

---

hexagrams that function with the binary principle of *yin* and *yang*. The binary interaction between *yin* and *yang* is considered to be the decisive cause for change.

22. According to Boddy, women in the Hofriyati culture in northern Sudan create their own social process, particularly in the culturally therapeutic *zar* ritual, with a particular emphasis on blood and fertility, and accordingly, they protect themselves from the over-objectification of womanhood demanded by the male-dominant cultural system. The *zar* ritual, particularly centered on an experience of the possession trance, provides a woman's context and assists her to be socialized apart from the male-dominant social system, the context that helps women to be reassured about their own cultural location in the male-dominant social context, as Boddy indicates, "through the anti-structure to grasp not only her context, but the context of her context."

with the development of modern science and institutional religions. In this regard, Durkheim's semantics are notable: "Sacredness is eminently a *représentation collective*, eminently a feature of *pensée* and *conscience collective*" (Durkheim 1995, 43). Similarly, in the shamanic consciousness rooted in the Korean collectiveness, the present is related to the past in the moral bond with the ancestral spirits, which is similarly noted by Durkheim: "The troop of the mythical ancestors became attached to the society of the living by a moral bond" (Durkheim 1995, 280). The moral bond and cultural continuity in the mediation between the ancestral spirits and the living kin in Korean shamanic tradition appear to be located in the representation of a collective common sense as becoming real, so as to be the "social fact" or "thing" that distinctively characterizes the ethnic particularities in the lives of Korean collectiveness (Durkheim 1982, 35). Therein, the shamanic intermediary in the form of spirits symbolically replicates *déjà vu* as "the part that evokes the whole of the collective consciousness," from the past to the present and from the dead to the living (Durkheim 1995, 231).

4. A Divination Ritual of M. Doryeong

M. Doryeong stood in front of the altar and bowed to the deities, after completing the disposition of the ritual implements on the small round table. He uttered a prayer to the deities on the altar: "Dear Deity-Grandmother, I am going to work now but without changing my dress. Please, help me to work in my dress now." He seemed to be uneasy about performing the ritual in his casual clothing, the dark blue sweatpants and a black T-shirt. After a few more bows with his hands put together in a prayer, M. Doryeong stood still, facing the altar for a while in silence, as if he needed to be assured of approval from his deity. He finally sat back before the small round divination table. Coming back to the table, he first picked up the folding fan. As M. Doryeong began flipping the fan, unfurled and furled, the female client instantly took several twenty-dollar bills out of her purse and put them on the table, as if she had been given a sign for a *bokche*, the fortune-telling fee. Once the twenty-dollar bills were placed on the table, M. Doryeong ceased fanning, as if he had been awaiting that moment, and shifted the bills into the little wood bowl, in which some bills had already been placed. It was unclear if these existing bills were from a previous client or if he himself had placed some bills in the little wooden bowl prior to beginning the divination. The little wooden bowl was placed over the *Iching*, the Book of Changes, as if protecting the monetary offering for the divination.

The *bokche* plays an important intermediary role to signal a ritual undertaking and is often bargained back and forth in the interaction between client, shaman, and spirit. Reasonable amounts of monetary offerings are always welcomed to help produce a good ritual outcome, in that they satisfy the deities or spirits and encourage productive communication. In this, the *bokche* is formally offered to the deities, but it is ultimately acquired by the shaman as the divination cost. The logic is that satisfying M. Doryeong with a reasonable monetary offering also satisfies the deities, in that the two are considered as interchangeable in this dynamic. So, there is some inherent ambivalence prevailing between M. Doryeong and the spirit. In other words, it is difficult to identify who is present and satisfied at the moment, whether it is the deity or spirit that is personified by M. Doryeong or M. Doryeong himself.

After the *bokche* had been placed on the table, M. Doryeong put the fan back on the table. He then picked up the long Buddhist rosary and put it around his neck, while placing the shorter rosary on his right wrist. While wearing the rosaries, he took the fan back from the table and held it in his right hand. He also grasped the brass gong in his left hand. Flipping the fan back and forth, while furling and unfurling it, he rested it fully unfurled on his chest, with his eyes deeply closed. Then, he suddenly opened his eyes and asked his client: "What's your lunar-calendric birthday?"

She replied promptly: "It's August 20, 1967."

His question continued: "Do you know the exact time of your birth?"

She answered: "*Sasi.*" *Sasi* generally indicates 9 to 11 a.m., associated with the snake symbol, in accord with the ancient Chinese zodiac (Covell 1983, 84).[23]

Then he started chanting a rhythmic lyric, which sounded to me more like humming than speaking. He hummed and chanted with his eyes closed, intermittently flipping the fan open and closed with his right hand and striking the brass wand with his left hand.

---

23. Birth time is determined by the twelve divisions of the zodiac signs. Every two-hour segment of twenty-four hours of a day is named by a different animal symbol. For example, *sasi* is 9 to 11 a.m., with the snake symbol; *sa* implies "snake" in the Chinese writing, although it is pronounced in Korean, and *si* means "time."

Baeg—du-San—shinRyeong—n—i—m, Halla-San—shinRyeong
—n—i—m, Jiri-San—shinRyeong—n—i—m, Tae—Baeg-San
—shinRyeong—n—i—m.[24]

His chanting, using the geographical toponyms of popular Korean mountains, continued for about ten minutes. Following that chant, his chanting shifted to call forth shamanic deities and spirits, such as *Samsin Halmeoni* (the birth or three spirits of grandmother), *Chilseongdang shin-ryeongnim* (the seven stars deity), *Yongwangnim* (the dragon king deity), and so on. After the preliminary chanting, calling forth various deities and spirits for about half an hour, his humming took up his client's details while reciting her name, birth date, and time: *Shin—ryeong—nim—deul.* Dear deities, here is a woman born in *sasi*, 20 in August 1967. Please, help me to divine for her.

Then he murmured a long sequence that sounded like certain pho-netic signs, "Uh—uhhh—uh." Meanwhile, his right hand was regularly flipping the fan open and closed, sporadically striking the brass gong. In doing so, he often shivered his shoulders, as if he were experiencing a chill, with his eyes firmly closed, so that it seemed that he was somehow envisioning something. As the fan was flipped, furling and unfurling, the image of the female deity drawn on the fan repeatedly appeared and disappeared, as if it symbolized the shift of persona, alternating between M. Doryeong and his *momju*. As he went on using the rosaries and the fan, as well as sounding the brass gong, the spirit seemed to shift, as if M. Doryeong were in a possession, all the while compounding two different realities and breaking the barriers between male and female, profane and sacred, visible and invisible, past and present, and even life and death. All these raised the question as to whose ego was in control at any given moment. Ambiguity pervaded.

M. Doryeong appeared to be communicating with someone or some spirits in his murmuring, with his eyes still enclosed, often flip-ping the fan open and shut in his right hand. His verbal articulation, now becoming more like whispering, was too soft and unclear to be under-stood. He seemed to be sobbing, shivering his shoulders intermittently, as he freed his hands by dropping the fan and the brass wand back onto the table. He seemed to be struggling against a strong physical force of

24. Translating the lyric in Korean: "Dear Whitehead-Mountain Spirit, Dear Halla-Mountain Spirit, Dear Jiri-Mountain Spirit, Dear Taeback-Mountain Spirit." All of the spirits that M. Doryeong called forth involved the names of major mountains in Korea.

some kind. Then he shifted and picked up the fan and the wand. His hand movement appeared to be faster and more vigorous, as if he were reaching the climax of the ritual performance. The brass gong sounded more loudly, and the fan flipped open and closed more quickly. Then all the movements and the tumultuous noise ceased. The tiny shrine was suddenly filled with an overwhelming silence. M. Doryeong stayed motionless for a few moments after the full cessation of his performance. His neck and arms were drooping. He looked exhausted and emptied. The fan and brass gong were loosely thrown onto the floor. Shortly after, he straightened his neck, seemed to open his eyes, and stretched out his arm to pick up a plastic water bottle that had been lying on the floor near the divination table. After drinking several draughts of water from the bottle, he finally spoke to his client: "You know a young man who died in his twenties, don't you?" The woman looked frightened. "His spirit is still moving around you. He didn't make his way to the other world. He couldn't leave you. He still loves you." Her mouth hanging open, the woman dumbfoundedly stared at M. Doryeong. He continued:

> Your uterus is mortally possessed by malicious spirits. So, it keeps driving good fortunes away from your life. Your ancestral spirits are upset and are harming you. You have to offer a *gut* for both him and your ancestral spirits. You have to offer a ritual so as to help him to go freely to rest in the other world. You need to do this. Until you offer a *gut*, nothing is going to be better for you. Has your life ever been better? So, tell me? Sorry, but your life has been getting worse. You have already been through a lot of pain, such as death, failure, illness, separation, and accidents happening to you and your family. Right?

Her eyes were tearing as M. Doryeong told her the divinatory message:

> Your ancestral spirits are very upset about your family, because they have been abandoned from the time since your great-grandparents died. Your great-great grandparents lived a socially prominent life by offering big *guts* to the ancestral spirits a couple of times each year. Your ancestral spirits had been pleased until then. But they began to restlessly afflict your family instead of giving good fortune, because they have been forgotten. They withdrew the blessings that were supposed to be given to you. So, a *gut* should be offered immediately to your ancestors . . . If you don't comfort your ancestors' hostility . . . Whatever efforts you put forth for survival, you will fail again . . . Your relationship with the man now is also going to be broken by the spirits

of the deceased man and of your ancestors. Did you notice that
I was severely shaking when I was chanting? The spirit of the
young man gruelingly haunted and grasped me to the full. It
took all of my strength to shake him off. All of the spirits kept
asking me to tell you to offer a *gut* for them.

As his comment continued, he often shivered, as if he were still grappling
with the spirits:

Now, I have told you all that I have heard and seen and what you
have to do. Whether or not you offer a *gut* is your choice. But
you have to remember that you need to act quickly. Unless you
offer the *gut*, these afflictions by the spirits will continue to come
on you and on your children as well.

When M. Doryeong had concluded the divination in this resolute
manner, silence heavily fell in the small room. Finally, the woman responded to M. Doryeong rather in a whisper: "So . . . What would be the
expense for the *gut*?"

"Three thousand dollars," M. Doryeong replied.

As she responded, "Uh—oh, my," her jaw dropped.

At the moment, he immediately proposed a deal to her, as if he were
awaiting the moment: "If you decide to offer a *gut* to your ancestors, I will
work for nothing to send off the spirit of the young man."

She barely articulated a response to M. Doryeong, seeming overwhelmed: "As a matter of fact . . . I don't have that much money. But—if I
have to . . . uh—umm—as you keep emphasizing . . . I will—think about
it."

M. Doryeong replied softly: "Sure, you do, *unni*.[25] You can call me
when your decision is made, OK?" M. Doryeong attempted to quickly
wrap up the session in a persuasive manner.

"Thanks," the woman said, looking weary. In all, she said very little
to M. Doryeong. Staring at him with her empty eyes, she stood up and
walked toward the door. She feebly said, while bowing to M. Doryeong,
"Take care!" Then she slowly walked back down the stairs. Her footsteps
were fading away one after another until she reached the tiny landing
space at the bottom of the stairs. Her footsteps sounded heavier and
slower than her steps an hour and a half earlier, when she had resolutely

---

25. *Unni* in Korean is a term used by a younger sister to an older sister, not by male
siblings. Its usage by M. Doryeong was odd, even perverse, being used by a man to
address a client/sister.

come up the stairway as if on a pilgrimage. It took some while until the entrance door opened and then completely closed, as she left the building.

5. Epilogue

The woman went back to the routine of her life, presumably bearing a sense of discomfort rather than some delightful news that she doubtlessly wished to gain from her divination. It was surely a difficult time for her as she went back to her everyday life, bringing with her the unexpectedly disappointing message given from M. Doryeong. The message given by M. Doryeong would leave an enormous psychological impact upon her for some while. Her mind would be quite devoured by the thought that her uneasy life was the result of afflictions caused by the restless spirits of her ancestors, as well as the matter of the deceased young man. In doing so, she would keep struggling to determine if she should offer a costly *gut* for her ancestors whom she had never met or known, as well as a *gut* for the spirit of the young man with whom she had had an intense relationship in her youth. So, what was it that had made the spirits of her ancestors and of the young man so displeased that they had afflicted her life with so much suffering?

An important clue for understanding this situation may be found by taking note of the culturally related neo-Confucian moral ethos that dominated the cultural politics of traditional Korean society. This neo-Confucian morality is deeply reflected in the ideology and ritual of traditional Korean shamanism as it emphasized the obligation of descendants to dutifully serve deceased ancestors in rituals. Furthermore, any premature death is believed to be an inauspicious sign, even a breach of a moral virtue, "a longer life with no illness," *mubyeong jangsu*. Early death prevents the person's proper carrying out of the moral duties of filial piety and loyalty. In this regard, although unfulfilled life expectancy does not constitute directly a breach of neo-Confucian moral virtue, an instance of premature death is considered as not only unfortunate and but also as morally shameful, in the perspective of traditional Korean shamanism. Premature death, in this regard, presents a contact point, through the unfortunate life condition, with the collectively shared common sense of *han* (N. Suh 1983, 64; Ro 2014; U. Kim and Choi 1995; A. Park 2004, 10–15)[26] as the culturally constituted reaction to such

---

26. *Han* is a collectively shared common sense within traditional Korean culture.

an instance. Deviations from the culturally ideal norm, particularly in relation to the life and death, are always troublesome, from the perspective of Korean shamanism. Such occasions are commonly believed to be the result of malicious reactions by unhappy spirits that vindictively stir up affliction in the lives of the living kin.

The *han*-ridden spirits can also afflict socially related individuals and even, in some cases, random persons who somehow come to the attention of the deceased. In addressing this situation, a remedy is considered in the form of offering the appropriate rites of passage or providing special ceremonies, in order to appease the unfortunate spirit and ritually correct the untimely death. Unless the remedial ritual is offered, the malicious actions of spirits will continue, so as to afflict the lives of the living kin. The ritual redress carried out within traditional Korean shamanism, then, accompanies ritual items of daily necessities such as food, clothes, and money that every living person requires for survival. In other words, the spirits are served as having needs comparable to the needs of the living. Meanwhile, in shamanic tradition, being neglectful about ritually serving the spirits, mostly ancestral spirits, is identified with a betrayal of the filial piety and loyalty that are highly valued moral items in the traditional culture of Korea. Also regarded as morally shameful, this forgetfulness not only displeases the ancestral spirits but also causes troubles for the related or living kin.

In this light, the female client's lifetime agony can be understood as resulting from a breach of moral virtue, forgetfulness on the part of her ancestors, a moral violation of filial piety and loyalty. In addition, the *han*-ridden spirit of the prematurely deceased young man is vindictive to her because of his closeness to her in their youth. The death of any young man or woman is an unfortunate but serious deviation from the virtue of having an ideal life—a longer life with no illness—as well as the moral breach of filial service, particularly in the cultural system of a male hierarchy. Thus, the premature death of the young man[27] not having

---

The importance of *han* was advocated as a central topic of the *minjung* theology that was developed during the *minjung* movement under a military dictatorship in Korea in 1970s. According to Nam-dong Suh, a pioneer *minjung* theologian, *han* represents "an accumulation of suppressed and condensed experiences of oppression." Thus, "accumulated *han* is inherited and transmitted, boiling in the blood of the people." It is also identified as the "emotional core of anti-regime action" (N. Suh 1983, 64). Young-chan Ro, a direct student of Suh, insists that *han* represents the culturally specific Korean spirituality (Ro 2012, 81).

27. Regarding the young man not having been in direct kinship with the female

been properly dealt with, together with negligence of the expected ritual services for ancestral spirits, can be viewed as the cause of the female client's affliction. These dissatisfied spirits have reason to be restless and consequently may harm the life of the woman (Haeoe Gongbo-Gwan 1996, 127). Despite the breach having been involuntary, the penalty for such a moral breach is punitively passed on to the living kin. The only way to remove present troubles and avoid potential problems in the future is a ritual remedy, in the belief of Korean shamanism. Such a ritual remedy could get her life back on track, according to M. Doryeong. From this perspective, the purpose of the admittedly costly ritual remedy is solely for the woman's welfare, restoring her to good fortune by pleasing the resentful spirits.

The sense of bitterness or resentfulness that rules the emotional condition of the spirits represents the culturally imposed cognitive response from within the Korean collectiveness, in regard to the experience of inexplicable life agony, that is, *han*. Misfortune in human life, in human existential reality, is understood as neither random nor "bad luck," in the Korean shamanic tradition. It is understood as the manifestation of restless spirits caused by morally undutiful service or violation of loyalty to the spirits, predominantly ancestral spirits. In this, living kin are blamed for their own sufferings in the present; they are also responsible for correcting the suffering of their deceased ancestors. Otherwise expressed, the cause of an unfortunate life for living kin is rooted in the sufferings of the ancestors, itself caused by that kin's neglect. Therefore, ancestral suffering has to be addressed first, to be able to recover good fortunes for living kin. The ancestral voices are heard and responded to through the shaman who is a culturally constituted spiritual agent, in the tradition of Korean shamanism. Imperatively administered only by a shaman, the *gut* ritual involves expiatory sacrifices to appease the spirits and repair the breach of morality, thereby countering the misfortunes of living kin and even calling forth good fortune for them in the future.

The Korean immigrant community in the U.S. is generally much more in line with functional Protestantism and is complicated by primarily or even solely identifying itself with the "mechanical solidarity"

---

client, it was not her responsibility to serve his spirit in ancestral worship, from the Confucian perspective. However, in the mixture of shamanic belief on this particular occasion, the premature death as the consequence of a breach of Confucian virtue can be understood as the cause of the female client's suffering; for in shamanic belief, the spirits act to afflict individuals beyond the range of kinship.

that is a feature of the traditional village community with its emphasis on ancestry (Durkheim 1933, 37–38; Lukes 1973, 148–49).[28] Given this context, it may seem irrational, in the shamanic worldview, to identify the misfortunes of M. Doryeong's immigrant female client as the consequence of unfulfilled moral bonds and abandoned loyalty to the ancestors. However, this shamanic analysis cannot be completely relegated to irrelevance in ordinary Korean immigrant women's lives that survive within the still-strong cultural legacy of the neo-Confucian moral ethos, alongside the traditional patriarchy. Connections with deceased ancestors associated with the familial bond do not easily disappear from the culturally minded Korean diaspora. However, given the divination by M. Doryeong, the diagnosis that led to prescribing a ritual remedy to counter the moral offences that caused subsequent spiritual afflictions in the life of the woman is puzzling in regard to just who the ritual recipient would be or who would benefit from the proposed ritual. Is the ritual offered to serve the ancestral spirits or to appease the traditional moral bond? Is the *gut* ritual offered to comfort the resentfulness of the Korean collective consciousness represented by existential suffering? A Janus-faced aspect is bound up with the characteristic of Korean shamanic ritual, in which it is hard to identify the ambivalent features separately. In this respect, the immigrant ritual offered to the traditional neo-Confucian moral ethos in Korean collective consciousness is actualized in "social facts" and vice versa, in seeking material success through physical enactment (Durkheim 1982, 35).[29]

In the meantime, an unusual observation was the cross-gender demeanor of M. Doryeong, while in the spirit possession of his female *momju*. M. Doryeong's vocal tones and bodily gestures often exhibited a blend of feminine characteristics. His cross-gender behavior was also marked by ambiguity as to who the performer was. Was the performer the *momju* or M. Doryeong? The interchangeability of the male M. Doryeong with his female *momju* was very observable in his speech and physical movements overall, not only during the time of an apparent altered state of consciousness (Brown 2001, 353; Gowan 1975, 23, 51; Boddy 1989, 4–27; Bourguignon 1973a, 42). The personae of M. Doryeong and his *momju* constantly alternated from one moment to the next, as the

28. Durkheim defines "mechanical solidarity" as "a solidarity *sui generis* which, born of resemblances, directly links the individual with society."

29. Durkheim emphasized social facts as *things* that share a common awareness of both tangible and intangible phenomena of the world.

presence of M. Doryeong himself represented symbolic significata in the cross-sexual enactments (V. Turner 1967, 28).[30]

The traditional emphasis in the study of spirit possession has been on the condition of the switch of the ego between practitioner and spirit. Yet, a discussion of specific cross-gender and cross-sexuality issues in the condition of spirit possession has not seriously taken place. In this regard, more extensive field research and further theoretical advances are expected to provide a more informed understanding of this specified subject. Such future study should open new perspectives to understanding the cross-gender and cross-sexuality features of spirit possession in the interaction with the practitioner or the possessed in general.

As a Korean immigrant male shaman who became the culturally constituted agent, M. Doryeong served to mediate the voices of spirits in the contemporary Korean immigrant community of the U.S., through the conduit of the traditional Korean collective consciousness from the past, from the world of dead, and from the invisible. His survival in the face of routine hostility of the predominantly Christianized Korean immigrant community helps to create a culturally alternative remedial mechanism, treating the manifold brokenness of those in the Korean diaspora who seek remedies and good fortune. In this, the traditional moral ethos continues being sanctioned for the sake of comforting restless spirits and thereby calling for good fortune through shamanic redress. Also imminent is that new deities and symbols will be consecrated in the pantheon of Korean immigrant shamanic practice, as new moral values are promoted in the new cultural context that the Korean immigrant shaman engages. In this regard, change is also imperative, bringing new spirits to be born in the new present, as manifest at the shamanic altar of M. Doryeong, as his practice continues in the life of Korean immigrant community.

30. Victor Turner explains the dominant symbol in three categories. The "unification of disparate significata" means that analogous meanings are interconnected and associated in a symbol. The cross-gender experience of M. Doryeong as a shamanic ritual practitioner can be also an illustration of cultural deviance from traditionally normative heterosexuality in the embodiment of blended gender personae.

5

Speaking the Unspeakable

Shamanic Charisma and the Collective Consciousness

THE SHRINE OF LEE Bosal and Kang monk shaman bustles with the constant footsteps of shamanic clients, special foods, divinatory messages, the wife shaman's clairvoyance, the shamanic hybrid with the Buddhist ritual, etc. All the routine activities at the shrine are associated with the shamanic gifts that freely permeate the unreal past and the real present, as well as the spirit and the body. In doing so, startling signs and divinations take a central role in creating an avenue for "peopling and ritualization" in the shrine of the two Korean immigrant shamans.

In this chapter, I introduce some narratives of shamanic activity and interpersonal dynamics in the shamanic shrine of two charismatic Korean immigrant shamans. This chapter also includes a concluding theoretical discourse that seeks to construe the individual shamanic gift and the ability to engage with the collective consciousness within a ritual context. My focus is on the shamanic gifts that play a central role for the shaman to function as a professional practitioner. Under the presupposition of the two elements that are essential in determining shamanic gifts—the individual charisma and a collective social sense—I utilize the first section of this chapter to illustrate how shamanic gifts are contextualized in practice by Korean immigrant shamans. These narratives may provide some examples of how shamanic gifts are intimately associated with the shamans' calling to be charismatic. The latter part of this chapter begins with a theoretical discussion of shamanic gifts by citing Choi's *younghum* and *noonchi* (C. Choi 1989, 236),[1] Weber's charisma, and Durkheim's collective consciousness. As shamanic gifts are important requisites to being a Korean charismatic shaman, it may be interesting to examine how Korean immigrant shamans contextualize the gifts to represent their role and then analyze each attributed context, which also frequently creates ambiguity in the shamans' representation of the spirits.

1. The Resident Female Shamanic Devotee, Kim

Kim repeatedly inhaled and exhaled cigarette smoke as she hunkered down on a small rock. She continuously threw pieces of garbage into the flaming furnace, intending to incinerate them. The furnace was a hand-built, small chimney made of cement bricks. It was located far across the field from the main shrine building but close to a creek that ran beyond a grove of trees. This creek ran along the remnant of a clay brick wall that was said by Lee Bosal to be the residue of a native Indian residence of times long past. At this time, after dinner, when the sun had almost set and it was getting darker, burning garbage was part of Kim's ordinary work. She burnt garbage and the trash after dark so as to avoid drawing the neighbors' attention. She was somewhat relaxed, sitting by herself in front of the furnace during a short break, after serving for a long day at the shrine. Watching the trash burning and drawing deeply on her cigarette, she was enjoying her only free time of the day, reflecting that:

> Ransacking garbage and trash for stuff to burn makes me feel sick, dirty, and annoyed, but I feel exempt from all burdens and noises when I am sitting here alone, all by myself, with no distractions. I feel like I am also burning up my sense of loneliness, hurt, anger, and anxiety along with the garbage in the flame, letting it be vaporized to fly away with the smoke . . .

Kim continued speaking about her circumstances prior to her relocation to Lee Bosal's shrine. She had had to quit her job as kitchen staff in a U.S. army camp a year before her planned retirement, which would have guaranteed her financial relief alongside her pension and medical insurance. Yet, her visit to Lee Bosal years before her possible retirement had completely changed her life. She had been advised by Lee Bosal that she should stay away from her son and her daughter-in-law. Moreover,

---

1. *Younghum* refers to spiritual power, whereas *noonchi* means social sensitivity, according to Choongmoo Choi.

she had had to hear that her son would be at serious risk unless she engaged in extended devotion and prayer. Kim had been living in her house together with her son and daughter-in-law, supporting them until that time. The couple worked as low-wage cashiers, having multiple health issues. So it had been a very difficult decision for her to quit her job and move out of her house, leaving them behind with low incomes and multiple health issues. She had been hesitant to make the decision. Yet, the reason for making a quick decision became even more compelling after she herself got an unexpected diagnosis of having diabetic sepsis. When she went back to Lee Bosal with her tremendous fears about her son's health issue and then her own health problem as well, Lee Bosal suggested that she should immediately move out of her house and stay at Lee Bosal's shrine for a three-year term of devotion, while helping out with all the domestic work associated with the shrine. According to Kim, Lee Bosal had insisted that her symptom of diabetic sepsis was not a medical condition but was given by the spirits and thus could be treated only by serving the spirits. Kim had had to accept Lee Bosal's offer, because no other option seemed to be left for her. Since then, her life at Lee Bosal's shamanic shrine was much more like a housemaid's, dealing with a continuous series of domestic chores, rather than having any private time for her own devotion. Regardless of her doubts, Lee Bosal often reassured her that the housekeeping work at the shrine was an essential part of her devotion in order to serve the spirits, according to Kim.

Kim was in her mid-sixties. She had known Lee Bosal for over ten years, which should mean that she knew Lee Bosal well in an interactive relationship. But, the character of their relationship had radically changed once the new figure, Kang monk shaman, appeared as a partner at the Lee Bosal's shrine. Kim commented:

> Kang monk bosses me around, treating me as if I were his own slave. What is more, he is very picky about everything that I have done in the shrine, and I often feel too distressed to deal with him. He wants all recognition to be given to him here, though the shrine belongs to Lee Bosal. This is so nauseating for me. But I have to endure until I have completed the three years of my devotion for my son's life. What can I do?

Kim's voice was desperate but determined. She liked to talk about her late grandfather who had been a shaman in Korea and who had left a number of his shamanic items to her when he died. His belongings that she had received included an old shamanic document, some hand bells, and a folding fan, which she had kept as her most precious treasures and disclosed to no one else, in keeping with her grandfather's will made at his death bed.

Her prior life, though not that great, had seemed smooth until her first husband's abuse began. The husband was a Caucasian, U.S. military man whom she met at the bar of a military camp in Korea where she worked as a waitress. His violence had eventually led to the end of their marriage not long after her relocation to the U.S. After the divorce that had left her quite alone, she had had a struggle with daily hardships and found it hard to survive in the face of cultural and language barriers. As time went on, she had gotten a job working at a regional military camp restaurant where she met and married another Caucasian man. She had not wanted to fail again, and she had thought that having a baby would help sustain a prolonged intimacy. She had wanted to settle down as a family in this foreign country. So she had been eager to become pregnant. But later, she had to acknowledge that her plan did not work out very well. Domestic violence and another divorce awaited her in that marriage. Regardless of her efforts to make her marriage successful, Kim had ended up having to raise her racially-mixed son as a single mother. Since then, she had worked hard to survive, returning to work at the military camp restaurant. Her son was then twenty-nine years old and married. She had felt somewhat relieved of her responsibility when her son had gotten married. She continued:

> My life plans never really work out. It's as if evil keeps track-
> ing me to destroy my *bok*.[2] What was suddenly happening to
> me was paralytic symptoms with my right leg about two years
> before my planned retirement with good benefits. So, I came to
> see Lee Bosal. Then, Lee Bosal's *gongsu*[3] was too frightening
> and urgent to delay action, so I immediately followed Lee Bosal's
> suggestion to move onto her shrine.

During Kim's narration of her life story, virtually all of the garbage turned into ashes. Then, the voice of Lee Bosal was heard from the shrine, calling her to come back in as if alerting her that her "break" was over now. Kim showed me a cynical smile on her lips as if saying: "See?..." Nonetheless,

2. *Bok* implies luck or good fortune in Korean pronunciation but in the Chinese letter.

3. *Gongsu* refers to the divinatory message of the charismatic shaman in traditional Korean shamanism. See T. Kim 1996b; Kendall 1993; Guillemoz 1993.

Kim acknowledged that she would continue committing herself to bear what was daily given to her until she would hear a great *gongsu*, a divinatory message, from Lee Bosal for her son's life. As usual, she was probably the first one to kowtow and offer clean water to the Buddhist and shamanic deities and spirits early in the morning at six o'clock, before anyone else got up. Kim was also ready to serve Lee Bosal and the other shamanic devotees, since she knew it was her religious legacy, which had been preciously inherited from her dear grandfather shaman.

2. Hybridized Practice, Subversive Divination, Cured Children

At Lee Bosal's shrine, it was a day of *baekjung* (C. Kim 2003, 36),[4] purportedly a Buddhist ritual kept annually on July 15 of the lunar calendar for sending the deceased's spirits "from this world, *iseung*, to the world of the dead, *jeoseung*" (R. Hwang 1992, 20). It seemed likely that there had been an argument between Lee Bosal and Kang monk shaman in regard to performing the *baekjung* ceremony in the shamanic shrine. Lee Bosal's muttering still continued at the breakfast table, somewhat unpleasantly disclosed:

> Why should the *baekjung* ceremony be performed in this shamanic shrine? It is not the shamanic tradition. We have our own ceremony for the deceased spirits in our own shamanic tradition.

Previously, Lee Bosal had spoken to me about her religious self-awareness as such: "Shamanism is my *shin-narim* [Guillemoz 1993, 27];[5] meanwhile, Buddhism is my belief." She clearly articulated a separation between her own shamanic vocation and her personal Buddhist belief. She primarily served the shamanic altar, but she also reserved a small, separate space for a Buddhist altar room, in keeping with her own belief, a room that was well supplied with various Buddhist decorations.

The Buddhist altar room was located across from the shamanic altar room on the second floor of the shrine building. Buddhist statues filled

---

4. *Baekjung* is the only day of the year for sending the spirits of the dead peacefully to the other world, whether from some hell or from still wandering in this world.

5. *Shin-narim* indicates the initiation by the spirit that typically occurs for the charismatic shaman, in traditional Korean shamanism.

the room. The big Amita Buddha statue in *gabuja*,[6] with gold plating, sat at the center of the altar, along with the *Ji-jang Bosal*, the light-being, on the left, and *Gwanseum Bosal*, the light-being, on the right of the Amita Buddha (Canda 1995; Popchong 1996).[7] The *Yaksa Bosal*, the Medicine Buddha, sat against the right side wall of the altar area. The *Ilgwang Bosal*, the Sunshine Buddha, sat to the left, and the *Wolgwang Bosal*, the Moonlight Buddha, to the right of the *Yaksa Bosal*. The mural paintings were all specially ordered from professional artists in Korea and delivered to her Buddhist altar in her shrine in the U.S. At about seven feet tall, the wood-carved, dark brown-colored *Mireuk Bosal*, the Buddha of the Future, was also separately standing at the far left corner, as viewed from the open front entrance of the Buddhist altar room. The *Mireuk Bosal* elegantly stood with a warm smile on its lips, holding a small jar in the right hand that was resting on its chest. A separate, small, wooden, round table was placed in front of the standing *Mireuk Bosal*, harboring a pair of candle stands, a bronze incense jar, a bronze raw rice bowl, and a water bowl on its top.

A relatively large-sized iron bell was placed on the right, next to the open front entrance of the Buddhist altar room. It had been donated by one of her clients whose son was cured from a paralysis of the lower body, according to Lee Bosal. The client who had donated the iron bell was a Harvard medical school graduate and a renowned doctor in the Mid-Atlantic area. All of his close family were core members of one of the Protestant Korean immigrant megachurches in the area. However, when he had faced the medical dilemma of his five-year-old son's sudden lower body paralysis, he had searched for alternative treatments. When he and his wife had heard from other people about Lee Bosal's success with shamanic remedies, they had decided to meet her, because of their strong concern for the physical healing of their son. However, the father, as a Western-trained doctor who graduated from an Ivy League medical school and as an evangelical Christian, was still cautious and suspicious when he and his wife sought the help of a shaman. It was something quite contrary to his scientific education and his public standing in the

---

6. *Gabuja* refers to the typical sitting position in the Buddhist tradition, also called the lotus posture. It is usually seen at the center of the inner room of a Buddhist temple.

7. The *Ji-jang Bosal* is Kstigarbha Bodhisattva and the *Gwanseum Bosal* as Avalokitesvara Bodhisattva. Both of them are Bodhisattva, from Sanskrit, literally meaning "light-being" or "the incarnation of compassion." In Korea, Bodhisattva is translated to *bosal*.

predominantly protestantized Korean immigrant community. So, the father had stepped aside but had sent his wife forth to arrange for the shamanic ritual. Lee Bosal said:

> I guaranteed to cure his son from the beginning when I first met them, because they were not destined to have a disabled son, according to both parents' *saju*.[8]

She regarded healing people from strange or unknown illnesses as one of her fundamental strengths, particularly in the case of children whose parents had consulted her. In this regard, Lee Bosal contended that her special gift was for retrieving children's well-being from various broken-nesses, since she was "spirited" by a strong *dongja shin*, a child spirit.

Two more anecdotal accounts intrigued me in this regard. About thirty years ago, when Lee Bosal was quite exhausted from fortune-telling, she decided to move on to a Buddhist temple to become a Buddhist monk instead of being a shaman. She even entirely closed her shamanic practice, disconnected from her social relationships, cashed out all the funds from her bank account, and offered these funds to the Buddhist temple. Lee Bosal encountered a famous female Buddhist monk, H. *seunim*, at the temple in Korea who taught her what it meant to be a Buddhist monk. Her teaching was that being a Buddhist monk did not mean just staying at the temple, but it meant serving and comforting other people with compassion. Lee Bosal was unable to agree with H. *seunim* at the beginning, but later, she took to heart what the *seunim* taught her. One day, following the lesson of H. *seunim*, she left the temple to walk in a nearby rural village. She felt thirsty, and then she saw some cold drinks in a refrigerator outside a small village convenience store, visible from the pathway. She very much wanted a drink but realized that she had not a single coin with which to buy a drink. Later, on the day's walk, Lee Bosal was delighted to find a residence where she could ask for a bowl of water to drink, as she felt quite thirsty. She gulped down a bowl of cool water that the resident had drawn from a well for her, but she saw a couple of earthworms stuck to the bottom of the bowl, which made her feel sick. At that moment, she suddenly spat out words to the woman who had rendered the fresh bowl of water for her to drink: "Is there a child here who is sick?"

---

8. *Saju* means the data of individual birth year, month, day, and time, which is believed to be the fundamental variable to determine one's own particular destiny in life (Y. Harvey 1979, 49).

She commented to me about this experience: "What on earth! I went up to the mountains having decided to quit practicing, but I realized that I was unable to get out of the wheel of my destiny."

Lee Bosal continued, saying that the woman who gave the water then asked her: "Are you able to do fortune-telling?"

Lee Bosal asked her own question again, not answering the woman's question: "Is there a sick child here?"

The woman said: "Yes."

Lee Bosal asked further: "Can I see the child?" Lee Bosal was then led to the room where the sick child was laid and demanded that the mother prepare some food and some ritual items for setting up a table. Lee Bosal continued with her anecdotal narration: "The little boy lived happily ever after, which was, in the long run, what made me come back to shamanic practice since that time."

A scientific account of the therapeutic reality of spiritual healing did not seem attainable in this case. Might there be a scientific blindness concerning unexplainable healings, even "miracles"? Is the label of super-stition a defense mechanism about such matters as shameful, ashamed, amoral, or pseudoscientific, which remain scary because they do not fit with "scientific" understandings (C. Kim 2003, 223)? In this regard, it may be helpful to listen to the way the Korean shamanic view relies upon the two worlds of the tangible and intangible: "The spirit and body are not discrete in Korean shamanism. They constitute 'a continuum, a mutually overlapping, interpenetrating, and conjunctive whole,' which is believed to make remedies possible, as in magic" (Hahm 1988, 62).

Another unusual disclosure in Lee Bosal's healing anecdotes was from her account of the process by which she determined the location of her current shrine building, so as to be able to move and settle in. She had envisaged the current shrine building a couple of times before her main steps in searching for it. Looking for a building similar to what she had seen in her vision, she made multiple tours around the northeastern U.S. She stopped by various realtors' offices as many times as possible, hop-ing to find the spirit-instructed location of the shamanic shrine building, with appropriate natural surroundings. About 2001, when she was still searching, she saw an intriguing picture that was posted in the list of local properties for sale at a realtor's office. Lee Bosal immediately made a tour around the property, accompanied by the realtor. The property was huge, but a flood had once damaged it. It was exactly the building that Lee Bosal had seen in her vision, and it was with a proper natural environment, with a nearby creek. The property had originally been the summer house of a judge who had decided to put it out for sale after the flash flood damage. Lee Bosal was sure that her *momju* would make a good bargain for her to purchase the property that would be the destined residence for her shamanic spirits. In the subsequent conversation with the property owner, she all of a sudden asked the judge if his child was sick with an unknown illness. The judge cynically laughed at her question but did not answer. He asked her immediately to leave his property. Later, after a series of persistent contacts, Lee Bosal made a deal that the judge render a bargain price to her for the property, with the stipulation that she would ritually heal his child. She described the situation as:

> The judge was laughing at my proposal from the beginning, but he was finally half in doubt when he accepted my offer. However, his attitude completely changed when he realized that his child came to be suddenly recovered. So, I could purchase this shrine at a reasonable price.

Lee Bosal did not mention what type of illness the child had and how it came to be cured. Yet, the location and the natural environment seemed to perfectly fit the physical conditions required for the shamanic ritual functions of the shrine. The shrine property was a three-story building surrounded by a big yard and bordered by an expanse of trees. The trees also helped to block the shrine from the view of the neighbors and to minimize the ritual noises that might bother them. Actually, each house in the forested area was at least a fair distance away from any neighbors, which could protect the privacy of each residence. Such privacy was particularly important for the shamanic shrine, with its various loud noises. A vigorous creek ran beyond the grove of trees across from the shrine, which provided a natural environment for water rituals (Y. Harvey 1979, 296; Jung Y. Lee 1981, 168).[9] In fact, based on my own research, very few Korean immigrant shamans in the northeastern region in the U.S. seemed to own such a sizable, impressive, well-laid out, and well-cared for shrine.

Though Lee Bosal offered a clear statement distinguishing her shamanic practice of *shin-narim*, initiation by the spirit, from her Buddhist belief, her ritual practice drew upon both traditions. It was unclear, however, the extent to which the mixture was due to her relationship

---

9. Lee Bosal serves the *yongshin* particularly devotedly in her shrine. *Yongshin* literally refers to the dragon king; in general, it involves the water spirit.

with Kang monk shaman or her own past. Historically, Buddhism and shamanism were more intimately interactive, sharing ritual environments from having been identified as politically unapproved religious dissidents under the Joseon regime (Vermeersch 2007; S. Hwang 1996; Y. Yoon 1996). In this respect, shamanism has a share in the collective Korean cultural mind along with Buddhism, despite the mainline Buddhist teaching and essential meditation system, *son* or *zen*, which differentiates Buddhism from traditional shamanic tradition (Y. Yoon 1996). The shamanic belief system involves a core value of *gibok*, which literally means "asking for luck or fortune" but, more meaningfully, signifies "praying for remedies of life anomalies."

The conflict cited above in regard to the *baekjung* ceremony might have been provoked solely by Kang monk shaman's initiative, without a full discussion ahead of time with Lee Bosal. Meanwhile, Lee Bosal often mentioned her respect for the Buddhist monk, indicating that "the *beopsa* is superior to the *mudang* in the spirit world of shamanism" (Jung Y. Lee 1981, 34).[10] No matter what she was actually convinced of, her caustic remarks mentioned above suggested that the Buddhist ritual could commandeer her shamanic shrine. Religion encompasses not only the text of transcendence but the context of imminence, the here and now, through an ongoing encounter with certain kinds of access to power that is considered to be supernatural. The bottom line was that Lee Bosal was "reluctantly" willing to surrender herself to the eminent power of Kang monk shaman, the power that she believed was coming from the supremacy of Buddhism. In so doing, the influence of Kang monk shaman's superiority was ultimately going to alter forms and practice of her shamanic rituals at her shrine. Lee Bosal frequently commented that "the spirits are very jealous." In this, the question arisen was if she would find her *momju* pleased by the intrusion and inclusion of Kang monk shaman's Buddhist ritual within her shamanic shrine and, thereby, the reduction of Lee Bosal to being a subordinate under his authority. Kang monk shaman had already attempted to control the rituals beyond Lee Bosal's *sin-narim*, initiation by the spirits.

10. *Beopsa* refers to the Buddhist monk who teaches the Buddhism. One of the ritual enactments, *gori*, from the full twelve-part traditional shamanic séance, is offered to the *bulsa*, the heavenly Buddha. *Mudang* refers to a female shaman in Korean.

3. A Symbolic Sign from the Past Delivered to the Present

Signs are critically important in the shamanic ritual, as they mediates their meaning between the world of spirits and that of the living. Just as a sign is related to certain particular circumstances of a specific time and space, it can also be indicative of a prediction or reflection of the future, an undercurrent of the present, and/or an impact from the past (Langer 2002). So, what the sign represents is access to meaning that is associated with specific narratives and contexts of particular events. Susanne K. Langer insists that meaning is functional, in that it is conveyed logically and affected psychologically in the form of sign or symbol (Langer 2002, 137). In other words, the meaning in each sign indicates more of a relation between one thing and another than its literal quality or property in itself, according to Langer's understanding of meaning as functional (Langer 2002, 138). Langer mentions that "even in the simplest kinds of meaning there must be at least two other things related to the term that 'means'—an object that is 'meant,' and a subject who uses the term" (Langer 2002, 142).

The awareness of symbolic signs was often intensively amplified in the ritual at Lee Bosal's shrine, which might have tremendous psychological impact on an audience whose sense of fear or power was stimulated, along with a triggered credulity. The primary reason for this response was articulated as the possibility of *bujeong*—actions of "the unclean spirits"—in the ritual proceeding, which could reduce the power of the ritual such that the ritual could not ultimately achieve its purpose (Jung Y. Lee 1981, 41). As an illustration, when the red bean rice cake was not smoothly steamed or the rice was not so well cooked, *seol ik da*, during the preparation of the ritual food table, Lee Bosal stood right before the stove, facing the rice cake or rice still being steamed in the pot, and kept bowing and *pison*, praying with rubbing the palms (R. Hwang 1996, 202), so as to appease the spirits, earnestly begging them: "*Shinryeong nimdeul, neogreobge yongseohae juseyo*" (Dear spirits, generously forgive me). In this situation, the inadequately cooked rice or rice cake was a symbolic sign of the spirits' dissatisfaction or complaint about certain components or proceedings in the ritual environment. Therefore, Lee Bosal pleaded with the deities or spirits for mercy, hoping for a successful ritual outcome. In respect to the reason for the sign, Lee Bosal did not forget, in advance, to ask the women who participated in the ritual preparation if anyone of them was having "a menstrual period" at the time, which might account for any problems.[11]

Signs also received significant attention particularly at the closure of the shamanic rituals, when Lee Bosal attempted to verify the satisfaction of the spirits with the ritual. She kept a careful eye on every item following the completing of each ritual, including such matters as the pattern and direction of the wax flowing from the burning candles and the appearance of the incense ashes on the altar, so as to assure and confirm for herself and her client that the ritual had been successfully completed. On one occasion, after having served a *josang gut* (Kendall 1985, 99; Kwon 2004), a shamanic ritual served to the ancestral spirits, Lee Bosal cautiously drew the attention of the ritual participants to a trail of tiny footprints on the pile of raw rice in a brass bowl that had been presented on the shamanic altar during the ritual. Lee Bosal's explication was that the trail of tiny footprints was a symbolic sign that the client's great-great-great grandmother was walking about, following her reincarnation in a human body. The client's great-great-great grandmother had been a dedicated shamanic devotee, engaging in offering big shamanic rituals a few times each year. Thus, the great-great-great grandmother's reincarnation, evidenced by the ritual sign of some footprints, signified to the client that the ritual had well served the client's ancestral spirits. The successful ritual held the promise of remedies and/or good fortune for the clients' family and their business, which would follow from the satisfaction of the client's ancestral spirits. "A sign is an operator, there being an intrinsic or natural connection between the sign and the thing it signifies," asserts Ernst Cassirer (as quoted in Morris 1987, 219). In this regard, the sign of the tiny footprints on the pile of raw rice in the brass bowl would continue to provide shamanic access to meaning in the mind of the client, indicating the significance of the ritual offering and the resultant efficacy of the ritual assurance, straightforwardly confirmed through the shamanic analysis of a symbolic sign from the ritual.

The ritual signs conveyed at Lee Bosal's shrine were often hard for the client to understand, unless there were a full shamanic analysis provided to them for each sign. As in the illustrations already given above, the not-so-well-cooked rice or rice cake was a symbolic sign that the spirits had been displeased by certain components of *bujeong*, a ritual

11. Association with the blood linked with the female gender is purportedly a worldwide ritual taboo, well attested in many forms of folk religious practices around the globe.

pollution. Also, the trail of the tiny footprints was a sign of reincarnation, which was identified to the clients as good fortune. However, the actual meaning of the enigmatically symbolic sign could be apprehended only when Lee Bosal reported her analytic account to clients. So, the shamanic interpretation of symbolic signs features a subjective aspect and therein may also provide room to be utilized for a shaman's own purpose, suggesting to the clients the need to offer additional rituals.

The next symbolic sign to be discussed here was pretty easy to follow, not requiring a special shamanic interpretation in order to grasp the relationship between the sign and its symbolic meaning. However, even such an easily comprehensible sign still triggered the mystery of the time and spatial contextuality in shamanic practice.

The D. couple, in their early forties, often visited Lee Bosal's shamanic shrine for a regular *gut*, concerning good fortune for their mobile phone businesses and a beauty supply store near a Korean immigrant community. On a summer day in August 2009, they arrived at the shrine in the evening somewhat after 6 p.m., having completed large grocery shopping for the ritual. Since the ritual had been planned ahead, the usual three assistants—Kim, Mrs. Yi, and Minja—were already in the kitchen for the cooking and the setting up of the ritual food table, a process that continued until about 11 p.m.

It had been a somewhat unsettled day for Lee Bosal, featuring a big argument with Kang monk shaman in continuation of their disagreement over the *baekjung* ceremony. Consequently, Kang monk shaman temporarily moved out by himself to the condo-consultation office, leaving Lee Bosal alone at the forest shrine. Because of his departure, Lee Bosal was in a troubled mood and was continually tossing out belittling comments about the behavior and then the absence of Kang monk shaman during the preparation of the ritual for the D. couple. The D. couple remained outwardly calm, while also frequently giving awkward looks to each other during the ritual preparation. The regular women's chitchatting in the kitchen was not heard that evening, leaving only the various cracking noises that echoed from the kitchen utensils and the washing in the sink.

As part of the preparation, Lee Bosal took out some new packs of hemp fabric from the special transparent plastic wrapping that would be used in making the *gopuri* (R. Hwang 1996; Bruno 1995).[12] As she spread

---

12. *Go* literally means "knot," according to the Chinese letter, but it symbolizes "hardship" or *han*. So, the *gopuri* is a combination of *go* as *han* or "resentment" and

out a lengthy rectangular section of white hemp fabric, she also stretched some black hemp fabric over the white one. Then Lee Bosal all of a sudden became dumbfounded, briefly muttering, "Oh—my." In the next moment, she showed to the D. couple the black hemp fabric, which had a hole in it surrounded by an ashy fringe. While her fingers were still marking the hole, Lee Bosal asked them if anyone in their family had died in a fire. The little hole still visibly bore the residual traces of the blackened ashy edge around it, giving the clear impression of having been burned. But the brand-new pack of black hemp was still giving the distinctive smell of having just been removed from the taped plastic wrapper.

As the D. couple leaned forward to look closely at the burnt hole, the husband replied to Lee Bosal that his grandmother had died in a fire when his house had caught fire during his adolescence. As he described the tragedy: "I was seventeen at the time. She was ninety-two years old. As my house seemed to explode with the fire, she, a disabled senior, could not be rescued and died in the fire."

Lee Bosal responded to him: "Imagine how much your grandmother's spirit had been resentful! Have you offered any *gut* ritual to comfort her spirit?"

The husband answered that his family had annually offered the ancestral service to her but not particularly offered any *gut* ritual to comfort her spirit.

Lee Bosal said:

> Look at this. Your grandmother's spirit attempts to inform me about her *han* to me. How accurate it is! This type of hole should not occur in a brand-new pack of hemp fabric. This occasion very seldom happens to me, no more than one out of ten thousand new packs.

The voice of Lee Bosal indicated that she was incensed at the moment, as she lifted up the fabric in order to show the hole clearly right before the very faces of the D. couple. They looked overwhelmed, while remaining silent.

Langer asserts that "a sign indicates the existence—past, present, or future—of a thing, event, or condition. . . . A scar is a sign of a past

---

puri, meaning "disentangling." In shamanic ritual, *go* is represented by symbolic ties of the hemp fabric in a ribbon shape. In this, different colors and distinct numbers implicate differently. When the tied, ribbon-shaped *go* is untied in a ritual, it symbolizes that a deceased person's resentment is released.

accident" (Langer 2002, 139). The burnt hole traced in the new set of hemp was a symbolic sign that was logically associated with the tragic death of D.'s grandmother in the fire. In this, the symbolic sign manifested its function for meaning in the psychological process of the D. couple by indicating an insufficiently recognized painful event of the past and the necessity of a remedy in the present. In doing so, it probed the significance of a symbolic sign during the preparation for a shamanic ritual, while thereby elaborating various semantic meanings for the function as well as the importance of rituals at Lee Bosal's shamanic shrine. A mystery was still residual regarding the question of how the symbolic sign of the burnt hole, signifying a tragic event of the past, had been powerfully transmitted to the present in the new hemp fabric that was selected for use as a *gopuri* at the D. couple's ritual for good fortune in the present.

Marking the unequivocal sign as a mere coincidence seemed incongruent, when it was bringing to light an engagement with the traumatic incident that happened to a grandmother in the early lifetime of a present client, pointing to unfinished business. Yet, "if everything signifies, the result will be either insanity or banality," as Jonathan Z. Smith asserts (Smith 1982, 56). Smith addresses this inscription particularly in his discussion of the significances created and valued in cases of accidental coincidence, which are settled in religion, especially in ritual, by the feature of regularity and repetition:

> Understood from such a perspective, *ritual is an exercise in the strategy of choice.* What to include? What to hear as a message? What to see as a sign? What to perceive as having double meaning? What to exclude? What to allow to remain as background noise? What to understand as simply "happening"? The priestess is exercising her sense of the *economy of signification.* (Smith 1982, 56)

Smith's reference to "insanity" perhaps offers some insight for what the Korean immigrant shaman carries to the otherness of the Korean diaspora, to be successfully routinized in the mainstream society in the U.S. What appears to be insane, mysterious, or miraculous could be interpreted as the superhuman power of spirits as significantly scoped by the charismatic shaman and taken up in the shamanic ritual, *jeom and gut,* fortune-telling and the shamanic ritual.

4. A Theoretical Implication

Speaking the Unspeakable:
Theoretical Implications of the Shamanic Gifts

Lee Bosal as a charismatic Korean immigrant female shaman was convinced of the quality of *jaeju*, the shamanic gift, as a feature of the shamanic practitioner. As she indicated, *jaeju* should be given by the deities, but *uishik*, ritual and food setting, should be learned from the shamanic teacher.[13] If properly paraphrased, a shaman needs gifts from above as well as skills from the shamanic relationship, particularly from the apprenticeship. Becoming a professional shaman in the Korean shamanic tradition presupposes specific qualities that mark her/him as different from ordinary people. The shamanic performance of divination and rituals cannot be properly enacted, unless the shaman has certain distinctive personal gifts that assist the ritual practice. A true shaman must possess at least a pair of gifts to be a professional shaman: individual charisma and the skill to quickly perceive various life conditions from the sense of collective consciousness.

Similarly, two particular features constituent of the shamanic gift are mentioned by Choongmoo Choi. The two qualities are critically expected from a successful shaman:

> "*Younghum*," in a Chinese loanword, is the spiritual power that produces the efficacy of ritual action. "*Noonchi*," a native Korean word widely used in everyday life, refers to social sensitivity—one's ability to understand a social situation, to make quick judgments about it and respond appropriately. (C. Choi, 1989, 236)

Younghum might be the foremost and indispensable quality for the *shinnarim* shaman, a charismatic shaman,[14] as the essential basis for the shaman's sensitivity and for the clairvoyance for fortune-telling, the aesthetic manifestation in the ritual, and communication with spirits. It is the given-to-the-chosen asset only for the charismatic shaman, not for the hereditary shaman (Ch'oe 1984, 230; Y. Harvey 1979, 5; Kendall

---

13. This pair of shamanic qualities, *jaeju* and *uishik*, were Lee Bosal's own specific words, when describing the shamanic gift used for her shamanic performance.

14. The *shinnarim* shaman is referred to in various ways, such as *gang-shin mu*, god-descended shaman, charismatic shaman, spirit-possessed shaman, etc.

1985, 37).[15] A *shinnarim* shaman is initiated by spirit possession, more specifically by *shinbyeong* as a shamanic sickness; whereas a hereditary shaman inherits through kinship. Thus, *younghum* is a certain unique quality not learned but given from above to the chosen shaman, by means of the spirit possession. Meanwhile, *noonchi* signifies a quick alertness to particularities in social circumstances, which is not automatically awarded but supposed to be acquired through shamanic training and relationships in the apprenticeship. One's *noonchi* takes for granted an ability to promptly grasp the client's contextuality, the social circumstances in general, and to capture significant indicators of the client's specific social and individual conditions in particular. Thus, this paired quality might be the definite requisite for becoming a *shinnarim* shaman, in order to be successful in her or his shamanic practice, according to Choi.

In summary, the aforementioned pairs share a similar structure while articulating different conceptions and are worth a deeper exploration, in order to investigate a theoretical perception of the shamanic gifts: an individual charisma and the acquired ability to grasp the range of the collective consciousness.

A Theoretical Implication of the Individual Charisma of the Korean Immigrant Shaman

Individual charisma refers to a supernatural gift given from above that is perceived as the sign of the shamanic call and received from the preliminary possession of shamanic spirits. It is a gift to enable a shaman's verbal, physical, and spiritual capacity to act, functioning as the essential means to practice shamanism. The characteristic of this gift is subjective, by means of the shaman's own individual experience. In other words, the shamanic attribute of gifts signifies primarily a dual sustainability—sacred and human—with the culturally collective Korean world. It combines the collective consciousness and the individual charisma. This heterogeneity of the shamanic gift is the indispensable feature in the professional life of each charismatic shaman, including the distinctive shamanic conduct in

---

15. There are two types of Korean shamans, the *shinnarim* shaman and the hereditary shaman. The *shinnarim* shaman is spirit-possessed, particularly initiated by *shinbyeong*, the shamanic sickness. Meanwhile, a hereditary shaman inherits by kinship, particularly from a mother-in-law. This type of shaman is found mostly in the southwestern part of the South Korean territory. Unless otherwise indicated, reference to a Korean shaman in this text is to the charismatic shaman.

immersion with each specific persona of spirit possession. It implies that the individual *momju* prescribes each distinctively personified talent or gift for the shaman, which differentiates each shaman's ritual performance and style of divination in each distinctive, individual spirit possession.

The comment of Tae-gon Kim seems a notable advance in this regard, as offering a foundational description for the individual charisma of the Korean shaman: "The ritual of the charismatic shaman unifies the spirit and the shaman, who originally were two separate entities" (T. Kim and Chang 1998, 15). Kim, in this citation, describes the aspect of individual interaction with the possessing spirits in its integrity. Max Weber clarifies the individual characteristic of charisma, as he states:

> The term ëcharisma will be applied to a certain quality of an individual personality by virtue of which he [or she] is set apart from ordinary men [and women] and treated as endowed with supernatural, superhuman, or at least specifically exceptional powers or qualities. (Weber 1947, 358)

Weber makes it clear in this discussion that there is a union of individuality and superhuman power in charisma. His remark prompts a threefold division, for an elaborated perception of the subjective experience involved: "A certain quality of an individual personality"; "apart from ordinary men [and women]"; and "endowed with supernatural, superhuman . . . qualities," which could be taken to identify a "leader" (Andreski 1984, 97).

Weber links his notion of charisma to "prophetic leadership" in ancient Israel, while elaborating its implications from the contextuality of early Western Christianity (Weber 1993, 328). In this, Weber asserts that the individual charisma has a groundbreaking quality and an underlying power that can transform the status quo of an institutionalized society (Andreski 1984, 108). Otherwise expressed, individuals who have radically dedicated themselves or, more specifically, been dedicated by sacred authority to the counterinfluences upon sociohistorical institutions are considered to be charismatic leaders who have the gift not by their own choice but "coming from above," according to Weber (1922, 328). With this, Weber associates the role of charismatic leaders with that of magicians, healers, prophets, heroes, or saviors, while considering all of them to be the agents of superhuman power (Weber 1971, 229–30).

The unique leadership of the Korean charismatic shaman can be identified with "the charisma given from above," as in Weber's description

(1922, 328). The individual charisma of the Korean charismatic shaman is initiated, as mentioned, particularly by the shamanic illness, *shinbyeong*, solely associated with the experience of spirit possession. The initiation illness comes involuntarily upon a shamanic candidate when an individual is possessed by an action of the spirits. The *shinbyeong* thus serves as an ordinary threshold for a chosen individual to become a professional shamanic practitioner in traditional Korean shamanism. Becoming a professional charismatic shaman begins with an individual experience of physical, mental, and/or life ordeals, such as sickness, a broken relationship, or a business failure. Simply put, the *shinbyeong* is the symbolic sign of being called to Korean shamanness. On this matter, the *shinbyeong* is the core element in the shamanic prescription that designates the shamanic candidate's holistic surrender to inhabitation by the possessing spirit. Therefore, the condition of spirit possession causes a drastic change in the behavioral persona of a certain individual due to this spiritual imposition (Chilson and Knecht 2003, 9). Once a shaman is possessed by a particular bodily deity or spirit, s/he is expected to continue serving the same deity as her or his *momju* throughout her or his shamanic practice, following the initiating ritual, *gut*.[16] Likewise, neither the *shinbyeong* nor the *momju* is chosen by the shaman but constitutes the gift given to her/him "from above." Apart from the charismatic gifts "from above," no one can properly perform shamanic rituals and divinations. Therefore, the *shinbyeong* that is undergone as part of the designation of an individual shaman is strictly a personal shamanic call, as is possession by the *momju*, which leads to individual shamanic servitude. In other words, becoming a professionally practicing charismatic shaman requires an individual gift of a charisma and an integration with the shamanic bodily governing deity[17] Thus, it may be appropriate to say that the shamanic body becomes an individual charismatic habitat. In doing so, the occupancy of the *momju* spirit becomes a therapeutic mechanism, while assisting in performing life remedies, physical healing, and discerning fortunes from anomalies that the Korean diaspora bring to the shaman.

16. Some distinctive methods are found in the categorization of *gut*, according to various scholars' definitions: either deity-centered or people-centered, either shaman-centered or people-centered (Yoon 1996, 190; Haeoe Gongbo-Gwan 1997, 128; Huhm 1980, 11; T. Kim and Chang 1998, 20; Yu and Phillips 1983, 146; and C. Kim 2003, 38).

17. In general, two types of shamans have existed in traditional Korean shamanism, but in this chapter, I continue focusing on the charismatic shaman who is initiated by spirit possession.

Lee Bosal was sent to live with a *shin-eomeoni*, a shamanic mother, when she was about ten years old. She got a *shinnarim*, a spirit possession, which allowed her to see things that others did not see, and she wandered about day and night. Her biological parents felt ashamed of her condition of apparent shamanic possession, and she became estranged from her entire family after she was sent away. After moving in with her *shin-eomeoni*, she was initiated in three separate shamanic rituals, while developing her own shamanic practice of divinations and rituals, accompanied by an apprenticeship with her shamanic mother. Nonetheless, she persistently battled against the shamanic call and managed to run away from her calling, even in the midst of her practice. After Lee Bosal completed high school, she met a Native American army sergeant who was stationed at a military camp in Korea. She thought at that time that it was a special chance for her to run away from her shamanic profession. Lee Bosal unconditionally followed the sergeant when he returned to his home in the U.S. She cohabited with him for two years and gave birth to a son. However, when her Native American partner could no longer tolerate her repetitively aberrant behaviors, as she wandered out late at night and randomly fell into a delirium or hysteria with him, he turned to another woman and ended the relationship with Lee Bosal. Even after breaking up with him, her shamanic symptoms went on. Nonetheless, Lee Bosal continued attempting to neglect her shamanic calling, not wanting to return to serving the shamanic spirits. In the meantime, she became involved with another man with whom she had a daughter. That marriage led her to a strong desire to seek to stay together with her new family and establish a good relationship. She even began attending a conservative Baptist church as part of sustaining her family. However, she soon realized that she was failing to succeed in this, as her shamanic symptoms never ceased. She failed to end her wandering behavior and screaming out in the late night, when everyone else was asleep. The harder Lee Bosal attempted to fit in with the church, praying eagerly for her life to be stable, the more she was troubled by the spirit possession that was regarded by her conservative Protestant church community to be demonic possession. She emphasized that she tried hard to change her destiny by getting away from her "calling" to the shamanic practice. As counseled by her Baptist pastor, she was once convinced that she could be victorious over the "demonic possession" and so even attended a regional Christian seminary to see if she could become a Christian minister, rather than returning to the shamanness. However, she had to acknowledge that her attempts to transform her fate all failed. Instead, her experience with spirits in the Christian church assisted her to clarify the direction that she had to accept: "I realized that the spiritual world in the Christian church was very different from the one that I was possessed by, which made me no longer able to sustain any other identity but becoming a shaman."

It had been several decades since she had finally settled down in the practice of Korean immigrant shamanism in the U.S., giving up her resistance to that call. She then looked content with her life as a shaman and was even proud of her shamanic practice. Perhaps, this was due to her total resignation from the effort to establish a conventional family life and avoid her calling to become a shaman. Moreover, she was even satisfied with the marginalized role as a shaman in which she brought healing and success to the lives of Korean otherness in the U.S. In contrast to M. Doryeong, the Korean male immigrant shaman discussed in chapter 4, who primarily worked with female clients from among the poorer immigrants, the clientele of Lee Bosal were mostly affluent, came from the educated elite and the upscale middle class, and were often Protestant Christians in religious affiliation, including males and non-Koreans. This wealthier clientele aided her financial condition, which noticeably contrasted with the financial condition of M. Doryeong.

A shaman is a subversive presence, generally, in the cliché world of the Korean immigrant community in the U.S. Weber's notion of charisma includes "a rejection of all ties to any external order" (Weber 1946, 250). Weber's emphasis in that remark fits together well with his discussion of the "prophet who was a man by virtue of his purely personal charisma and by virtue of his mission" (Bendix 1960, 89). The prophetic personalities that ignite changes in the established authority of religious and social arenas are then, according to Weber, brought about by the phenomenon of the prophetic practices of power, divination, magical healing, and counseling by virtue of personal gifts (Weber 1968, 253–55).

Weber's notion of charisma, in this regard, delineates a portrayal of the Korean shaman in two major attributes. The primary feature is the woman-stream leadership running in the man-centered society. Similarly, the shamanic tradition inhabits a counterculture to neo-Confucianism as the cultural prescription in Korean society. In doing so, the charismatic leadership of female shamans as cultural agents is considered subversive of the masculine ordinariness in Korean culture, wherein the role of intercessor or impact-maker is ordinarily the privileged entitlement of males.

Meanwhile, new trends in the inland Korean world are altering the shamanic footprint, by frequently producing modern, educated, professional, younger male or female shamans, in contrast to the traditionally poorly educated, female environment of the earlier shamanic arena. However, the situation of Korean immigrant shamanism in the U.S. is still mostly shaped by the traditional shamanic trend, as with the first-generation immigrant female stream. The impact of a mainstream Protestant immigrant environment, along with nostalgia for the traditional Korean environment, cannot be overlooked in this regard. Further ethnographic research will help to articulate the recent trends of Korean immigrant shamanism, in general, in the Protestant grassroots Korean immigrant community in the U.S. This research can also be resourceful in a comparison of the recent, more open trends of Korean shamanism in the homeland to the development of Korean immigrant shamanism in the U.S.

The other subversive feature that delineates a portrayal of the charismatic shaman is the shamanic kinship that is granted to the initiated shaman. The charismatic shamanic kinship is not cohesive with hereditary legal rights, but it is in accordance with the bond affected with the *momju*, the bodily governing deity, and the senior shaman who presides over the apprenticeship of the shamanic neophyte. That is, the shamanic candidate acquires a spirit-given family relationship with the shamanic teacher to be the *shinttal*, the shamanic daughter, or the *shinadeul*, the shamanic son, to the *shineomeoni*, the shamanic mother, in the case of female shamanic teacher, or the *shinabeoji*, the shamanic father, in the case of a male teacher. Discretely differentiated from the genetic line of descent in the Korean traditional family structure, the shamanic kinship is godly and granted "from above" in relation to the shamanic possession and initiation associated with the shamanic apprenticeship (Weber 1968, 58; Weber 1993, 65).[18] It is accorded sacredness for the shamanic spirits' sake.[19] The shamanic family relation is, then, quintessentially marked by

18. The shamanic kinship often becomes an abusive arena associated with the hierarchical practice of powers and control and with economic advantages, as it is granted to charismatic shamans sequentially, by the initiation in traditional Korean shamanism. In this regard, Eisenstadt's notion of Weber's charisma is noteworthy: "The routinization of charisma takes the form of appropriation of powers of control and of economic advantages by the followers or disciples in the process of traditionalization or legalization" (Weber 1968, 58).

19. Kinship is entitled to the shamanic parent, the shamanic daughter, and/or the shamanic son, regardless of age and gender differences. For instance, in the case that

a matriarchal discipline, whereas the status quo family structure prevails as an exclusively male hegemony in both traditional Korean society and Korean immigrant community.

In this regard, M. Doryeong, the Korean immigrant male shaman, explains his own odd experiences in the predominantly female shamanic domain that he had to face as a male shaman. He had always been the only male among the ritual staff, which brought him enormous difficulties in terms of resting, sleeping, or changing clothes, when the entire group stayed together during the duration of the ritual.[20] As an added difficulty, he frequently had to deal with romantic rumors whenever he performed rituals for female clients, having embarked on his own independent practice of shamanism. Meanwhile, there was the curiosity of his feminized behavioral pattern and vocal tone, as if his feminized shamanic persona reflected the impact of his female superiors, such as M. Doryeong's *shin-bumo*[21] and his *momju* spirit, the bodily governing deity. M. Doryeong mostly socialized with male friends but also enjoyed working at the nail salon for his part-time job, according to him. Although the role of M. Doryeong when in his household is that of a dominant male, in keeping with the traditional Korean family structure, he is a subaltern under the female order, in the traditional shamanic arena.

Meanwhile, it is puzzling as to whether the radical feature of the shaman's charisma can serve to transform the status quo in the same Korean immigrant community in which the Korean immigrant shaman is severely stigmatized. The primary public reason for such a strong sense of condemnation towards the shamanic practice is its polytheistic pantheon, an element that generates instant hostility from the avowedly monotheistic Protestant church.[22] Along with this Protestant dogmatic resentment, there is also the traditional mainline neo-Confucian moral

---

the educated aged female is akin to the uneducated younger shamanic parent, kinship still demands respectful behavior in the shamanic hierarchy, regardless of the condition. The shamanic kinship is not cohesive with the bloodline but with the spiritual integrity of the *momju* and the shamanic teacher.

20. A certain number of staff are required in order to compose a traditionally formal shamanic ritual, such as shaman, drummer, gonger, flute player, etc.

21. *Shin-bumo* refers to the shamanic parent, mostly implying one parent, such as *shin-eomeoni*, a shamanic mother, or *shin-abeoji*, a shamanic father; but it can also refer to both shamanic parents, in other cases.

22. The condemnation of the shamanic practice is usually from the Protestant church, rather than from Catholics, within the Korean immigrant community.

ethos of male dominance, which is part of the Korean immigrant collective consciousness and which also fuels antagonism towards the shamanic practice. These perceptions promote public suspicion on the part of the Western Protestant religious hegemony as to the credibility of folk religious charismatic leadership and power. Then, as Weber insists that the charisma barely copes with the public suspicion due to its subjective feature and its source "from above," this also leaves aspects of the Korean immigrant shamanic charisma characteristically unproven and implausible (Weber 1947, 328). Furthermore, the factor that the Korean immigrant shamanic remedy is initiated by an individual encounter between the shamanic individual and the client, without reliance upon any form of structured community, can also elevate public suspicion. Therefore, the subjective and seclusive character of the charismatic shamanic practice contributes to the public perception that the Korean immigrant shamanic remedy is at best only individually therapeutic for those immigrant clientele who desire to repair their lives from the wretched brokenness or ordinariness of their life in a new land and to achieve good fortune, ultimately, materialistic success. The Korean charismatic shaman carries out individual remedies using mysterious, subjective therapeutic power, effecting micro transformations, but not affecting the status quo of the Korean immigrant community. This is a feature that differentiates shamanic charisma from prophetic charisma, the latter of which is directed in large part to the whole community and is discussed by Weber who hatched his rhetorical discourse of charisma out of a Western mainline Christian background.[23]

Both Lee Bosal and M. Doryeong often encountered inhospitable treatment by the Korean Protestant immigrant churches located close to their residences. They often faced hostile preaching or intimidation from the conditionally formed evangelical mission teams dispatched from the Korean Protestant churches. The primary purpose of such mission teams

23. The communal nature of the shamanic ritual was critical, particularly in the life of the traditional Korean village community, as with the village *dang gut* in the agricultural community or the *byeolshin gut*, particularly in the eastside ocean village in Korea. Some of them are still performed in the modern life of the inland Korea, though mostly in rural areas. But such shamanic engagement is rarely seen in the diasporic context of the U.S. The main reason for this is that the shamanic ritual takes place in isolated locations, so as to avoid public attention. Meanwhile, a recent trend of Korean shamanism, commonly, in both inland and diasporic Korean communities, is towards more of a ritualless pattern, which seems to help it encroach upon the crowded urban center, attracting the public simply to fortune-telling.

was to evict the "profane" shamanic superstitiousness from what was regarded as the "sacred" Protestant environment. In doing so, the teams often utilized verbal and physical abuse, breaking or defacing identifying signs and materials or pouring forth furious verbal condemnation of the shamanic presence. As an example, Lee Bosal mentioned the local dry cleaning store, whose owner was an elder in a regional Korean immigrant church and refused to launder the "demon-possessed" Lee Bosal's clothes. So, she had to take her laundry to a rather distant cleaner. M. Doryeong was once menaced by local church elders who threatened to jeopardize his shamanic business by reporting to the local police department that he conducted the shamanic practice in his apartment without having obtained a legal permit. At the same time, both shamans shared a "popular secret" with me that, in their shamanic practice, the majority of their clients are current churchgoers, including church elders, even ministers, and their wives. In this, as the Korean collective effervescence has moved onto the ethical monotheistic Protestantism in the public life of the diaspora, the hunger of the first-generation Korean immigrant cultural mind is, in private, yielding to the shamanic ethos, in asking for *bok*, good fortune, while looking sideways in their eagerness to search for the "demon possessed" to be their "culturally postulated defense mechanism" (Spiro 1987, 159).[24]

Meanwhile, Weber's concept of routinization is an essential element to be addressed in the discussion of charisma. Weber indicates that the destiny of charisma may be fully transformed when it leads to a routinized structure, losing the element of the primacy of a sacred gift (Andreski 1984, 108). That is, beginning with the subversive counterbalance to an established authority, the quality of charisma is "gradually superseded by other forms, indicating a decline of charisma in a context of a reiterating pattern of the routinized institution" (Bendix 1960, 327). The shamanic remedy starts with the purpose of transforming ordinary life conditions, but its ritual invocation turns back to the ethos of the traditional esprit de corps (Grim 1984, 235; Covell 1983, 11). Even when the shaman calls forth ancestral spirits during the ritual, an ancestral victimhood cries out, in keeping with the contemporary cliché under the neo-Confucian moral order that is linked to the Korean patrilineal power structure (Kendall 1984).

24. Melford E. Spiro concentrated his research on a Burmese Buddhist community, leading to his conclusion that "religion serves as a highly efficient culturally constituted defense mechanism."

For example, the female ancestral spirit often delivers her *han* in shamanic ritual—the Korean collective sense of resentment (U. Kim and Choi 1995; Jonghyun Lee 2009; A. Park 2004, 10–15)[25]—during the altered state of consciousness of the shaman (Bourguignon 1973a, 42). In her article "Wives, Lesser Wives, and Ghosts," Laurel Kendall portrays at length the tensions provoked between the deceased first wife's spirit and the living second wife (1984).[26] Wives were common victims within the traditional polygamous family structure in Korea. Particularly in the case of the first wife, the addition of younger wives and concubines might make her position terribly painful in the male-dominant family structure. A misogynous atmosphere also pervaded in the polygamous relationship, escalating rivalry and jealousy among the women themselves as they competed for attention from the male household and sought power over the other women. Particularly, the first wife often became embittered when abandoned by her husband and forced to yield her position to younger wives. So, the wretched emotions of the abandoned first wife restlessly survive in the presence of her spirit after she dies. This can be the cause of afflictions in the life of the second wife who directly supplanted the first wife's position and usurped the love of husband (Kendall 1984). This polygamous situation, no longer very prominent, provides a brief illustration of women's life in subservience within the male-dominant marriage system in traditional Korean society, where wealthy males could afford many wives and/or younger concubines. Typically, by means of abstinence and self-denial, the first wife stepped aside to be like a housemaid in charge of house management or entirely neglected, in the face of new women who were favored by the male head of the house. This situation constituted a difficult, *han*-ridden life for the first wife (A. Park 2004, 10–15)[27] Although her life was "silenced" within the male-dominated household, her death promoted her position and enabled her spirit to create restlessness in the living world. The potentially embittered life of a first wife gained status as a spirit to be able to control the well-being of the living male's household, including the favored women. As a spirit, the deceased first wife is expected to be sincerely and loyally served in rituals, and so, she gains power as a spirit. In this regard,

25. See ch. 1 about *han* for more information.

26. As Laurel Kendall notes, the *keun manura* is the "big wife" or "major wife," who is distinguished from the *jageun manura*, the "little wife" or "concubine," also called *cheop*.

27. See p. 27 for the significance of *han*.

the shamanic ritual, *gut*, can come into play as a means of comforting the *han* of the deceased first wife, opening an important space not only for projection of the distressed spirit of the deceased first wife, as enacted by the shaman, but also for vindication of the forbidden lives of Korean women behind the world of male supremacy. Moreover, it is usually a female shaman, someone who is also culturally condemned and socially deprived, who serves the ritual that satisfies and comforts the restlessly resentful spirits of women in general.

Han reflects deep resentment, addressing a wounded heart from the life experience of living as a wife of a polygamous husband; or living as a barren woman unable to fulfill her procreative role of giving birth to a son so as to extend the virile heritage; or living as a daughter-in-law routinely mistreated and abused under the patriarchal privilege of family-in-law, particularly of the mother-in-law; or ritualizing the *han*-ridden spirits as a *mudang*, etc. Or the deceased elderly spirits might vent inimical thought because of an unpleasant grave site or unfaithful service by the living descendants who give up offering dutiful shamanic rituals. In this regard, although the shamanic charisma is directed to repairing life troubles, the remedies take place only by calling forth and comforting the spirits, in keeping with the ancestral status quo that is established in the male-line order. That is, the shamanic remedy comes to fruition when the ancestral spirits, relative to the ordinary structures of authority, are ritually appeased. In doing so, the shaman then serves as an intermediary between ancestral spirits and living kin, in conjunction with the culturally constituted collective consciousness. To this end, the shamanic body and consciousness take on the role of being a conduit so as to "transform" the life of Korean diaspora, so that various forms of anomalies are dealt with by restoring harmony in the collective Korean consciousness. More specifically, the ultimate goal of the shamanic remedies, effective through the Korean immigrant shamanic ritual, is to assist the Korean diaspora in successfully integrating into the new mainstream society by reproducing the bond with the traditional status quo of the ancestral authority in the present, in keeping with Weber's notion of routinization (Andreski 1984, 108).

Korean shamanism in the immigrant context is no longer welcomed by the community as a means for celebrating collective consciousness or in thraldom to ancestral worship. Instead, it plays an alternative role to ensure *bok*, luck or good fortune, so as to lead Koreans in diaspora to successful lives in the U.S. In spending about three thousand dollars or more for each ritual, in investing valuable time that could be used for economic activities, and in striving to satisfy the seemingly abandoned spirits in rituals, the Korean diaspora, predominantly the first generation, is focused on enriching their lives by drawing upon the charisma of Korean immigrant shamans who maintain connections to the spirits of their native land. Accordingly, in spite of the predominantly protestantized life of the Korean diaspora, Korean shamans are repeatedly called upon to join the transnational migration to the U.S.

A Theoretical Implication of Korean Collective Consciousness Addressed by Korean Immigrant Shamans

Weber's notion of charisma provides a benchmark to understand the subjective character of the shamanic gift. As Tae-gon Kim also insists, the Korean charismatic shaman obtains individual gifts for her or his ritual performance, in connection with spirit possession (T. Kim and Chang 1998, 15), which are visibly manifested through the shamanic enactment in each unique form of shamanic behavior and persona. In this, the charismatic gift is regarded solely as the subjective experience of the shaman. Meanwhile, alongside the subjective nature of the shamanic experience, the content of the spiritual invocation as manifested in the shamanic enactment seems to be controversial, reflecting the ambivalent character of the charismatic gift. The ambivalence is featured in the concurrence of the subjective and collective status quo, when the shaman coherently engages the ancestral spirits during the spirit possession (Andreski 1984, 108). Weber asserts that an ultimate result of charisma may well be a routinization, which state is much more collective than individual, and more traditional than transformative. Thus, this subject matter compels us to examine the ambivalence of the collective aspects of the charisma that the shaman represents, alongside the charisma's subjective nature.

The research carried out by Roger and Dawnhee Janelli provides multifarious ritual illustrations tied to the moral implications of ancestral worship as a collective cultural practice in traditional Korean society (Janelli and Janelli 1982). Those instances that deliver moral implications in the varied life conditions of the descendants are also similarly represented in the shamanic ritual during the interactions of the shaman with ancestral spirits. As those occasions foreshadow various causes for spiritual bitterness toward living kin, the backdrop of these ancestral spirits conveys the grassroots of the traditional moral ethos derived from neo-Confucianism. The personae of the spirits impersonated in the *gut*, the Korean shamanic ritual, preliminarily demonstrate the animosity of the ancestral spirit(s) rather than the desired empathy, an animosity that is believed to harm or afflict the lives of living kin. This is well illustrated in the case of cremation of deceased ancestors, as opposed to burial in a properly oriented cemetery, since burial is much preferred in the traditional moral ethos. Moreover, suicidal, accidental, or premature deaths are regarded as defying the virtue of disease-free and lengthy life in the neo-Confucian moral ethos. Lack of faithfulness on the part of living kin in offering regular ritual services to the ancestral spirit is believed to break the moral code of filial piety, *hyo*, which also applies in traditional Korean shamanism. Random change, such as moving ancestral remains or grave sites, is resented by the spirits, unless done on the right date and time, at an approved location (Janelli and Janelli 1982, 156–60). Accordingly, the highlight of the Janellis' discussion of shamanism is the emphasis on the hostile reactions of the ancestral spirits in cases of a living kin's moral deviance, provoking brokenness, illness, or even accidental death. In this, the key to transforming the ancestral spirits' resentment falls upon the living kin's subservience to the relational moral ethos, which is mostly achieved by offering rituals, with abundant food tables, to the spirits. In order to understand the grassroots reason for why Koreans believe such specific instances to be the cause of ancestral hostility and the resultant misfortune experienced by the living descendant, it is necessary to examine some particularities of the Korean collective consciousness.

Durkheim provides a helpful insight in this regard, as he asserts: "The troop of the mythical ancestors became attached to the society of the living by a moral bond" (Durkheim 1995, 280). A moral cohesion between ancestral spirits and living kin is inconspicuous but is actualized in cultural practice as observable "social fact" through the collective common sense, as discussed previously (Durkheim 1995, 369). Also, consideration of neo-Confucian politics demonstrates how social politics alter a cultural construct and practice. Meanwhile, it is also noteworthy that moral references are not forever stagnant, but gradually "processual," slowly altering the cultural implications and practices in a different time and space and even within a common cultural location (V. Turner 1995, 13). Clifford Geertz also probes this aspect, commenting on how culture is differently interpreted by different symbolic references in differing contexts (Geertz 1973, 127). As cited by Geertz, the Azande in

Africa believe all natural disasters to be the result of "hatred," while the Melanesian Manus put heavy emphasis on "secret sin" as the cause of life misfortunes, and the Javanese believe that the ultimate source of evil is uncontrolled desires (Geertz 1973, 131). In these cases, at least, each culture obtains a specifically different moral reference that is engendered by its individually apprehended worldview.

The moral referents for the occasions of ancestral worship, such as discussed by the Janellis, have long been significantly applied in the traditional inland Korean culture. Those traditional referents are also still widely and culturally impacting the Korean immigrant collective consciousness in the predominant practice of Protestant ethical monotheism. Yet, the contextual shift in the life of Korean diaspora has also provoked a different cultural interpretation that, if continued, will ultimately alter the cultural practice. Indeed, the new cultural experience in the shifted context is associated with the demand for cultural assimilation, i.e., cultural change. Given this demand, the traditional moral implications of the Korean collective consciousness become cultural controversies, at various levels, and lead to conflicts in the immigrant adaptation. For example, cremation, moving, or selling a grave site is no longer a taboo topic in the life of Korean diaspora, since funeral and burial systems are multivariable in the U.S. None of these issues is considered in relation to economic profit or increasing fortune in the U.S.[28] Thus, the Korean diaspora has become much less obsessed with the burial or grave site relative to displeasure and misfortune coming from the ancestral spirits (H. Yoon 2007) Moreover, a busy lifestyle, the tendency toward independence, the nuclear familial setting, and moving linked with work opportunities—all help to produce a different life setting and a lesser sense of the Korean collective consciousness on the part of the Korean diaspora that feel unsettled and alienated from one another. This leads to some relaxation of the traditional dutiful servitude to either parents or the ancestral spirits, in relation to the traditionally quintessential moral ethos of filial piety and loyalty.

---

28. Grave sites are often cashed in and reckoned as an economic resource, in view of governmental or regional development projects or housing or factory developments. Yet, this occasion is not morally employed in the life of the protestantized Korean diaspora in the U.S. Still, the moral issue of either cremation or burial of the deceased can still be an emphasis in the lives of Korean diaspora reliant upon their belief systems and/or preference.

The impact of the evangelical Protestant atmosphere should not be overlooked in this discussion. Its cultural influence upon the life in the Korean immigrant community strongly promotes altering the cultural behavior and practice of the Korean diaspora. The mainline Protestant environment has influenced changes in the pattern of dutiful servitude to the ancestral spirits, emphasizing, instead, Christian memorial services. In this, life as reckoned with Protestant Christianity tends to be geared more towards the present and the future, rather than the past, which encourages reshaping and reinventing the characteristics of the hierarchical bond with ancestral spirits. However, when life conditions are troublesome and unresolved, the Korean diaspora are often driven to serious consideration of reestablishing traditional ancestral bonds, even in their immigrant life chosen for making a new beginning. They then search for a shaman.

Certain instances, such as suicide, accidental or premature death, and mental illness, continue to seriously challenge the cultural mindset of the Korean diaspora in regard to the conception of the actions of spirits. Particularly, occasions of mental illness have frequently been a hot spot in the Korean immigrant community in the U.S. because of associated physical abuse, deadly accidents, or violent deaths. In the cultural judgment, there has existed a strong tendency to consider that psychological or psychiatric symptoms or illness are the result of the spirit possession or actions of evil spirits. So, mental illness and psychological disorder are perceived as a matter of cultural shame and accordingly veiled in the Korean diaspora, often to great harm. Patients in the Korean immigrant community with mental illness or personality disorders are frequently excluded from professional medical treatment because of this cultural perception. One of the most traumatic results can be found in the incident of the Virginia Tech campus massacre in 2007. When the severe anxiety disorder of the twenty-three-year-old second-generation Korean immigrant college senior was not properly treated by an official medical process, his symptom triggered him abnormally to use a gun, brutally shoot, and even kill many friends and peers on campus (O'Connor 2007).

Many in the Korean diaspora attempt to search for an alternative way to deal with an occasion of mental illness or psychological disorder. One alternative, occasionally resorted to by the predominantly Protestant portion of the Korean immigrant community, has been ritual exorcism performed by charismatic Christian healers in lieu of medical treatment.[29] However, its outcome has often been tragic, provoking the imposition of heartbreaking injuries for the "patient," as discussed in chapter 3.

Despite the impact of Protestantism in the lives of the Korean diaspora, shamans are also sought out for a ritual rendezvous with the ancestral spirits. The Korean immigrant shaman plays a role, as "the part evokes the whole" (Durkheim 1933, 231), reestablishing a connection with the Korean homeland as a viable alternative or in addition to life in the U.S. In doing so, the shaman summons forth the traditional collective status quo to the local Korean immigrant community of the global world. The shaman typically provides such rituals privately, in keeping with the desire of the clientele to remain secretive, rebooting the bond of the client with the ancestral world in order to invoke the supernatural powers on behalf of Korean otherness in the U.S. As the Korean collective consciousness is rejuvenated in ritual performances, the shaman becomes the ritual border-crosser for the spiritual cohesion of the past with the present, the dead with the living, ancestors with their descendants, resistance with assimilation, and Korean with American. In this regard, the shaman as a mediating individual has to overcome "a reality to be conquered" in order to call forth the "whole" for the Korean diaspora (Lehmann 1993, 72).

Durkheim insists that "a personal agent is profane" (Durkheim 1995, 83). Thus, a personal agent would be inadequate to convey the significance of sacredness in association with a collective agency (Durkheim 1995, 83). The statement by Durkheim is illuminating, in that charisma as a gift given "from above" to the Korean immigrant shaman becomes also profane property, since its manifest nature is essentially subjective, in accordance with Weber. Meanwhile, Durkheim highlights that the ancestral spirits represent a collective "social fact" (Durkheim 1995, 94), which means that the sacred is the main source of the shamanic charisma. In this, the shamanic charisma creates ambivalence in intermediating the subjective experience with the collective sense of ancestral spirits, so as to attain remedies.

Yet, the rendezvous of the two opposites means that they are not inherently contradictory or mutually exclusive, as Durkheim affirms that the "individual is the double of an ancestor, the factor by which they share the *same nature*" (Durkheim 1995, 280). So to speak, the individual

29. See ch. 3.

is not a separate entity from the collective unity but rather exists as part of the same organic whole. Certainly, the notion of Anthony Giddens is convincing, as he asserts that Durkheim may aim to demonstrate the optimism of the cult of individual in the social process, as Weber insists in one of his remarks about charisma (Giddens 1978, 15; Thompson 1982, 83).[30] The same nature, in the words of Durkheim, reflects the collective consciousness which is felt and shared in the collective effervescence that encompasses the collective cultural and moral experiences of individuals. The same nature is lived through individuals, as manifested in social facts, by which the collectiveness is identified as valuable, just as the sacred or god (Giddens 1978, 351). Thereby, Durkheim's sense of collective consciousness transcends its generational barriers and geographical shifts as sacred, while is also being slowly and partially altered, as its moral implications, subsequent cultural behaviors, and cultural practices are modified in the shift of time and space (Durkheim 1982, 59).

On this matter, the Korean immigrant shaman as an individual charismatic agent is not exclusively aligned with the Korean collective consciousness in the life of the Korean diaspora. S/he acts as a conduit to interplay with "the cult of the individual," so as to reproduce the traditional moral ethos of Korean "mechanical solidarity," a feature of the traditional village community with its emphasis on ancestry, and therein to assist others in adapting to the cross-cultural context of the U.S. (Durkheim 1933, 37–38; Lukes 1973, 148–49). In so doing, the practice of the Korean immigrant shaman engages the in-between brokenness in the life of otherness toward healing, for routinization in mainstream society, and reconnects the culturally located therapeutic mechanism to the global community. While reinventing the collective cultural references to the immigrant community in the U.S., the Korean immigrant shaman fills the geographical and collective mental gap of the Korean diaspora by bridging the present with the past, life with death, the living with the ancestral spirits, neo-Confucianism and Protestantism, in the transnational life of the Korean diaspora in the U.S.

30. Durkheim perceived the "cult of the individual" as the moral ideal of a culture of organic solidarity.

6

The Call to Korean Diasporic Shamanism

A CALL TO KOREAN shamanism signifies undergoing not only the condition of spirit possession but also an apprenticeship under the direction of a senior shaman. The two categories, spirit possession and training, often interact ambiguously, and therefore it is difficult at times for the observer to identify whether the apprentice is under the control of the possessing spirit or the order of the senior shaman. This chapter discusses the routinely interactive dynamics of the shamanic attendees and trainees at Lee Bosal's shrine, underscored by the ambivalent character of a call to Korean immigrant shamanism. In addition, at the end of this chapter, a counter-discussion is presented, in an attempt to reimagine the traditional Korean feminist discourse that too easily idealizes the images and roles of *mudang*, a female shaman, as compared to the realities of the *mudang*'s practice and life.

1. The Shamanic Apprenticeship

To encounter a resident shamanic novice who is actively pursuing an apprenticeship is a rather rare experience within the context of the Korean immigrant community. Laurel Kendall has referred to the circumstances of a shamanic apprenticeship, which include the details of emotional and physical difficulties that a shamanic candidate undergoes in the training process (Kendall, 1996a; 1993). Meanwhile, Kum-hwa Kim, a globally renowned Korean female shaman, grumbles about the intolerant manner of contemporary shamanic trainees (S. Yi 1992).[1] Kim

1. Kum-hwa Kim is a charismatic shaman in the northern style, in the most

161

insists that contemporary shamanic candidates are unable to handle the traditional pattern of shamanic apprenticeship, such as she herself had undergone with enormous hardship for over a decade after she was called to become a shaman (S. Yi 1992).

The change of life environment and new demands in the immigrant context also change the pattern of the shamanic apprenticeship. The basic reason that one rarely encounters a resident shamanic apprentice in the immigrant context in the U.S. is probably not the weakness and/or lethargy of persons who consider becoming shamanic novices. It is more likely the economic demands on the senior shaman to provide the time and residential space to work with apprentices, and the parallel demands on the apprentice to set the time aside and have the financial means to pay for upkeep while staying at the shrine, without earning any professional income during the apprenticeship. It is an expensive process for both the apprentice and the senior shaman, particularly in the immigrant context. Traditional shamanic training in the Korean homeland featured a long-term residence, without proper employment or family life. This fashion of traditional apprenticeship is not very compatible with lifestyles in the immigrant context in the U.S. However, according to my informants, a succession of short-term stays is frequently possible at an immigrant shamanic shrine, should the senior shaman be able to provide appropriate time and space for the apprentice. The duration of stay varies, particularly utilizing various prayer periods/cycles, such as for the forty days' prayer or the hundred days' prayer that is entirely reliant upon the senior shaman's instruction. Overall, the possibility of pursuing a shamanic apprenticeship in the immigrant context requires the shamanic novice to be able to meet the financial needs and to have the time available. It also demands that the master shaman have the available space and the willingness to mentor the apprentice.

In case of M. Doryeong, the Korean immigrant male shaman, he himself went to his female trainee's house for teaching and performing rituals. It was because his tiny shrine room was not suitable for any type of training that he was unable to provide the adequate environmental

---

colorful and ecstatic shamanic tradition in Korea. Her shamanic ritual performance has been globally recognized as a form of art. "The official demonstrator of the *gut*," the shamanic ritual, sequentially after her ritual performance of *pung-eo-je*, a ritual for a big catch of fish, was designated as Intangible National Cultural Property in 1984. Kim had performed over twenty *naerim gut*, a shamanic initiation ritual, for shaman novices by the time the interview was conducted in 1992.

condition; the room was spatially small, with no additional space for his female apprentice to stay. Moreover, the location of his shrine was in the middle of a densely residential area, and he was nervous for any complaints about noises during the training. His time frame for extra work at the nail salon during the weekdays, which produced immediate income for his survival, could not be disrupted by any other activities either. So, retaining a shamanic trainee was simply impossible for M. Doryeong.

Meanwhile, the living conditions of Lee Bosal were rather different from most other shamans, as Lee Bosal had abundant space and sufficient funds to provide for resident shamanic trainees at her shrine. Nonetheless, I met only one shamanic trainee, Jiyon, at her shrine, setting aside Kim, who was not an apprentice but a resident devotee there for her own long-term prayers, while staying at Lee Bosal's shamanic shrine.[2] According to Kim, another resident shamanic trainee had stayed at the shrine for about a year and a half prior to Jiyon's arrival.[3] However, the prior apprentice left without completing her training because of constant conflicts with Kang monk shaman, which also resulted in disruption of the intimate relationship between Lee Bosal and the trainee. The previous apprentice never came back to Lee Bosal's shrine, even for a very brief visit, according to Kim.

A Shaman Trainee, Jiyon

Jiyon[4] was a Korean immigrant shamanic trainee, commuting back and forth from her residence to Lee Bosal's shrine for her shamanic training since her shinnarim *gongsu*, a divinatory message about her initiation to become a shaman, that was performed by Kang monk shaman in 2010 (T. Kim 1996b; Kendall 1993; Guillemoz 1993). Jiyon first met Kang monk

2. Regarding the presence of Kim, consult ch. 5.

3. I use an alias in order to protect the identity of the shamanic apprentice.

4. I met and interviewed Jiyon during my stay at the Lee Bosal's shrine in the summer of 2010. She subsequently left the shrine, ending her shamanic training, days before I myself left the shrine. Jiyon explained to me later during our phone conversation that she left the shrine due to the uncertainty of her call to shamanism, which she thought had been exaggerated by Kang monk shaman. Also, Jiyon had learned the true reason why Kang monk shaman moved to the U.S., and she had experienced his routinely violent behavior, abusive verbal attacks, philandering style, and controlling personality. Jiyon told me that she no longer had any trust of confidence in his direction.

shaman when he showed up at Lee Bosal's condo office while she was having a meeting with her in that office. It was a time when Jiyon was under immense emotional pressure, due to her extended unemployment that completely depleted her savings and threatened her desires and hopes for the future. Her visit to Lee Bosal was to seek some solace and experience some optimism that, even though invisible at that moment, could give her hope for possible fortune in the near future and thereby help her survive the immediate situation. She wanted to hear something that could give promise of changing her life, ending her sense of being incapable of experiencing anything positive, and releasing her from financial and relational distress. All clients may expect to hear words of good fortune when they search for shamans. So, Jiyon was terrified beyond her naïve expectation when she heard the commanding divination from the newly-met Kang monk shaman who told her that she was destined to become a shaman herself and needed to have initiation.

Jiyon's former life had gone basically well until her husband had been diagnosed with cancer and had died about a year later. Since the beginning of his cancer diagnosis, his dismay had only increased during the year's treatment, all of which overwhelmed her with worry about the future. Jiyon had lived with an elementary-school-aged son as a single parent since her husband died. Although her church community was strongly supportive, and her pastor explained her suffering as part of God's purpose, she was unable to fit in, feeling a sense of isolation with her individual experience of radical hardship. Her experience of hardship prompted some reasonable doubt about her Christian faith, shaking somewhat her lifelong religious belief that had been part of her life ever since she could remember. Moreover, her unemployment seemed to her equivalent to a death sentence, not giving her hope of supporting herself and her young son. So, it was conceivable in the Korean cultural mind that her crushed life condition was a sign of *shinbyeong*, the shamanic illness, and a signal to the call to shamanic practice. As Kum-hwa Kim asserts:

> *Shinbyeong* can hit anyone, young or old, rich or poor. It is true that women who suffer from the psychological pain of economic hardship and family difficulties are most likely to contract *shinbyeong*. (S. Yi 1992, 50; see also Ch'oe 1989, 232; Kendall 1985, 208)

When Kang monk shaman firmly announced to her that she was born to be a shaman, it was a heartbreaking claim upon Jiyon and hardly attractive for her.[5] Yet, in a contemplative manner, Kang monk shaman shared his reflection on his own experience of a stream of surrender: first giving up his youth to the call to the Buddhist monkhood, when he was seventeen years old; then abandoning his dream of becoming a Buddhist scholar, when he experienced the shamanic spirit possession; and, finally, giving up his life to the practice of shamanism. After he had had a sudden experience of spirit possession in the midst of his Buddhist studies at a prominent Buddhist university in Korea, his life had never been the same. He had quickly sought to be initiated as a shaman, no longer being a solely dedicated Buddhist monk. This had led him to move out of the *Buddhist* temple that had been his home for decades, since his adolescence, to a location on the fringe of the capital city, Seoul. He started an urban Buddhist shrine on the fourth floor of a modern commercial building, where, for a while, he performed a combination of Buddhist and shamanic practices.

Still quite confused, Jiyon attempted to calm her ongoing vague feeling of uneasiness caused by what she had heard from Kang monk shaman. Since that time, he had added to his pronouncement by unleashing a stream of similar *gongsu*, a divinatory message, to Jiyon, in an attempt to make her move immediately to prepare to enter the training process, as well as the rituals for initiation:

> Your husband spirit is still around you, not able to leave to *jeoseung*.[6] His spirit continues to be unsettled and is tearing your life apart. Unless you offer a ritual to comfort and send your husband to *jeoseung*, his *han* will continue to harm your life and even your son.

As he continued to divine, he told her that, within two years, her son would quit school and wander about, unless she quickly offered a ritual, so as to comfort the spirit of her husband. Should she question or neglect the *gongsu*, it would designate a woeful outcome for both of them, according to Kang monk shaman. Jiyon felt entirely besieged by this series of dreadful divinatory messages communicated by Kang monk shaman, particularly in regard to her young son. His *gongsu* finally was

---

5. Jiyon was brought up in a basically Protestant Christian environment, in which, she said, she had never explored any form of fortune-telling or any other folk religious practice at all in spite of her interest in cultural diversity and distinctive religious practices.

6. *Jeoseung* refers to the world of the dead.

too frightening for her to deal with, and she totally surrendered. As she recounted the story, for her, then, the only choice appeared to be to offer the ritual. Kang monk shaman again beseeched her to act quickly, by saying that she had to know that it was a very urgent matter. He also said that the sooner she acted, the better. Asking her to come back the following day and be ready to offer the ritual for her deceased husband, Kang monk shaman strongly urged her to make a cash deposit for the ritual on the very next day. That was the high-pressure beginning of Jiyon's apprenticeship at Lee Bosal's shrine.

Jiyon's first encounter with Lee Bosal had taken place six years prior to the meeting with Kang monk shaman, at a time when she was undergoing financial hardship and personal distress. By word of mouth, Jiyon had heard that Lee Bosal was a spectacular *shinjeom* shaman (Covell 1983, 54),[7] and her curiosity had prompted her to meet Lee Bosal. Being Christian, Jiyon had been anxious about such a meeting with a shaman. Nonetheless, she had also been curious about the fortune-telling of the shaman.

The first impression of Lee Bosal was very powerful for Jiyon and completely overturned her general preconception about shamans. Lee Bosal's personality was cozy, inoffensive, and even comforting. Bit by bit, Lee Bosal uncovered a whole stream of revelations for Jiyon by articulating, in the conversation, an amalgamation of her life experience, alongside Lee Bosal's own personal anecdotal moments. Lee Bosal seemed to be more like a familiar neighbor whom Jiyon routinely greeted and with whom she felt at ease in speaking about her everyday life, without any sense of disapproval. Lee Bosal did not indiscriminately pressure her with random suggestions of rituals or frighten her with directly negative notions about Jiyon's circumstances. Instead, Lee Bosal attempted to create a comfortable, companionable space during the conversation,

---

7. *Shinjeom* refers to spirit divination by the charismatic shaman while under spirit possession. Divination, in the practice of Korean shamanism, functions as a threshold for the more expansive ritual performances that may be remedial or therapeutic, as mentioned in ch. 4. So, the very first thing to be pursued, when meeting with a shaman, is normally going to be a divination. In facing various life conditions of affliction or uncertainty, either because of adversity or eagerness for good fortune, the ordinary cultural remark incorporated into traditional Korean collective mind is *"Jeom inna chireo galgga?"* (Shall I go for a divination?). In this regard, whether it is either playful or seriously invoked in the mind or out loud, the common remark in this type of sublinguistic interplay provides a culturally significant insight into the traditional Korean collective consciousness.

easing her along. So, it was not difficult for Jiyon to be receptive to what
Lee Bosal told her about her life and agonizing experiences. The impression Jiyon formed at the first meeting with Lee Bosal was that she was
quite exceptional. Jiyon was very much intrigued and started thinking
about further opportunities to meet with her in the near future. But a
subsequent encounter with Kang monk shaman entirely disrupted her
openness to Lee Bosal, according to Jiyon. Whatever he said about her
life, including his repetitive insistence that she had been called to become
a shaman, made her feel offended by the way he spoke to her. Meanwhile,
Lee Bosal slipped in only a word edgewise, as the reaction to Kang monk
shaman's emphasis on Jiyon's call to a shamanness.

On the following day, feeling devoured by fear and distressed by a
complex sense of anxiousness, Jiyon hurried over to Lee Bosal's shrine.
In compliance with Kang monk shaman's instructions, she had brought
three cartons of Marlboro cigarettes, three bottles of Johnnie Walker
Scotch whiskey, and three packages of candies, along with the amount of
four thousand dollars in cash, as the fee to be carried out on her behalf
for a sending-off ritual for her deceased husband. Jiyon was anguished
about the ritual expense, an amount that was excessively large and would
have been about a month's salary if she had still been working as a full-
time agent at the foreign company. However, the intensity of her anxiety,
particularly for her son's life, made it impossible for her to disregard what
Kang monk shaman had prescribed for her, and she was quite aware that
having such a ritual would require a large financial sacrifice.

The amount of money that is required plays a critical role from the
very beginning of the contemplation of a ritual, and a kind of bargaining
or negotiating with the shaman continues throughout the ritual (Kendall
1983, 156; Bruno 2007b, 49; J. Kim 1996).[8] The client bargains with the
shaman to pay less, while desiring a maximum level of satisfaction from
the ritual outcome. Meanwhile, the shaman does not easily retreat from
her or his request as s/he wants to serve a richer food table to the spirits,
as an inducement to provide better fortune. So bargaining continues,
even in the midst of the ritual to indulge the cravings of the spirits. In this

8. As to the material aspects of rituals, the discussions of Laurel Kendall and Antonetta L. Bruno are noteworthy for an understanding of to what extent a monetary
offering is involved in traditional Korean shamanic ritual. Kendall utilizes the image of
"a greedy god" in Korean shamanic ritual, so as to highlight the relationship between
the material aspects and the ritual effectiveness. Meanwhile, Bruno details how the
monetary transaction is distributed within and beyond the ritual setting in Korean
shamanic practice.

regard, Lee Bosal seemed not to be hesitant to bargain for higher ritual expenses with her clients. As part of her rationale, she often stressed that the shamanic ritual costs benefitted the market economy, in which the preparation expenditures on ritual materials injected cash into the marketplace. She also insisted that most of the ritual expense was spent on purchasing ritual items rather than accruing to her own personal account.

When Jiyon handed over the ritual fee to Kang monk shaman, a big grocery shopping trip followed. All the shrine attendees, as a group, went out to a Korean grocery market, in order to purchase appropriate ritual materials, such as fresh fruits, vegetables, fish, meat, rice, steamed rice cakes, Korean rice wine, and even a steamed pig head. Lee Bosal and Kang monk shaman rushed about the store, picking up items as if they were very well acquainted with various sections of the store. They seemed to know exactly where to look for the variety of items that they were seeking in the large store, H-Mart in the Korean immigrant community.[9] They looked carefully at each item that interested them so as to select the best, freshest goods, setting aside any damaged items as they sought what was appropriate for the spirits. The major food shopping was followed by a brief visit to a nearby small Korean store[10] that specialized in some ritual items such as steamed rice cakes, ground rice flour, steamed red-bean, and steamed pig-head. The store owner was a longtime client of Lee Bosal and therefore was eager to help her select and pack specific ritual items. Next, although Jiyon had already brought some cigarettes and some Johnnie Walker, they stopped at the liquor store and the tobacco stop, both important for having the particular kinds of whisky and cigarettes that were mostly consumed by Kang monk shaman.[11] For this reason, Kang monk shaman seemed to be quite picky at the liquor store, wanting above all the particular Scotch whisky Johnnie Walker, as well as at the tobacco shop where he insisted on his favorite brand of cigarette, a red Marlboro. Finally, there was a brief stop at the local grocery store to get various candies for serving the children spirits and some packages

9. H-Mart, named Hanarheum, is the Korean grocery store chain in the northeastern U.S. There are also some other chains of Korean grocery stores, such as Hanyang Mart or Assi Store, in the Korean diasporic community in the U.S.

10. There are small Korean grocery stores, in addition to those big grocery markets as cited above. The small grocery shop is a food market for homemade, traditional Korean food, indispensable for the Korean diaspora who can purchase various Korean ethnic foods for their tastes while saving time and effort for cooking.

11. The alcohol and cigarettes were initially served on the altar to the spirits but ultimately ended up as part of Kang Buddhist monk shaman's share.

of Italian breads that were Kang monk shaman's favorite. It was already quite dark when all arrived back at the shrine, fatigued, but with a heavy load of ritual items packed into the back of the van. Shopping for all the ritual materials can easily consume an entire day, or at least from early afternoon to about 9 to 10 p.m. in the evening.

Upon returning to the shrine, the varied and heavy load of shopping items was moved to the kitchen, located on the second floor, which involved negotiating a full flight of tilted stairs. The items were then washed, cut up, cooked, arranged on plates, and organized by the female attendees for the ritual, according to the specific recipes and the particular requests for the food table, all in accord with Lee Bosal's ritual traditions of Korean shamanism. The procedure for ritual preparation often required the attendees to stay up until the next morning when the ritual was served about midnight, following a long day of ritual preparation. When the main ritual took place on the following day, the female attendees continued to prepare until 2 to 3 a.m. before finally being able to go to bed.

The *Yongshin*, the Dragon King Deity

Upon return to the shrine after the long ordeal of shopping, Lee Bosal and Kang monk shaman were in a hurry to make a trip, with the others, to the *yongshin* altar (Covell 1986, 56–72).[12] Visiting the *yongshin* was always the first stop for Lee Bosal when she returned to the shrine from her condo office or local errands. She often emphasized that the *yongshin* spirit was her strongest energy source amongst the many spirit possessions. She received the *gongsu*, the divinatory message, more accurately in the *yongshin* spirit possession than in any others. The *yongshin* altar was some distance across from her shrine building, behind the cluster of trees that lay beyond the wide, bare lawn that surrounded the three-story mansion. A local creek flows through piles of crude rocks deposited on both sides, skirting the trees behind the cluster. The location was very satisfactory as the environment for the *yongshin*, the water spirit, whose altar was always set close by a stream of water. According to Lee Bosal, the creek area had been a village site for a Native American tribe. There was also the remnant of an old clay brick fence or wall alongside the creek,

12. *Yongshin* is the dragon king deity literally in Korean, but it means the water deity generally in Korean shamanic tradition.

seemingly connected with a residence in the past. In keeping with this, Lee Bosal herself often remarked that the Native American spirit was the most vigorous among the sacred energies, and thus her *yongshin* altar, located close to the historic Native American site, produced a very strong and indeed superhuman power of the spirit. Considering that Lee Bosal's first husband was a Native American and that the title for the three-story shamanic shrine property also listed his son from that marriage, it was quite interesting that she had obtained that particular property for her own shamanic practice.

The outdoor *yongshin* was not a formally constructed altar. At first glance, it did not look like a proper altar. It was marked and decorated somewhat crudely with stones and pieces of wood, and was adjacent to a small landing place that dipped down to the creek. A thin, grey, rectangular-shaped stone was supported by two thick wooden pillars, erected along with a pile of small rocks, and covered the top of the *yongshin* altar in lieu of a tabletop. Some food and three packages of candy were served on top of the stone altar surface. The lower level of the altar, with an open-front nook roofed by the flat stone cover, provided a protective shelter for a pair of lit candles and some burning incense. In addition, glass lamp holders, framed by lustrous cast iron, were set at each end of the open-front nook, while also enclosing the candle lights of the *yongshin* altar.

The three packages of new candies had been prepared by one of Lee Bosal's devotees, Mrs. Yi, who prepared most of the candies served in the rituals, since Lee Bosal was convinced that the *dongja-shin*, the children spirits, loved Mrs. Yi and candies as well. The Yi couple were first-generation Korean immigrants, then in their late forties, with three children. Mrs. Yi was a housewife, having a degree in dance from a college in Korea, whereas Mr. Yi was a businessman and an alumnus of Columbia University. Living in a town near the city, their previous life fit well with the prevailing pattern of the protestantized Korean immigrant community, in solidarity with other Korean immigrants. The Yi couple first met Lee Bosal at a desperate time for them, as their finances had completely run out after Yi's construction business had failed, back in 2007. Before meeting Lee Bosal, the Yi couple had attended a local Korean immigrant church with which Mr. Yi's parents were affiliated. They had prayed hard, hoping for some recovery in their financial situation, but the condition of Yi's business had continued worsening nevertheless. When the financial life of the Yi couple had continued on a downward slope, they had been concerned about what had gone wrong for them, and they had come to question their Christian allegiance as not compatible for them. Having heard that Lee Bosal was a very accurate fortune-teller, they had decided to meet with her. Their first consultation with Lee Bosal had fully convinced them to become loyal devotees in her shamanic shrine ever since.

Their conversion to following shamanism, prompted by their frightening financial downfall, completely altered their routines. They frequently drove many hours back and forth from their residence to Lee Bosal's shrine. In order to help in serving rituals, they often drove to the shrine in the early morning and stayed until the next morning. They responded quickly to either Lee Bosal or Kang monk shaman whenever they were invited to help. The Yi couple had the full confidence of Lee Bosal and Kang monk shaman not only for their dedication to shamanic belief but also for the fortune they would acquire in the near future. Mrs. Yi was a good cook, equal to Lee Bosal. So, Lee Bosal could confidently rely upon her for preparations of the ritual table. Mrs. Yi was also the most active kowtower during the ritual, for which Lee Bosal and Kang monk shaman gave her full credit and which pleased them very much. In brief, the Yi husband and wife were among the most favored and reliable devotees for both Lee Bosal and Kang monk shaman.

However, one might be curious as to how they felt about their conversion, if they were comfortable and confident in their shift to an entirely different belief system from the Protestant faith, and if they felt any conflict between their dedication to folk religious practice and their lives in the global world in the U.S. It was also curious as to how their shift away from the Protestant church may have affected their familial and social relations in the life of the immigrant community. Mr. Yi mentioned, in this regard, as we were en route to do some small shopping at a local grocery store in September 2010:

> I think religion is my own choice, whatever is suitable for me. The Protestant church did not work for me, though I tried hard through prayers and dedication. But this shamanism works well for me. It looks promising to me. I feel comfortable while taking part in the shamanic rituals. . . . But frankly, my parents do not know what I am now involved with. I have not told them anything yet. They still pray for us as the first thing they do every day, during the early morning prayer meeting at the church.

Yi appeared somewhat diffident when he spoke about his parents who seemed to be dedicated Protestants and very active in a local Korean Presbyterian immigrant church. Religious affiliation often provides the primary condition for a sense of communal solidarity and belonging in the immigrant context. In this regard, deviation from the mainstream religious affiliation can often threaten the associated beneficial networking and social web, which can engender a stream of destructive losses, sense of isolation, and disadvantages for survival in the immigrant life.

In preparation for the ritual, Lee Bosal set up the *ohbang-gi*, the five colored, rectangular fabric strips wrapped on arm-length, thin bamboo rods, and placed them on the flat stone altar top of the *yongshin* altar (Jung Y. Lee 1981, 196–98).[13] The *ohbang-gi* belonged to Lee Bosal and would be used only in the case of a divination. In fact, each shaman uses distinctive shamanic items and materials for divination, such as old coins, raw rice, charms, fans, etc. The specific shamanic items and materials used for divination are associated with each shaman's distinct gift and vary for each shaman, in keeping with the distinct persona of each *momju*. In the meantime, for Lee Bosal, the *ohbang-gi* was the most important item that she used for divination.

Lee Bosal gave a sign for summoning the ritual attendees to the *yongshin* altar: "Let's kowtow." As if corresponding to the ritual summoning, Mr. Yi lit the candles and the incense. Jiyon, Kang monk shaman, Lee Bosal, and the Yi couple stood in a row before the *yongshin* altar, facing the creek and hearing its trickling sound, as a backdrop for the ritual. Once the altar seemed to be ready, Kang monk shaman began banging the brass *kkwaenggwari*[14] and chanting, as he stood before the altar. Lee Bosal continued praying a *pison*, praying with rubbing the palms (R. Hwang 1992) and standing next to him, after kowtowing three times before the altar to salute the *yongshin* deity. The Yi couple began kowtowing. Jiyon was also instructed to kowtow three times while kneeling in Buddhist fashion, bowing to the *yongshin* deity first and then kowtowing four times to the spirits of four directions, once in each direction. Once Jiyon had offered the seven kowtows, Kang monk shaman suddenly stopped chanting and banging the gong, as if giving a sign to Lee Bosal that it was time for a divination. Seemingly receptive to his sign, Lee

13. Lee Bosal always carries the *ohbang-gi* around for her divination. With its five symbolic colors, white means the king of heaven, yellow the ancestral spirit, light green the military general spirit, red the mountain spirit, and light blue the star spirit. In particular, the green strip also signifies the call to be a shaman, and the red color, when picked up, represents good fortune, according to Lee Bosal's interpretation.

14. The *Kkwaenggwarhi* is a circular-shaped Korean traditional instrument, a gong. Made of brass, the player bangs it with a wand, while holding the string handle attached to the gong.

Bosal started jumbling the *ohbang-gi* with both hands, after picking them up from the altar. The first selection was made by the day's main character, Jiyon. She picked up two flagged sticks, using just her left hand, as following Lee Bosal's instructions.[15] Jiyon's selections were the white and the yellow. Following Jiyon's picks, Lee Bosal began offering her *gongsu*, which included a strikingly unexpected message for Jiyon. Lee Bosal stated that a woman had died of tuberculosis right after giving birth to a baby, as she ejected a stream of blood though her mouth. The woman was identified as Jiyon's mother, whose spirit appeared to stand right there before her, holding hands with her father, according to Lee Bosal: "My daughter, I have missed you so much. You grew up nicely. I will give you a fortune. I will let you make it out. I will also help your son . . ," as voiced by Lee Bosal, apparently in the spirit possession of Jiyon's mother. Jiyon herself burst into tears. Later, on the following day, Jiyon told me about her personal curiosity about her birth, as addressed by Lee Bosal's message. There seemed to be some secret about her actual birth, once she discovered, while in high school, that her blood type did not match that of any of her family members. Jiyon then wondered if it were possible that her internal uncertainty about her birth was consciously or spiritually transferred and so was brought up by Lee Bosal in the divination, or if it was truly the spiritual appearance of her late parents. Jiyon was very tearful while speaking about her own curiosity.

2. Some Male and Female Attendees at Lee Bosal's Shamanic Shrine

Minja, an Unpleasant Presence at the Shamanic Shrine

Minja and Kim were cooking in the kitchen when the others arrived back from the *yongshin* altar. On that particular day, both Kim and Minja were asked to stay at the shrine building to prepare dinner, while the others went out to visit the *yongshin* altar. When everyone else was leaving to visit the *yongshin* altar, Kang monk shaman suddenly put a question toward all the women: "Is there anyone who is having a menstrual period now?"

---

15. According to Lee Bosal's practice, a woman uses her left hand, whereas a man uses his right hand when picking up the *ohbang-gi*.

Minja replied to him by whispering: "I am, *seunim*."[16]

As soon as Minja answered, Kang monk shaman coolly responded to her: "So then, Minja, you should stay here. Don't come to the *yongshin* with us today. It can upset the deity, polluting the ritual. Stay here. Why don't you prepare a dinner with Kim?" He then turned towards her and said: "Kim, you better stay with Minja here and cook dinner together, OK? And serve us a meal when we get back from the *yongshin*."

Kim seemed to be upset when she was commanded to remain inside the shrine building, unexpectedly being in the company of Minja. Kim had wanted to go to the *yongshin* with the others, because she had been told that rituals and prayers were the main reason for her stay at the shrine. She did not want to be left out when other people were praying in a ritual and having an opportunity to hear additional *gongsu*. She knew that Lee Bosal always gave *gongsu* at the *yongshin* altar and did not want to miss Lee Bosal's message, which might offer certain updates about her son.

Meanwhile, Minja seemed delighted, as usual, to stay behind and work, regardless of Kim's disappointment. Upon the others' arrival back at the shrine, Minja immediately asked Kang monk shaman if her prayer had been said at the *yongshin* altar. He merely nodded to her as he walked past her towards his bedroom, without saying anything.

Minja, in her late forties, was a devotee at Lee Bosal's shrine. She lived in a rented studio room close to where her ex-husband and her teenage son lived, in the midst of a crowded Korean immigrant community. Although Minja worked days at a local nail salon and nights at a bar, she often showed up at the shrine to help out with the pre-ritual and post-ritual cleaning, notwithstanding the distance of about one hundred miles from her studio room. She called Lee Bosal *eonni*, meaning "big sister" in Korean, which seemed to reflect an intimate relationship with her. Their relationship had begun with a client-shaman encounter and subsequently developed into a close friendship, sharing personal stories with each other, particularly during the time when Lee Bosal went through her divorces. Kang monk shaman was not at ease with Minja's presence at Lee Bosal's shrine and attempted to restrict Lee Bosal's intimacy with Minja, acting like a jealous person. Minja kept mostly in a good mood, in spite of the emotionally charged atmosphere at the shrine. It was unclear as to whether she was disinterested in other people's moods, or ignorant

16. *Seunim* indicates the Buddhist monk in Korean.

of the dynamics while sitting around with them, or determined not to let others ruin her joy at being there. Her foremost concern was to meet a wealthy man who could satisfy both her materialistic goals and her physical desires for the rest of her life. Whenever she showed up to help at the shrine, she mentioned the names of new male acquaintances to Kang monk shaman, the males to whom she was attracted, and repeatedly asked if one of them could be a good match for her. At another time, she asked Kang monk shaman: "*Seunim*, when will I meet the right man? May I have a good fortune to marry a really wealthy man?"

Kang monk shaman seemed to feel annoyed by her repetitious questions, but he attempted to respond coolly to her: "Soon . . ."

Kang monk shaman, however, sharply attacked Minja's personality and demeanor when she was not present, saying: "Such a prostitute . . . She has already had a seven-day sequence of men for her sexual pleasure, while she repeatedly asks me the same question, when she is going to meet the right man. What a crazy woman!" Kang monk shaman described her as a sex maniac who needed professional treatment.

The occasion of Kang monk shaman's most extreme antipathy toward Minja took place when he ordered a change in the kitchen utensils in the shrine to the use of disposable utensils. In this, he was targeting Minja, arguing that he could no longer endure the risk to his health and his cultic purity by sharing table utensils with her in the shrine. The very thought of possible contamination disgusted him. So, he ordered exchanging the glasses, cups, and tableware immediately for disposable items, complaining directly to Lee Bosal that Minja's promiscuous behavior would taint his health. Lee Bosal remained quiet, with a forced smile on her face, as her response to Kang monk shaman's insulting remarks about Minja.

Nonetheless, Kang monk shaman also frequently made a meaningless promise to Minja to offer a *bulgong deurrida*, a Buddhist prayer, for her. Minja apparently had no idea about what Kang monk shaman did or said regarding her when she was not present. In fact, Minja had been one of the loyal, committed attendees for Lee Bosal, responding to demands for her time and presence, in order to help out with the rituals at Lee Bosal's shamanic shrine. Minja was the first individual to whom Lee Bosal comfortably turned for help whenever a big ritual was scheduled at the shrine, and she quickly responded, regardless of whatever personal problems she might be dealing with. Lee Bosal was quite pleased to have Minja in her company, and Minja had never refused her requests, according to her. In addition, Minja was an important outlet for Lee Bosal, as she provided a welcome audience to talk out loud about such womanly issues as sexuality and desires with which she struggled, outside of her professional practice as a shaman. Minja's presence seemed to be, at the same time, a necessary evil for Kang monk shaman, especially because of her willingness to help with the chores that rituals required, offsetting his sense of disgust towards her. Lee Bosal responded in silence to Kang monk shaman's condemnation of Minja, as she persisted in keeping Minja as an intimate companion, conducting their conversations about women's worlds privately. Minja was the one person whom Lee Bosal could approach about anything, privately and comfortably, with no fear of interference with her professional practice, an important area that Kang monk shaman, in my observation, just did not understand at all.

Mr. Yi and Mr. Jeon, Disfavoring Institutional Religion

One evening, when a dinner was ready, so as to feed the attendees in the shrine prior to a ritual, Kim, Jiyon, Mrs. Yi, and Minja carried out food to the tables. A square type of Korean food table, the top of which was decorated with mother-of-pearl, was set for the men and Lee Bosal, who sat around the floor. A bigger, plain, brown, rectangular table was set up separately, next to the men's table, for the females at the shrine. Meekly sitting next to Kang monk shaman, Lee Bosal served every spoonful of food to his mouth, adding food from the side dishes that were served on the table onto the spoonful of steamed rice. Meanwhile, Mr. Yi and Mr. Jeon were feeding themselves, carefully moving around their spoons and chopsticks while picking up food from side dishes, taking care to avoid contact with Lee Bosal's chopsticks over the various dishes on the table. Mr. Yi and Mr. Jeon were seated at the master's table solely because of their maleness, and they placidly listened to what Lee Bosal and Kang monk shaman spoke to each one of them.

The women's table seemed to be quiet. Only the noises of chopsticks and spoons bumping the dishes and bowls broke the stillness. The women seemed to be in a hurry to finish their dishes quickly, so as to get back to the work of cleaning up the two dinner tables and washing the dishes, before starting the ritual preparations. In the meantime, Kim was the only person who continued moving back and forth from her dinner table, being constantly summoned by Kang monk shaman, who kept demanding for the men's table more side dishes, water, seasonings, teas, etc.

As the dinner was being served, Kang monk shaman started to re-peat the same remarks to Mr. Yi that he had already spoke to him a few times in regard to his recent business proposal. Kang monk shaman told Mr. Yi that the one-hundred-million-dollar business proposal would not go smoothly. So, it would take time and require a lot of patience before its completion. But no matter how difficult the proceedings were in the interim, he had to be patient and not give up, because the proposal would ultimately be successful, according to Kang monk shaman. In the mean-time, Kang monk shaman did not forget to mention his anticipated re-ward in connection with Mr. Yi's ambitious business proposal. He smiled and said to Mr. Yi: "I promise that I will help you to successfully launch the business. So, then, the Chairperson Yi will dedicate a nice small Bud-dhist shrine for me, right?" Kang monk shaman looked to have his own Buddhist temple in exchange for his promise of success for Mr. Yi's busi-ness. Having experienced failure in his attempt to establish a small Bud-dhist temple in the area, some years before, his goal as a self-determined Buddhist monk of owning a temple was stronger at that time than it was before. He wanted to construct an elegant Buddhist shrine on the big, empty front lawn of Lee Bosal's mansion shrine.

Though an exaggerated example, this kind of exchange was fairly common at Lee Bosal's shamanic shrine, especially in cases involving high finance, like Yi's business proposal. The clients are expected, and even di-rected, to provide some portion of their success as a form of appreciation, ostensibly to the shamanic deities but, in fact, to both shamans, for the good outcome. Both Lee Bosal and Kang monk shaman attempted to in-clude some kind of deal when there was a big promise in their *gongsu*. Lee Bosal had previously mentioned to me a number of instances in which she had received appreciations from her clients after the promised good fortunes truly came about. So, the question was whether this sort of deal in the shamanic promise had brought her the financial prosperity that supplied the affluent life condition that contrasted with many other im-migrant shamans. This seemed to be at least partially the case, as she told me that most of the expensive pieces of furniture and special decoration in her shrine had been dedicated by her clients. Moreover, it was also curious how Lee Bosal and Kang monk shaman managed to have wealthy clients with whom they were able to make deals and how the shamanic promise could be assured to come true. In this regard, it was assumed that the announced good fortune did not always come about. So, then, how do shamans and clients deal with such apparent failure?

When listening to what Kang monk shaman promised to Mr. Yi about the hundred-million-dollar business proposal, it sounded entirely unreasonable and illogical, because the Yi couple currently had no significant financial resources or reserves to commence the multimillion-dollar business. Lee Bosal told me that she often provided the gas for the Yis' luxurious white car, because their pockets were empty and they could not afford even to pay for the gas. Nevertheless, all the wishes finally did come true, although it was entirely incomprehensible as to how it happened. Mr. Yi's business venture was launched in the summer of 2012, and it immediately prospered, being located on the edge of the so-called Koreatown. As Mr. Yi's business succeeded, he later proceeded to build an impressive Buddhist temple for Kang monk shaman in the front yard of Lee Bosal's mansion, as he had promised from the beginning.

Returning to the dinner mentioned above, after Kang monk shaman's brief course of instruction addressed to Mr. Yi, Lee Bosal began speaking to Mr. Jeon, while she continued serving Kang monk shaman with the side dishes on the spoonful of steamed rice. Making eye contact with Mr. Jeon and smiling, she said:

> It seems to be good for you to make time today, right? You were not listening seriously when I told you before to immediately start a hundred-day prayer, were you? But now look at what has happened to you. You had a bankruptcy within a month. Now tell me. Do you have any dollar bills in your pocket now?

Mr. Jeon compliantly reacted by checking his pockets, front and back, before replying to Lee Bosal: "I have two twenty-dollar bills. That's all I have now."

Lee Bosal continued: "Take them out and show me."

Mr. Jeon hesitantly took his hand out of his pocket with two twenty-dollar bills and spread them out to show to Lee Bosal.

Lee Bosal said:

> Is this all you have now in your pockets? I see that. So, now you must decide to begin a hundred-day prayer after losing everything. It is too bad about your loss, but you have to do something now to recuperate your financial condition right? Once you complete the hundred-day prayer, you will hear good news about your financial condition. Your life is now downtrodden, but I will take care of your *gwanjaesu*[17] that causes the failure in

17. *Gwanjaesu* means misfortune related to public authorities, such as bankruptcy,

your current financial and public standings. When you sincerely complete the hundred-day prayer, you will see my promise come true with your own eyes. You will recover everything and you will be in a CEO position soon after that.

Mr. Jeon seemed delighted, and he verbally expressed his many thanks with repeated bowing to Lee Bosal. He usually was a quiet person, responding mostly by facial expressions in conversation with or to questions put by either Lee Bosal or Kang monk shaman. Mr. Jeon was in his early fifties, educated at one of the top universities in Korea, Yonsei University. He had owned his own financial firm nearby for years, since his immigration with his family to the U.S. in 1990s. His life seemed to have been pretty good until the bankruptcy. He had become, ever since then, a fully dedicated attendee to Lee Bosal's shamanic practice, as he sought to achieve success through a long-term prayer. He often took advantage of the Yi couple's trips to Lee Bosal's shrine, eagerly participating in weekday rituals and traveling back and forth with them to the shrine.

Mr. Jeon rarely spoke of his religious thoughts, particularly his disenchantment with the Protestant church that most of his relatives and close friends attended. But one time, when Mr. Yi, Mr. Jeon, and I sat around having an ordinary conversation during a break from the ritual, Mr. Jeon briefly expressed how much he disliked institutionalized religion, specifically the Protestant church that prevailed among the Korean diaspora in the U.S. He particularly underscored the controlling, dogmatic system as very bothersome, as he viewed it as an unreasonable power structure seeking to brainwash the congregation.

However, these controlling issues may also be disclosed at the core of the Korean shamanic practice, even with the shaman as called to the profession in the state of spirit possession and trance, on behalf of the deities or spirits. Simply put, the shamanic practice cannot exist unless the deities or spirits control or condition the shaman in spirit possession. The divination and ritual take place in compliance with the commands of the spirits, often in an altered state of consciousness on the part of the shaman. Only under control of the spirits can the shaman divine or transmit messages for redress or good fortune to the client, so as to proceed to the desired outcome. In this regard, control issues certainly prevail also in the tradition of Korean shamanism as much as in other religious traditions, although their application is distinctive in each

---

being laid off, incarceration, etc.

individual religious tradition. Moreover, considering the clients' desire to achieve successful remedies or good fortune from the rituals, the clients are also conditioned by the shaman or shamanic conduct necessitated in the compliance with the shaman's instruction. In this, Mr. Jeon, as an educated financial manager, might have not sensed that he was under the direct control of both shamans and their deities in his shamanic dedication. Or he might have attempted to suppress and endure the control issue at Lee Bosal's shamanic shrine, since he was granted the promise for immediate success in the future, and he really hoped to achieve it. That is, it was questionable if he would still have been eager to dedicate himself to shamanic practice without the given promise by both shamans for an instant remedy and his success.

Mr. Jeon, on the whole, said little but committed himself to be more under the command of both Lee Bosal and Kang monk shaman. In my observations of his bonding with them, his interest seemed to be more in the instantaneousness of his fortune as announced and the remedy of his current condition of failure. The issue of instantaneousness is certainly the most intriguing in the practice of Korean immigrant shamanism. The presence of shamans is mostly forgotten in routine times, but it is sought urgently in various life crises, so as to obtain an immediate remedy or good fortune. As noted by Karen McCarthy Brown, Haitian immigrants tend to leave Vodou behind in the ordinary immigrant context in the U.S. but seek to contact the Vodou priest immediately in times of life crisis (Brown 1991, 5). Similarly, the Korean diaspora seek out the shaman to learn the cause of misfortunes and thereby be able to remedy the effect of spiritual afflictions. In times of life crises, when the Korean diaspora feel discomfited by the theological yearning for salvation, they often seek out the shaman.

3. The Field-Worker

The Menstrual Period

In connection with another *yongshin* trip in late September 2010, Kang monk shaman repeated the same question to the women just before going out the door: "Is there anyone who is having a menstrual period now?"

I had already learned that the menstrual period might function as a strong ritual taboo in the Lee Bosal's shrine. Nonetheless, I had no prior expectation that my own feminine privacy could be a target of the ritual taboo. As an observer doing the field research, I had faithfully followed the strict rules that the couple, Lee Bosal and Kang monk shaman, had established for my presence at the shrine in general and in the ritual setting in particular. The rules were specified primarily by Kang monk shaman. I was strictly prohibited from taking pictures, making tapes or video recordings, writing down notes, or using a computer in any fashion during the times at Lee Bosal's shrine. Any formal interview of a shrine attendee was prohibited, unless both Lee Bosal and Kang monk shaman gave explicit permission. I was expected to share in the domestic chores and to help with the pre-ritual and post-ritual cleanups, in coordination with the female attendees, during my stay in the shrine. In other words, Kang monk shaman was unwilling to allow me to be present only as an observer. No autonomy, no freedom from the ordinary schedule for rituals—or for anything else—was allowed without specific sanction, particularly from Kang monk shaman. So, various boundary issues were already strictly set for my presence at the shrine, altogether presenting various difficulties for my field research, as many other ethnographers frequently experience.

It was a rather embarrassing moment for me while pondering how to reply to Kang monk shaman's unanticipated question about menstruation while surrounded by a group of people, including some male attendees. I felt that all of the eyes seemed to be looking at me for my response to the rather private question. It was a moment requiring an instantaneous reply to Kang monk shaman's question, and I was hesitating. It was one of those moments as a researcher for which I was not prepared: I could not lie, and yet I had not expected to be so called forth. Thus I, as indifferently as possible, just replied to him: "I am."

Kang monk shaman concisely responded to me, indifferent to excluding me from possible ritual observation in the *yongshin*, by simply saying: "Stay here."

Although I should have anticipated such a response, his abrupt response made me suddenly feel naked, as if my feminine privacy had shamefully become known to all the shrine attendees, including some male participants. More than that, his cold, brief command made me instantly feel offended, as being judged unworthy to join with the others. I knew that I did not have to take the exclusion personally, because I fully understood that it was a matter of the ritual taboo rather than of me as a person. I had to accept the couple's rule, because I was not in the position to decide my role in their world. However, I could not help my emotionally uncomfortable reaction at that moment.

The female menstruation taboo linked with various folk religious traditions is well known, even to the general public, around the globe (Dennis 2004, 226; Hoskins 2002, 317).[18] The commonality of this form of taboo illustrates the liminal demarcation of boundaries between the sacred and the profane in connection with the menstrual period (Durkheim 1995, 412–13). Widely regarded as impure, dangerous, and polluting, the female menstrual condition is commonly isolated from the realm of the sacred in both traditional and established religious practices. However, regardless of my scholarly knowledge, the sense of shame immediately aroused as the reaction to the circumstance surprised me in my own self-awareness. More than that, facing the literal application of the female menstrual taboo in my necessary fieldwork, particularly in the immigrant context, was quite embarrassing, involving as it did the privacy of my own monthly physical cycle, which was part of my own well-being as a woman. Then, I was to be set aside as an impure, dangerous, and profane threat, which paralyzed my presence, at least temporarily, in the shrine.

Kang monk shaman habitually expressed his sarcastic view of my "academic" research into Korean immigrant shamanism. He repeatedly spoke to me like this:

> Shamanism is not a theory but a practice. So, it cannot be fully comprehended when it is studied in theories and books. The reality of shamanism is acknowledged by the practice, which is very different from what you learn in theories. . . . When I studied Korean folklore and folk religions in my master's degree, I thought theories and readings were pretty much everything that I had to learn. But later, I realized that it was an entirely different story from what I discovered in practice, once I was unexpectedly caught in spirit possession. Shamanism is never correctly understood unless you are fully involved in accessing the spirits.

18. Menstruation has been considered as dirty or polluting in many traditional societies throughout the world. In some societies, women are even forbidden to cook for their husbands during their menstrual period because of fear of polluting them. Note an illustration of Janet Hoskins, indicating her field experience of menstrual taboo as a female anthropologist: "The Huaulu of Seram have extremely stringent menstrual taboo, and as a woman among them, I was required to comply strictly. I spent five to six days each month in a menstrual hut on the edge of the village, refrained from eating big game, and bathed at a special fountain which was forbidden to men" (Hoskins 2002, 317).

So, your academic research focused on the theoretical basis,
even over a long period, will become useless in this regard. I am
telling you.

Dealing with his criticism and his sarcasm was a common feature of
my time as an observer at the Lee Bosal's shamanic shrine. Frequently
expanding on his ideas, meanwhile, as he consistently sought to belittle
the academic value of my fieldwork, he incorporated all of this in his
routine reactions to my questions or expressions addressed to him or to
Lee Bosal. He invariably reiterated his comments, by which he sought to
persuade me to his point of view, as he commonly dodged my questions
instead of offering reasoned responses. His typical comment was: "I told
you that the kind of research you are doing now will never give you a
proper understanding of the practice of Korean shamanism." He tried
to convince me to seek out the experience of spirit possession. He was
never at ease with my role of being solely an observer doing field research. Perhaps I overreacted, but I frankly could not escape a sense that
my feminine physical condition of having a menstrual period at the time
of a special ritual seemed to be part of the interplay with Kang monk shaman's belittlement of my academic fieldwork. That is, my physical condition reasonably satisfied him to ignore my role solely as a field-worker
and to bar me temporarily from observing his shamanic practice involving spirit possession, especially as associated with the *yongshin* altar, the
most powerful spiritual site at Lee Bosal's shamanic shrine.

In the meantime, my curiosity also concerned why the issue of
female menstruation was still regarded as a strict taboo in the couple's
practice of Korean immigrant shamanism, whereas religious hostility
towards Christianity could easily be set aside for the sake of the larger
shamanic clientele. The couple's immigrant shamanic arena seemed to
negotiate with the predominantly Protestant public of Korean diaspora
and modify its discomfort about Christian clients participating in shamanic rituals. In this, the female gender issue related to the traditional
taboo of menstruation seemed to be more strictly employed, particularly
at Lee Bosal's shrine.

Preserving the taboo of woman's menstruation seems to help
serve masculine authority, particularly at Lee Bosal's shrine, while
reinforcing the stereotypical image of women as subordinates under male
leadership.[19] The space of Korean shamanism, a predominantly female

---

19. I never heard if Lee Bosal herself submitted to this menstrual restriction. However, I assume she had reached her menopause.

venue, is apparently gendered and therein often paradoxically closed off periodically from women in the shamanic practice of Lee Bosal and Kang monk shaman. Sacred spaces, such as ritual sites, are always accessible to men, whereas profane spaces, such as the kitchen and the sites for domestic chores, are accessible only to women at Lee Bosal's shamanic shrine. And all this while, the majority of clients are women, as well as the clients' shaman, Lee Bosal.

The Field-Worker's Call to Become a Shaman

About 11 p.m. one night, after the shamanic altar and the separate food table had been mostly set up by the female attendees, the male attendees were sitting around the table in the connection room[20] and watching the female attendees, as they bustled back and forth between the kitchen and the altar. The night ritual was mainly for Jiyon to *shin eul bullida*, "call out the spirits," a ritual performed particularly for a shamanic candidate, so as to identify the specific possessing spirit. It was part of the shamanic training for the neophyte before entering the main shamanic ritual of initiation in Lee Bosal's shrine. Kang monk shaman commented at the beginning of the ritual: "It is a perfect time for a ritual, since it is dark and a right time for the spirits to be working." Most shamanic rituals begin after sunset, especially around midnight, at Lee Bosal's shrine. In this regard, Kang monk shaman explained that the spirits were believed to be very active in the middle of the night.

Lee Bosal asked all the attendees and particularly her shamanic novice, Jiyon, to continue kowtowing to the deities on the altar during the ritual. Kang monk shaman would play a threefold role simultaneously as chanter, drummer, and gong player, whereas Lee Bosal emphasized kowtowing and, alternately, *pison*, rubbing the palms in prayer (R. Hwang 1996). The invocation of spirits went on for some, with explosive noises that were interspersed with the ceaseless kowtows of the ritual attendees who were constantly shifting between kneeling down and standing up for the Buddhist bows offered to the shamanic deities. Everyone was then sweating, as the room was warm. The light of candles kept flickering on the altar, while the incense fragrance densely filled the room.

---

20. The connection room was located at the center, giving access to the Buddhist altar room, the kitchen, and the shamanic altar room.

All of a sudden, Kang monk shaman randomly stopped his three-fold role and walked out to the connection room. Then, he returned to the altar room and resumed playing. He repeated that particular shift a few more times. As he restlessly stepped back and forth between the altar room and the connection room, Kang monk shaman had a very serious look, as if he were deeply engaged in some thought. All the attendees looked exhausted, but they were fully awake, due to the tenacious kowtowing and almost mechanical noises. They exchanged puzzled looks with one another when Kang monk shaman would intermittently cease his threefold role, and the space finally became remarkably quiet. At one point, Kang monk shaman summoned Lee Bosal to pick up the *ohbang-gi*, as if he had something in mind. This action usually signaled that it was time for a divination.

Lee Bosal took the pack of the *ohbang-gi* out of the big, tall jar that stood at the corner of the shamanic altar room. She began, as usual, shuffling the five colored strips, which adhered to the long, thin bamboo rods. Tightly holding them in both her hands, Lee Bosal handed them to Jiyon, as if asking her to pick out two strips with her left hand. Jiyon picked a white and a yellow, and a shamanic interpretation began to be conveyed by Lee Bosal for Jiyon's two choices. According to Lee Bosal, Jiyon was under the possession of a military chieftain spirit that retained one of the highest ranks amongst all the shamanic deities. In this regard, Lee Bosal continued to reassure Jiyon of her calling: "You cannot neglect your shamanic calling but should accept it."

Lee Bosal then, to my surprise, approached me, while I was standing next to Jiyon, and asked me to pick two strips, using my left hand, while she held the pack in her two hands. My selections were a white strip and a red strip. As I showed her my choices, Lee Bosal began speaking a *gongsu* for me:

> The deity is going to give you a calling to be a shamanic teacher. You will travel all over the world to talk and teach about shamanism, holding the microphone in your hand for broadcasting. Your shamanic profession is different from ours. Your calling is for the teaching of shamanism, not for ritual enactments. Your name will be known to the public, which will make a big fortune for you.

As favorably responding to Lee Bosal's *gongsu*, Kang monk shaman jumped into her procession, while adding to her shamanic analysis. He attempted to rephrase Lee Bosal's message by indicating:

You will make a huge amount of money, like a duck sitting on
the water. Water means money. You will be sitting on the pile of
money. But remember that you have to be initiated as a shaman
first of all to acquire all of the fortune.

His interest in divination and the ritual usually seemed to be centered on two issues, making monetary wealth and discerning the call to
shamanism. Moral values or humane concerns were of no interest to him,
at least in these moments. Kang monk shaman once spoke about how
the shamanic deities would be displeased if their money were used for
some other purpose that was unrelated to serving them. For example,
he insisted that the shaman should never lend money to anyone, even
though the poor approached her/him to ask for help. If they lent or gave
out money, they would be punished by the deities, because the deities
would not like the assets they earned to be consumed for others' sake.

Actually, Kang monk shaman repeatedly emphasized that I had to
be ritually initiated as a shaman first before becoming a public shamanic
teacher. He also pressed his instruction by emphasizing the instantaneous
need for the initiation ritual: "You have to start *shin eul bullida* [calling
out the spirits] as soon as possible, because you have no more time to
spare now." It was hard for me to understand why I had to suddenly hear
all of this unexpected *gongsu*, why I had to *shin eul bullida*, and why I
suddenly had no more time to spare before doing so. As if Kang monk
shaman were aware of my embarrassment and my lack of enthusiasm
and sought to address my issues, he insisted that I had belonged to shamanism since my birth, regardless of my lack of such recognition. Thus,
I should realize the urgency of accepting the shamanic deities before it
became too late, since my time would be up soon. Tons of questions came
to my mind that night, in response to the divinatory message initiated by
Lee Bosal. Nonetheless, I had to set aside until later all of the curiosity for
myself, when Lee Bosal and Kang monk shaman sought to conclude the
night's ritual.

The Interruption of the Marriage of Lee Bosal
and Kang monk shaman

Lee Bosal and Kang monk shaman gave me permission to stay on at the
shrine as an observer, following their wedding ceremony in a municipal
office near the city, in which I served as translator during their vows. Such

permission was rarely granted to anyone, and their invitation greatly assisted my field study that had begun in early August 2010. Nonetheless, though given permission to stay in the guest room at Lee Bosal's shrine, there were associated stipulations. I was asked to give a great deal of time to helping with the chores, including all the daily activities, such as cleaning the shrine, setting up the meals, shopping for rituals, and serving the morning altar ceremony, which was rather like the expectation of Kim as a stay-in devotee. As every step of my movements in the shrine was strictly stipulated, particularly by Kang monk shaman, a severe scolding followed any time that Kang monk shaman was not satisfied. Ultimately, the tight daily timetable resulted in my being quite exhausted, producing a sense of confusion, without making any progress with my field research. Nonetheless, I decided to stick with an optimistic sense, considering the theme of "the anthropology of experience" (V. Turner and Bruner 1986), while trying to convince myself that staying on might be a special opportunity to build up an intimacy with the shamanic couple, which would lead to a better understanding of their practice. I indeed challenged myself, thinking of the possible benefits of additional engagement, activities, conversations, and observations during my stay in the shrine.

In the meantime, the shamanic couple were having an intense, lengthy quarrel that began one day after lunch. My thought at first was that their fight was an ordinary enough process for a newlywed couple, so as to win more attention to each other. But actually it turned out to be something else. Their quarrelling involved rehearsing a stream of hidden, unpleasant anecdotes that exposed the personal history of Kang monk shaman.[21] Lee Bosal was getting more aggressive in verbalizing those details, as she attempted to humiliate him. Kang monk shaman for a moment resorted to physical abuse as part of his defense. He began threatening Lee Bosal and displaying physically violent behavior along with verbal abuse, including curse words. Faced with this, all the other attendees at the shrine seemed to be frozen into a prohibitive silence. As the mood took a turn for the worse following the physical threats of Kang monk shaman, Lee Bosal seemed totally overwhelmed, stopped her inveighing, and was silent. As for Kang monk shaman, no one could dare interrupt his physically and verbally abusive treatment of Lee Bosal. No one could break through the tension that was, at that moment, fully

21. The anecdotes involved Kan monk shaman's affairs with women, and that was the basis for a sequence of lawsuits filed against him by various of his female clients from the time of his Buddhist shamanic temple in Korea.

under the control of Kang monk shaman. In fact, the couple's fighting, which was lightly treated as a joke at the beginning, had now produced an overall sense of general tumult for all those at the shrine. After a while, Lee Bosal was asked by Kang monk shaman to go into their bedroom. No one knew what transpired inside their bedroom, but all could recognize later that there was a special chilliness between them for a while afterwards. When they encountered each other in a hallway of the shrine building, they turned their backs to each other. Lee Bosal spent most of the time in the shamanic altar room, whereas Kang monk shaman mostly locked himself up in his old bedroom that was behind the shamanic altar room on the same floor.

Meanwhile, I encountered an additional unexpected challenge during the period of the couple's cold war, being caught in an odd, in-between position, as each one attempted to pull me over to their own particular space during their fight. Each one wanted me to be present at their own particular altar space for individual shamanic training, creating a very challenging situation. My position under that specific condition turned out to be immensely uncomfortable. Nonetheless, I decided to try to view the competing invitations as offering an opportunity to more fully experience shamanic practice, somewhat in keeping with the emphasis of Kang monk shaman. I tried to avoid engagement with the quarrel and to focus on experiencing more of their practice. So I attempted to set aside my academic reluctance and worked with Kang monk shaman who aggressively tried to lead me into a state of possession, as he called upon the spirits and asked me to dance while emptying my mind so as to receive them. Meanwhile, Lee Bosal would frequently yell out or scream, while sitting in the shamanic altar room or visiting the *yongshin* altar nearby the creek, giving full vent to her anger and resentment, ostensibly addressing the deities but actually targeting Kang monk shaman. Her screams boomed out from the *yongshin* altar loudly enough to be heard by Kang monk shaman and others at the shrine building, despite the distance.

I started seriously reflecting on all the happenings of the last days at the shrine, particularly concerning my so-called calling to become a shaman, which was repeatedly being confirmed by both Lee Bosal and Kang monk shaman. My own resistance to that sudden but repeated confirmation led to confusion and disorientation as I focused on the purpose of my presence at the shrine, which was to engage in a field study. I became anxious about my academic project and did not want to shift from being an observer to becoming a shamanic novice. I thought that it could interfere with and possibly undermine my project. I decided that I needed to clearly reassert my role as an ethnographer and resist the shamans' efforts to draw me into their professional shamanic circle.

After a week or so, the couple got back together again, recovering their bond. This personal resolution prompted them to be even more actively engaged, now in a united effort, in the training and formation of their potential shamanic novices, particularly me, as they joined in the goal of producing a formally educated female Korean immigrant shaman. After dinner one evening, as Lee Bosal divined for all the shrine attendees, she also gave me a special *gongsu*. The couple had been interested in my projected professional career following my potential initiation, envisaged as taking place in the near future. Lee Bosal repeatedly assured me that I would be a teacher of folk religion, whereas Kang monk shaman still stated that I had to become a shaman, which seemed somewhat deviant from the divinatory message of Lee Bosal. She adamantly maintained her *gongsu* against Kang monk shaman's alternative: "I am telling you that you are a teacher. Be a good teacher."

Curling his lips, Kang monk shaman reluctantly corresponded to Lee Bosal and myself, saying: "All right. So then, be a teacher. But you should be first initiated, before becoming a teacher."

Going back to the guest room, in which I stayed at the shrine, I was absorbed in reflection on my experience that night, particularly in regard to the shamanic training sessions, Lee Bosal's divination, and the subsequent conversation. It had been a very strange experience, such as I had never had before, unleashing a stream of questions in my mind. I had danced, cried, and laughed in accord with Kang monk shaman's directions. I had been in a half-conscious state of mind, but my physical and emotional expressions had been almost automatically driven by the instructions of Kang monk shaman. He had continued emphasizing that I should empty my mind. When he had slipped a folding fan into my hand, a pink-colored one with decorative white feathers around the edge,[22] I had laughed happily, like a child character in the fairy tale. When he had called for the spirit of my ancestor, who, he said, died prematurely of some sickness, I had all of a sudden shed tears. My physical response had been more like a puppet being controlled by a puppeteer, although I had still been conscious enough to hear the drumming and chanting of

22. The folding fan in the pink color with the feathered edge was referred to as the fan of the heavenly female angel.

Kang monk shaman and see the *pison* and kowtows of Lee Bosal during the enigmatic experience.

On that particular night, for some reason, Kang monk shaman had handed over the gong wand to Mr. Yi, who was to play the gong and participate in the ritual. Usually, only Kang monk shaman or Lee Bosal handled the ritual instruments in the shamanic shrine. Handing over the gong wand to a client who would then assist in the ritual had never happened before in the shrine during my fieldwork there. It seemed that Kang monk shaman had attempted to improvise an episodic performance that night, including his favorite client as a gonging assistant, who would be able to attest to his ability to control the spirits. Meanwhile, Mrs. Yi, Jiyon, and Kim had been exclusively and continually focused on their own prayers, while kowtowing toward the altar.

After a period when the space was filled with heavy, loud noise, Kang monk shaman had suddenly ceased, as usual, and asked me to go back upstairs and to take a shower with saltwater, then to return to the ritual.[23] As soon as I had returned to the shamanic altar room, having followed his instruction of a full shower with saltwater, he had resumed drumming and chanting. As before, Mr. Yi had also taken up his role as a gong player, strongly playing in his own rhythm while sitting on the floor in the connection room. After a while, Kang monk shaman had tried to slip a shamanic folding fan into my right hand and a bundle of shamanic charms into my left hand, while again asking me to completely empty my mind and just allow my body to move about as it desired.

Kang monk shaman had focused on trying to identify the spirit that might possess me. Although two brief sessions had been performed prior to his attempt at night, he had still been struggling to identify my so-called *momju* spirit, the bodily governing spirit. He had seemed to be very upset and continued spewing rage towards the unknown spirit that was supposedly possessing me at the moment: "Who are you? Whose spirit are you? Show me who you are." His harsh scolding and threatening had been spit out toward the unknown spirit: "Disclose your identity. I will hurt you, unless you show me right now who you are." He had directed his complaint upon the spirit but actually on me, as he had argued that

23. The purpose of taking a full shower with saltwater was to eliminate some negative elements and make my bodily condition clean, to be ready for the spirit ascension, according to Kang monk shaman. When Kang monk shaman could not identify the specific spirit that was supposed to possess me, he complained that I was not willing to empty my mind.

his lack of success was because my mind was not properly empty but was filled with miscellaneous thoughts. The ritual session for *shin eul bullida* that night had ended in chaos, fueled by his anger. His attempt to conduct an episodic ritual had failed, leading me to feel offended and rather terrified, due to his ceaseless blame and complaints in a controlling style.

Nonetheless, all the ritual attendees had sat around after the session, welcoming a break, so as to release themselves from the tension and the uncomfortable mood as they quietly sipped hot tea and hot water. Eventually, his rage had lessened and his smile had returned, as he reflected on the ritual. He had begun describing what I looked like during the ritual, as he continually blew off cigarette smoke into the air. According to him, I had danced like a *manshin*,[24] comfortably draping the bundle of charms on one of my shoulders while my entire body was relaxed, like an experienced shaman in the dance. He had said that my footsteps in the dancing matched perfectly with the traditional order of the shamanic dance steps (Covell 1983, 42; Huhm 1980, 41–52). He felt convinced that my footsteps in dancing were not faked but directed by him in the power of spirit. I would be a big-name shaman once properly trained, he had assured me.

The episodic event that night was, indeed, difficult for me to understand. If his description was correct, I wondered how I could have perfectly followed the order in the traditional shamanic dance, which I had never learned, let alone investigated. Moreover, I could not understand how my emotional shifts would have been able to control my physical movements during the ritual, laughing at one moment and crying at another moment, or how Kang monk shaman could have controlled my physical and emotional states, making me feel like a puppet. My curiosity pushed me further and further but did not reach any convincing conclusion about these matters. Certainly, Kang monk shaman's skill was something given "from above," in keeping with Weber's hypothetical remarks in his reflection on the traits and roles of the charismatic leader (1947, 358–62). Or perhaps it was "the actual path of the power of a spirit," as Edith Turner proclaimed after her experience of an incomprehensible moment in the Ihamba healing ritual in Zambia (E. Turner 2006, 22).[25]

24. *Manshin* refers to an expert, skillful, senior shaman, particularly the female shaman, in the tradition of Korean shamanism.

25. Edith Turner mentions her experience of the Ihamba spirit in the introduction of her book, *Among the Healers*, that "there is no better way to start learning about spiritual healing than with a story. . . . I am only one of many who tell stories. On my

Turner was an experienced anthropologist, mostly working together with her husband, Victor Turner, until his death in 1983. On a
return trip to Africa, where she had previously worked many years with
her late husband, a strange phenomenon completely changed her experience of spirits, something she saw in an Ihamba healing ritual, unlike
anything she had seen previously in that place. According to her, she was
immediately "hooked" by a suspicion at the moment about the traditionally social-scientific understanding of such rituals, finding conventional
social science to be at a loss in understanding what she had seen (E.
Turner 2006, 21). She articulated her new perspective through anecdotal
illustrations, writing:

> So when I consider the Ihamba tooth, which was the resultant,
> the trophy, the material prize gained from the long morning of
> ritual, and wonder about its appearing at the end—after what I
> saw, after what the doctors said about its journeys in the body—
> what then? The tooth did become present; I do not know how. I
> have to say that by the year 2005, I have seen so many material
> things alter under the circumstances of power and spirit that I
> grant the Ndembu doctors the truth of what they say. (E. Turner
> 2006, 22–23).

Why the experienced social scientist, Edith Turner, was convinced
that certain spiritual phenomenon were "real" years later, but had not
been "visible" during her previous fieldwork with the same community,
became a lingering question for me.

In this regard, note that Turner is not the only one who had experienced forms of the spirits during fieldwork, but there are similar anecdotes from other anthropologists. As such, I. M. Lewis introduces some
illustrations as he states:

> S. T. Kimball, for instance, records how he encountered a ghost
> in the course of his fieldwork in Ireland. . . . Paul Baxter told me
> how he had become so thoroughly imbued with the spirit of the
> Boran pastoralists he was studying in northern Kenya. . . . Simi-
> larly, Rosemary Firth reports how on the eve of her departure
> from Malaya, where she had been working with her husband,

---

trip to Africa I found that spirits were real, for I saw one with my own eyes at the height
of an Ihamba healing ritual" (E. Turner 2006, xxi). Turner also provides a description
of the image of the Ihamba spirit that she saw, saying: "As far as I was concerned,
everything they said was vindicated by the actual sight of the spirit form, gray, quite
definite, and fuzzy, like a thick cloud of guck."

Raymond, she had a terrifying nightmare. She dreamed that she had become "a Malay peasant, a woman crouching over the fire to blow up the embers for an evening meal." (Lewis 1986, 5)

Meanwhile, I still felt confused when I reflected on my own ritual experience at the shrine, in light of the prototypical call to shamanism. The general sense is that, in traditional Korean shamanism, a shamanic call is determined by the condition of *shinbyeong*, that is, the so-called shamanic illness, the representation of various kinds of physical and life brokenness. That is, the condition of spirit possession is associated with misfortune in life. In response to this, the initiation and the shamanic apprenticeship lead to becoming a professional shaman. Nonetheless, I realized that the manner in which Kang monk shaman led me to the supposed shamanic calling was opposite to that of the prototypical shamanic call that I had learned about from my shaman informants, as well as through my scholarly research. In brief, there was no sign of spirit symptoms derived from possession, the so-called *shinbyeong*. There was none of the expected suffering with spirit possession in advance of Kang monk shaman's repeated assurance of a call and his unsuccessful attempt to identify the spirit that was assumed to possess me. At some point, I was also struck by Kang monk shaman's half-jesting comment that a female shaman with a doctoral degree would be a great representative for Korean immigrant shamanism. Moreover, considering that he had previously trumpeted his special ability to control and condition the world of the spirits while traveling in and out of the two different worlds of life and death, he might also have been able to create calls to shamanism. Consequently, putting all these pieces together, I decided that it was now the right time for me to leave the shrine, which I did at the beginning of May 2011.

A Countering Discourse to Some Traditional Korean Feminist Perspectives on the Female Image of *Mudang*, the Female Shaman

The shamanic practice has been frequently located as a cultural otherness within the male-dominated society. Moreover, it has often been socially viewed as the number-one religious stigma, particularly during times of stressful shifts in the Korean political regime. The female domination of the Korean shamanic domain is not a reflection of some kind of philogyny, the fondness for or worship of women, in its tradition, nor does it reflect a safe haven. Rather, the image of the shaman has been disparagingly negative since the reign of neo-Confucianism, a society where women were widely ill-treated within the culturally distinct gender system, which, together with strengthened class distinctions, contributed significantly to a rupture of social integrity under the ideological practice of the neo-Confucian literati in the Joseon dynasty (Guksa Pyunchan Uiwon Hoe 1994, 195–203).[26]

The traditional image and role of the shaman, then, particularly the predominant female shamans, were interpreted and celebrated by some Korean feminist scholars, particularly from within the Christian sector. Building on the awareness of *minjung* or the ordinary and oppressed people, in the sociopolitical movement of the 1970s to 1990s, the primary concern of Christian feminist scholarship was the oppressed experience of women, in agreement with much of the radical feminist discourse (Donovan 1985, 156).[27] The scholars endeavored to unveil and disclose the marginalization of Korean women, apart from the stereotypically subordinated images promulgated by the male-dominant structures that were particularly accentuated under the military dictatorships in modern Korean society. In this regard, in the attempt to reconstruct images of Korean women, some feminist scholars advocated the female shaman as the representative role model of superhuman agency, by which the traditionally submissive image of the Korean woman was replaced by the image of the superhuman maternal healer for all, including for the male-dominant society.[28]

Highlighting the reconstructed images and roles of the female shaman, three schematic frames can be cited as epitomizing feminist hermeneutics: the divine healer and liberator, the matriarchal care-giver, and the cosmic intermediator. Hyun Kyung Chung identifies the character of the *mudang*, the female shaman, as the "big sister" of the female *minjung* who had been disenfranchised in the traditional society of Korea (H.

---

26. See ch. 2.

27. Radical feminists were convinced that "male supremacy and the subjugation of women was indeed the root and model of oppression in society and that feminism had to be the basis for any truly revolutionary change."

28. By contrast, some Korean male scholarship suggests that female dominance in the traditional shamanic arena was a deviant form, derived from the formerly dominant grassroots masculine tradition of shamanism (Ch'oe 1984; Jung Y. Lee 1973). Seemingly, they refuse to agree with the superhuman power of the female shaman.

Chung 1990, 66). She elaborates on the character of the big sister further in describing her as a female Jesus who is in charge as the priest of *han* and who cares for the well-being of the *minjung* in general (H. Chung 1990, 66; A. Park 2004, 10–15).[29] Meanwhile, Soon-Hwa Sun portrays the *mudang* "as counselors, healers, clowns, teachers, priests, and intermediaries between the spirits and humans" (Sun 1991, 350). Manja Choi further highlights the image of female shamans as Korean goddesses (M. Choi 1991b): "Independent and powerful, preserving life and sustaining survival, having profound wisdom, acting as saviors, demanding justice and furnishing hope" (Kwok 2000, 73). The image and role of the female shaman, intriguing and impressive in reality, are hypothetically made much more sophisticated and elaborate by these interpretations, as the female shaman becomes not only a spiritual mother but also a superhuman goddess who cares for the healing and watches over the well-being of all ordinary people. In fact, greatly exaggerated and reconstructed as an ideal in this attempt of a Christian feminist hermeneutic, the image of the *mudang* was shifting from the long-enduring, much more ordinary stereotype that has been favored within male supremacy. In this, the female shaman, who, in fact, had survived at the fringes of male dominated society, began to receive a great deal of attention from the scholarly world (S. J. Lee 2001; M. Choi 1991b; H. Suh 1991).

The real-life condition and image of the *mudang*, regardless of scholarly reconstruction, persists unaltered as basically desolate, a reality that can be observed particularly in the Christianized environment of the Korean community and the culturally pervasive bias, rather remote from the romanticized images that are promulgated in some speculative Christian feminist discourse. More than that, some critical points are still unfortunately disregarded in those Christian feminist discourses. The proper understanding of the image and role of the *mudang* requires liberation from the perspectives of male dominance and differentiation from the highly idealized portrayal given in those feminist discussions.

As for the reality of the *mudang*, at least two additional points must be included in this discussion. The first concerns the male gender specificity of the shamanic deities served in the predominantly female-led ritual tradition of Korean shamanism. As these shamanic deities or spirits are not only distinctively served in each ritual segment but also collectively

---

29. Again, *minjung* refers to the ordinary people in Korea who endure oppressive life situations, while *han* as the collective psyche of Koreans was advocated as the theme of the *minjung* movement from the 1970s through the 1990s.

honored in the shamanic pantheon, they are characterized in association with an impersonated masculine persona, with appropriate costume and equipment for each ritual scene, by which the shaman, particularly the female shaman, performs each ritual segment differently.[30] The majority of the featured Korean shamanic deities are masculine in gender, enacted in spirit possession or trance through the performance of the shaman.[31] Moreover, the associated shamanic props or devices, such as the swords, military uniforms, and flags, among others, that the impersonated deities or spirits carry about in their particular ritual segments also reproduce personae and power relations in terms of the old male-dominant hegemony in Joseon society (Haeoe Gongbo-Gwan 1996, 65; Jung Y. Lee 1981, 213).[32]

There is also a female deity or spirit, called *samsin halmeoni*, who is the spirit of childbearing. *Halmeoni* signifies the grandmother in Korea, the older female who finally gains respect and serves a social function when she grows older and her gender is basically neutralized. Only when she becomes a senior in the cultural hierarchy can she function to be a female guardian of family tradition. Meanwhile, the title of the female deity, *samsin halmeoni*, is thought to originate from the prototypical male shaman king Dan-gun as the putative progenitor of the Korean nation (Jung Y. Lee 1981, 167). The importance of the male gender in the discussion of the vast majority of the shamanic deities with reference to the realities of the *mudang* is that she, in her shamanic practice, operates under the control of all these masculine spirits, representative of a male-dominant cultural system and its morality. The image and role of a *mudang* are certainly identified by her practice while under the control of

30. The traditional, charismatic shamanic ritual is purportedly composed of twelve ritual segments. But I have not seen the entire twelve segments fully performed by a diasporic shaman wearing the ritual costume in any ritual in my fieldwork.

31. For example, the *sanshin*, the mountain spirit, is portrayed by an image of a senior male accompanied by a tiger, one of the most important among the shamanic deities, for which the shaman wears an old military uniform of old Joseon society and carries flags in her hand. The spirit of *byeolsang*, the star spirit of another world, is identified by a warrior's helmet, *cheolip*, in the performance of the shaman, an imitation of male military dress from the time of the old Joseon society (Jung Y. Lee 1981, 32). The *daegam* represented not only the title of a powerful governmental officer but also the male head of a high-class household with an authoritative and greedy persona in the Joseon society (Huhm 1980, 76; Y. Harvey 1979, 195).

32. These props include such items as crescent-shaped swords, tridents, and even military flags, used in the ritual to threaten the evil spirits, but they were military equipment to keep ordinary people in line during the Joseon period.

the spirits. That is, the role of a *mudang* is reliant upon spirit possession by a predominantly masculine group of deities. From the perspective of the *mudang*, it is the spirits that make it possible for her to become a shaman and who allow the shaman to enact the particular personae and demeanor so as to represent and even to embody the spirit's dominant male social relationships and moral ethos. The *mudang* understands herself as acting under the control of the various spirits or deities that possess her and acknowledges the male-dominant world.

Related to the first point, the second remark arises from the character of spirit possession, the mechanism of which is strangely ignored in the advocacy of the role of the *mudang* by those Korean Christian feminists. Spirit possession is an essential condition for the practice of the charismatic shaman, a ritual phenomenon in which the consciousness of the shaman is seized in such a manner as to be altered by the particular possessing spirits (Bourguignon 1973a, 42). More specifically, the call to become a charismatic shaman in the Korean shamanic tradition initially requires spirit possession, which is characterized as ego-exchange between the shaman and the spirits (Brown 1991, 353; Gowan 1975, 51; Bourguignon 1973a, 23; Boddy 1988b). According to John Curtis Gowan, the cognitive state in the condition of spirit possession or trance is "escalated by the action of the id's impulses and the super-ego's moral verdict during the host's ego-excursion," a "sandwiching effect" (Gowan 1975, 51). In keeping with Gowan's account, one can argue that the action of the spirit occupies the consciousness of the charismatic shaman and supplies the form of moral judgment that allows for adherence to the cultural strata of the masculine moral ethos, particularly of the neo-Confucian society. Again, note that all the behavior, the personae presented, and the particular costumes and props enacted or utilized in the performance of the *mudang* while in possession or trance are purportedly under the control of the spirits and not the shaman's autonomy, in the state of switched egos. Also, the images and roles that are explicitly performed relative to the spirits in shamanic enactments exclusively relate to the cultural patterns and masculine moral ethos of the Joseon society. A similar illustration can be found in the annual Haitian marching band of *Rara* (McAlister 2002, 3–4).[33] The particular costumes and various tools used

33. Elizabeth McAlister refers to the *Rara* as "the yearly festival in Haiti that, even more than Carnival, belongs to the so-called peasant classes and the urban poor. Beginning on the eve of Lent until Easter Week, the season's ritual events combine the symbols and tropes of Afro-Haitian religion with the plots and personae of the

in the mocking behaviors shown during the march reflect the painful history of African slavery mixed with oppressive political Catholicism, which is powerfully imprinted in contemporary cultural practices and ritual performances. The ritual costumes and props of traditional Korean shamanism also reflect traces of the military organization and social stratification of the neo-Confucian ideology that prevailed, especially in the early Joseon dynasty. In this regard, the ego of the *mudang* is directed to switch and thereby to provide a conduit for the restless masculine morality of the spirits, the personae of which are firmly attached to the power relations of the male supremacy of the past.

On the whole, the Korean Christian feminist scholarship that was cited fails to take into account these two basic points, which must be included in any critical analysis or reconstruction of the image and role of the *mudang*, the charismatic female shaman. In contrast to the Korean feminist hypothetical advocacy, the Korean female shaman has no autonomy or power to independently undergird the therapeutic remedies for the lives of people but is always operating under the control of the restless spirits, under the predominantly masculine pantheon and moral ethos.

Spiritual subjugation is the destiny of the *mudang*, for the *mudang* is chosen and called for servitude to the masculine pantheon, carrying on a very old power system with its associated moral ethos, brought back to life, as it were, in her ritual impersonation. When a shamanic remedy is sought through a ritual, in the belief that the deities or spirits vindictively and restlessly act upon the lives of living kin but can be persuaded to offer help instead, the shaman calls forth the deities or spirits for bargaining and appeasing in a state of nonself under the altered consciousness. The cause and effect of the spirit affliction and the curative pedagogy for the remedy are pursued in terms of the core values of loyalty and filial piety, just as these values are emphasized in neo-Confucian social relations. Unless she serves them, together with that morality, she cannot offer remedies or good fortune to her clients.

It is not surprising thus that not even one of the shamans whom I interviewed expressed any exuberance about their call or took pride in their shamanic practice with its servitude of deities but rather exhibited a kind of resignation to what had occurred. All of my informants emphasized that they had to be thoroughly compliant to the orders of the spirits

---

Christian narrative and rehash them in local ritual dramas. Their content is generated from various moments in the history of the Atlantic world, from the European Middle Ages to the contemporary condition of global capitalism in the Americas."

within and beyond their practices. Lee Bosal once told me, "Disobeying orders means getting consequences from the deities." Meanwhile, the matter of submission seemed to apply not just to the shamans, associated with their call to the world of spirits, but also to the devotees in their shamanic practice. As introduced earlier in this chapter, the environment of Lee Bosal's shrine seemed very much gendered, which was, in fact, more assisted by the presence of Kang monk shaman.

The image of the *mudang* as "big sister" or "goddess" glamorizes the shamanic role and ignores the suffering of the shaman, which she has to encounter, together with the condition of subordination to the masculine order of the past. The *mudang* is "chosen" to be possessed by the spirits from the beginning of *shinbyeong*, the shamanic illness, and "called" to serve the masculine pantheon and moral ethos for the whole period of her shamanic profession. In ignoring this, Korean feminist scholarship disregards the reality of the *mudang* in particular and of Korean women in general, replacing that reality with an ideological reconstruction of the women's role and image.

However, the advocacy of the feminist Christian scholarship may not be completely dismissed, considering that such discussions suggest more critical thoughts about the life of the female shaman, particularly Korean women who have lived through traditional male dominance. The cultural location of the *mudang* can provide a place for women's concerns and women's voices, in ways not obtainable in the more male-dominant neo-Confucian social arena and Christian worlds. In this regard, it is worthy to note that Korean shamanism predates both and provides a place of resistance—or, at least, of coping.

7

From the Dead, From the Living

The Spirits Summoned to the Korean Diaspora

RITUAL IS OFTEN REFERRED to as culturally contextual (Hahm 1988, 60–62; Kister 1993; Chilson and Knecht 2003, 116; V. Turner 1995, 167; Grimes 2000, 5; Van Gennep 1960, 6; DuBois 2009, 7, 146; Bell 1992, 15).[1] In the Korean shamanic world, all kinds of misfortune, including unsuccessful, unhealthy, unpleasant, and agonizing life occasions, are perceived as being the result of vindictive actions by the spirits. These vindictive actions, running against the normative "good" and "healthy" life, should have a ritual response, as they are believed to derive from unhappy spirits. The counterforce is the therapeutic shamanic ritual, through which a medium can readily transform or remedy such dire predicaments in the immigrant context. The shaman, in this respect, purports to be someone who, in spirit possession, can correctly diagnose the cause of trouble with its negative effects and with reference to each specific distressing occasion. Thereby, the shaman also directs a ritual enactment focused on each particular breach of well-being and on mediating a positive relationship of the living with the spirits.

The ritual arena of Korean immigrant shamanism is richly filled with various items and constant enactments, such as with the scents of traditional Korean food and burning incense; the boisterous sounds of chanting and instruments; and the constant movement of kowtows, the

---

1. Ritual experiences and analyses have been studied in many different disciplines. One thing commonly found in ritual is that each ritual embodies, more or less, distinct social, cultural, and historical specificity, by various means.

pison (R. Hwang 1992), and/or, often, the dancing of the shaman. Contemporary cultic settings in the practice of Korean immigrant shamanism still actively preserve divine spirits in the unique images and authoritative personae that prevailed in the social power strata in the past. These deities or spirits are given warm receptions, e.g., through various material ritual components such as delicious, freshly prepared food, a pile of money, and physical reverence. As the deities or spirits are summoned to this feast from the past and from the world of death, indeed, heartbreaking real-life narratives are often disclosed in the communication between the spirits and the living, through the mediation of the shaman. Negotiations are conducted and favorable promises are often granted by the spirits, once the spirits are basically appeased, to the living kin who live in a world of otherness in the immigrant life in the U.S. In this regard, reestablishing a bond between the living and the ancestral spirits through the offered banquet is supposed to lead to immediate, practical, and visible remedies or good fortune, including materialistic success, for the immigrant descendants in the here and now. The main objective of the Korean immigrant shamanic ritual is, therefore, far remote from routine worship, from transcendental hope, or from developing the ethical sophistication of the clients. The focus is solely on well-being and materialistic success.

This present chapter includes a description of some illustrative ritual occasions. It introduces the shamanic belief, reflected in the rituals observed, that the world of the deceased is intimately connected, like a deadlock, with the world of the living in the practice of Korean immigrant shamanic ritual. This discussion also includes various ritual settings, including roles and movements of all the ritual attendees who were involved in the overall composite group in the rituals at Lee Bosal's shamanic shrine. Reviewing the ritual setting may guide to observation of any significant differentiation from the traditional practice of Korean shamanism. Moreover, the interactive dynamics of the attendees may also provide a significant glimpse of Korean immigrant life within and beyond the ritual context.

Ritual in general was not an everyday affair at Lee Bosal's shrine, whereas most of the ritual time was given over to summary ritual forms[2] that were targeting the immediate redress of various life misfortunes through attaining good fortune. Rituals such as the sizable, week-long

2. As part of the form of summary ritual, particularly of the shamanic costumes, Lee Bosal and Kang monk shaman never fully dressed up in the ritual by wearing traditional Korean shamanic costumes. They performed rituals in their casual clothing.

gori gut with twelve ritual episodic segments, found in very formal shamanic ritual practice, were not likely to take place at Lee Bosal's shrine, since Lee Bosal concentrated on rather briefer rituals. The ritual, after hours of preparation for food and tables, was enacted usually at midnight, either entirely in her indoor shrine or transitionally at the outdoor altar, *seonangdang*, from some initial indoor enactment.[3]

1. Rituals for the Shamanic Apprentice, Jiyon

A Ritual for Sending Off the Spirit[4]

The midnight stillness abruptly replaced the fierce loudness in the altar room, when Kang monk shaman suddenly abandoned his threefold ritual role as chanter, drummer, and gong player. He immediately rushed to address a question to Jiyon: "Has your son ever undergone a seizure while he was a baby?" When the *gongsu*, a divinatory message, was communicated to Jiyon, Jiyon became mute again. Her eyes alternately stared at Lee Bosal and then at Kang monk shaman, for she was already quite overwhelmed by the startling divinations being poured out upon her. Jiyon hesitated for a while before replying to Kang monk shaman. His question had been an additional shock, tersely addressed to her, and she needed some time for reflection on her son's infant years as to a possible seizure. Watching Jiyon while she was contemplating her answer, Kang monk shaman grew impatient at her slowness and left the altar room, violently throwing the drum and gong wands on the floor. He walked out and sat at the table in the connection room. Seemingly upset by what he regarded as Jiyon's deliberate lack of cooperation, Kang monk shaman motioned her to sit down next to him while he lit a cigarette. He began to harangue her, as Jiyon quickly sat down next to him, warning her that she had to listen to him very attentively:

> I began this ritual to send your husband's spirit safely off from your life. But, your ancestral great-grandfather suddenly appeared in the midst of the ritual and told me that your son was

3. *Seonang* refers to the village tutelage deity, while *seonangdang* refers to the village shrine. "Built at the entrance of a village or on a hillside," its symbolic meaning in tradition is protection of the village from evil spirits, misfortunes, and adversities. As a sacred site for personal prayers or rituals, it includes an old tall tree tied up with five colored fabrics and stacked stones next to it (*Encyclopedia of Korean Folk Culture*).

4. This ritual occurred at the end of 2010.

in trouble. So, I was unable to continue. That was why I stopped
the ritual enactment, as I had to ask you if you remembered
your son having a seizure when he was a baby.

He continued speaking to Jiyon that her son had suffered minor brain
damage when he underwent a seizure in his babyhood. The seizure
would lead to the breakdown of his liver function, and he would develop
epilepsy within the next two years. Jiyon was terrified by this pronouncement, crying immediately. She now quickly responded to Kang monk
shaman by asking what could be done to prevent that. He responded
that he had just then heard about this from the ancestral spirit of her
maternal great-grandfather who had been a learned herbalist as well as a
geomancer, a *feng shui* practitioner, in his lifetime. Kang monk shaman
added that he had no immediate answer as to what could be done to
avoid the impending problem. He just hopelessly shook his head while
blowing a cloud of cigarette smoke into the air. He then said: "I will have
to ask your great-grandfather about what can be done for your son." Putting out the cigarette butt in the ashtray, he got up to return to the ritual
that had been so abruptly interrupted.

Kang monk shaman resumed his ritual role, sitting back on a cush-
ion and picking up the sticks for the drum and the gong. The altar room
suddenly again reverberated with explosive vibration and intensity. The
incessant movements of kowtowing by the attendees, particularly Jiyon,
started up again, and Lee Bosal resumed the *pison*, praying with rubbing her palms together. Everyone resumed their roles in the ritual. Kang
monk shaman looked very absorbed and emptied, virtually unconscious,
as the ritual reached a deepening and ripening mood. He was still playing
forcibly and rhythmically, beating the drum and the gong, but his chanting shifted to more of a humming mode. He seemed to be slowly shifting
into another part of the world. His bodily motions continued, but his
mind seemed to be flying away to a world of a deep tranquility, leaving
a vacuum behind. It might be that he was traveling in the world of the
spirits in order to obtain an answer for Jiyon from her ancestral spirits.
He had previously stated that he was able to travel and engage the spirit
world. His lips were moving, muttering something. But it sounded quite
different from his routine ritual chanting. It seemed to involve some kind
of interactive engagement with someone else, but it was nothing like a
conscious recitation. Perhaps it was only a meaningless ritual rhythm,
noise from his vacated consciousness.

Traveling into the world of spirits is purported as a prototypical feature of the shamanic gift, particularly in the tradition of Siberian shamanism. Yet, it is rarely mentioned in connection with Korean shamanic tradition. The apparently special gift of Kang monk shaman, in this regard, is most easily associated with his long-term experience with the Buddhist sword dance, a type of religious exorcism that is quite distinct from traditional shamanic ritual, according to him. He had once briefly mentioned that he had been engaged in the ritual practice of the Buddhist sword dance during several decades of his stay at the traditional Zen Buddhist temple on the Korean mountain.[5] When observing his shamanic ritual practice in connection with Jiyon and recollecting his earlier remark of engagement in the Buddhist ritual that I had heard from him, it seemed apparent that his individual gifts for shamanic practice were distinct and unique, in contrast to Lee Bosal who was a traditional shamanic practitioner from the beginning. In this regard, the couple appeared to be a rather special combination for professional shamanic practice, to the extent that each one's gift could complement the other's.

When Kang monk shaman was deeply absorbed in dialogical interaction with the spirits during a ritual, all the attendees had to stay in intense silence. Even a minor disruption would lead to a furious scolding, waking him up from his interaction with the spirits. According to him, engaging the spirits required his full attention because of the delicacy and sensitivity of the contact. Meanwhile, during the ritual, Lee Bosal also seemed unconscious, her appearance hollow and unfocused, her pupils dilated, and her physical movements in slow motion. The main ritual participants—Kang monk shaman, Lee Bosal, and Jiyon—strikingly exhibited not only a peak level of shamanic vibrancy but also a paradoxical tranquility in spirit possession in this particular séance. All the attendees were dripping with sweat while continuing the ceaseless motions of kowtows. Meanwhile, Kim kept supplying tissues and damp towels, particularly for the three main performers of the day's ritual. The air in the altar room heated up, becoming thick and dense with moisture, joining with the loud noise, the endless physical salutations, and even the curious unconscious tranquility of the two shamans.

---

5. He was trained and became a resident monk in the Beopju Buddhist Temple on Songni Mountain, a representative, traditional Zen Buddhist temple in South Korea.

The Additional Requisition for a Ritual

After the ritual had gone on for several hours, Jiyon received an additional divinatory message from Kang monk shaman. This new message sounded far more frightening than the prior *gongsu* regarding Jiyon's son. Kang monk shaman announced that her son had been born with a short life span. His voice seemed magnified as he spoke to Jiyon:

> Do you know? His father, your husband, sent you to here in order to save his son's short life span. His spirit has been rubbing his palms to the *chilseong* deity[6] so that his son's life span might be lengthened. He has even asked the *chilseong* deity to take his own unfulfilled life span from his untimely death and use it to extend his son's life. He has ardently prayed that his son's life might be prolonged, so that he could have a healthy and long life span with a lifetime of good fortune.

Kang monk shaman also attempted to reassure Jiyon, saying:

> You may have been feeling that you were driven by a certain impulse when you recently, all of a sudden, started repeatedly visiting this shrine. Of course, you certainly feel like that. That's it! It is because he sent you here. Now, as I tell you, your son's life span needs to be extended.

Then, he proposed an additional ritual to Jiyon. A ritual referred to as the *myeongdari* ritual (Chung et al. 2013)[7] needed to be offered to the *chilseong* deity, in order to lengthen her son's life span (Covell 1986, 79–80). Kang monk shaman again stressed the urgency of the ritual, saying: "It should be done sooner if you would like to get it done. You may understand how urgent this is for your son." Jiyon seemed quite frightened as she listened to Kang monk shaman's *gongsu*, followed by his specific recommendation for an additional ritual preparation. She burst into tears and was very agitated. She felt that she could not ignore the ritual in spite of her very difficult economic situation. Caring for her son was her foremost concern and the center of her life as she had frequently emphasized.

---

6. The *chilseong* deity literally means the "seven stars deity," known as a life-giving deity in the tradition of shamanism (Covell 1986, 79–83; Jung Y. Lee 1981, 101).

7. *Myeongdari* originally refers to the "life bridge," which is composed of silk or cotton. The purpose of the *myeongdari* ritual is for blessing a newborn baby or child with a long life span. The date of birth, name, and address of the child are inscribed on the fabric in ink. During the ritual, the shaman calls out loud the child's name while holding the *myeongdari* in her/his hands (Chung et al. 2013, 234–35).

The ritual had to take place, following the instruction of Kang monk shaman. It seemed to be essential.

When Kang monk shaman announced that the *myeongdari* ritual should be performed very soon, the basic ritual expense would be an additional fifteen hundred dollars that should be presented in a sealed, clean white envelope, tied with a thin gold string, and offered to the *chilseong* deity. An additional five hundred dollars would be required for setting up the food table and supplying the ritual items that would be demanded particularly for this sequential ritual proposed by Kang monk shaman (Bruno 2007b, 48–49; Kendall 1996b, 514).[8]

In the meantime, Jiyon was harboring a stream of questions in her mind. Her husband had been cremated, as allowed with a Protestant Christian funeral, at which time she believed that his spirit was resting in the loving arms of Jesus. In contrast to her confidence, however, Kang monk shaman had told her that his spirit had been restlessly wandering around, unable to find rest in the other world. So, Jiyon had proceeded to offer a sending off ritual for her husband, following Kang monk shaman's instructions. But the most urgent message given to her was not the completion of a sending off ritual for her husband's spirit but, instead, an increasing concern about her son. Feeling exhausted and hopeless, she was unable to identify any way to get rid of her fear, particularly about her son, given the stream of disturbing divinatory messages that had been communicated to her by Kang monk shaman. Jiyon was even doubtful of the situation, unsure as to whether she was pursuing the right direction in considering the sequential ritual for her son.

The present ritual was resumed after the proposal of an additional ritual had been given to Jiyon. The altar room was reanimated with the resumption of the loud noise, the repetitive kowtows, the dripping sweat of the participants, and tearing eyes, particularly on the part of Jiyon. As the resumed ritual in the altar room had continued for about an hour, it came to a complete pause at a signal from Kang monk shaman. It was time to move on to the outside *seonangdang*. The ritual offering at the *seonangdang* would mark the closure of the day's ritual, but the duration of the ritual at the outside altar could be hardly predicted.

---

8. The ritual practice of Korean shamanism very much involves "the monetary and material transactions as a means of communication" between the spirits and the living (Kendall 1996b, 514).

The Sending-Off Ritual at the *Seonangdang* Altar

An open-front, square structure, about five feet by five feet, had been built to hold the *seonangdang* altar. The outdoor structure framed by wood with a metal backing looked durable enough to sustain the altar, even under a severe storm. It was also up against a big, tall oak tree. Nonetheless, it still seemed questionable that the solidly constructed wood block could protect the *seonangdang* altar if there were some serious flooding, as had once ravaged the entire area and created a disaster, because of the naturally low-lying ground of this section of the forest. The open front of the structure faced the main entrance door, a glass door, of Lee Bosal's mansion shrine, which was symbolically protected by a pair of stone, midsize, mythical lion statues sitting on each side of the entrance. The altar itself was about ten feet away from the entrance door. Some tree trunks, rested against the altar support structure, were tied with the long pieces of five colored fabric strips, such as white, yellow, light green, blue, and red. Those five colored strips (Jung Y. Lee 1981, 196–98), symbolizing the shamanic spirits, were also tied to the corner of the inside wood structure of the *seonangdang* altar. Supported from inside the wood frame, the altar was structured by a three-tiered wooden shelf. A transparent glass box, about fifteen inches square, was placed at the right end on the top shelf. The box contained a bundle of shamanic charms, tied with the five colored fabric strips, and a shamanic folding fan. A dried-up pollack fish was hanging from the other side of the corner on the same shelf. On the second tiered shelf of the altar, there was a set of small bronze cups placed at the center that was used for serving rice wine. Two candle holders sat at each end next to the cups. A thick-walled bronze incense jar was placed on the lowest shelf, with a few bags of candy piled next to it.

Once the outdoor entrance lamps were turned on, Lee Bosal, Jiyon, Kim, Mrs. Yi, and Minja carried out some food to set on the *seonangdang* altar. Kang monk shaman handed a lighter to Jiyon so that she could light both candles once the food was set up on the altar. Jiyon also lit the incense contained in the bronze incense jar. Meanwhile, other ritual attendees were also allowed, one after another, to light the incense, which was routinely prepared on the altar next to the incense jar. Jiyon then poured rice wine from the bottle into the bronze cups and placed them on the second shelf of the *seonangdang* altar. As usual, Jiyon was advised to kowtow three times to the *seonangdang* and four times to each of the deities of the four directions by following Lee Bosal's instruction. Kang monk shaman began forcefully banging the gong to signal the start of the sending-off ritual at the *seonangdang* altar, while standing by its center. Lee Bosal, standing next to Kang monk shaman, alternately began *pison* and bowing while other attendees stepped aside and quietly watched the ritual proceedings from a distance. Kang monk shaman's chanting and gong playing started up again, breaking the midnight tranquility in the forest. Soon, Lee Bosal's actions of *pison* and bowing smoothly shifted into dancing.

The performances of dancing, chanting, and gong playing went on for about a half hour and then suddenly paused. Lee Bosal turned her face to Jiyon, who was earnestly praying *pison* while standing some distance behind Lee Bosal, and began impersonating Jiyon's husband while in spirit possession. Lee Bosal then addressed her:

> Hey, I am sorry. I am very sorry. I left all the heavy burdens on you. I am really sorry. You have been through a lot. I will retrieve your life back. So, I will come back to you after *do reul dakda* (training oneself spiritually).

Jiyon burst out crying while Lee Bosal was impersonating her husband's spirit. Lee Bosal's voice was heavy and thus sounded quite unlike her own normal voice during the impersonation. Her eyes looked hollow and completely dark, the pupils of her eyes dilated, as she spoke to Jiyon in the spirt possession. Jiyon replied to Lee Bosal but, in fact, to her husband's spirit, with watery eyes: "Don't come back. Go and rest now."

At this very moment, Kang monk shaman moved closer to Jiyon and took on the role of her husband, hugging her from behind. As he had his arms around Jiyon's waist, Kang monk shaman said to her: "Your husband loved hugging you like this, right? He was like a sweet mama's boy to you, wasn't he?" Jiyon nodded in reply, with tearful eyes. He continued:

> He still loves you. That is why he is still around, unable to leave you. He is alone in love, while you are no longer interested in him. . . He is now wearing a light khaki London Fog jacket. It was one of his favorite coats, right?

Jiyon broke into shoulder-shaking tears. Meanwhile, as if attempting to prove his gift, Kang monk shaman continued describing the image of Jiyon's husband, detailing his facial appearance, height, body shape, vocal tone, physical behavior, personality, and even routine habits. Jiyon was silent, seemingly overwhelmed, with a startled look on her face as her jaw dropped, indicating her incredulity about the accuracy of the descriptions.

All the eyes of the attendees busily shifted back and forth from Jiyon to Kang monk shaman, absorbed in the flow of their interaction.

The night's ritual at the *seonangdang* altar seemed to be immensely irritating and puzzling for Jiyon. She seemed to be haunted by Kang monk shaman's sketch of her husband, wondering:

> How was he able to correctly identify my husband's favorite coat? The light khaki London Fog jacket was his favorite. How was he able to portray my husband's appearance that well, although he had never seen him before? How could he possibly describe my husband's routine habits, which no one could really know unless having lived with him?

Jiyon was more curious about Kang monk shaman's ability to sketch her husband than about her husband's unexplainable spiritual presence in the ritual. Jiyon's husband seemed to be accurately described by both Kang monk shaman and Lee Bosal, though no one at the ritual saw his presence during the ritual. Lee Bosal, in her spiritual impersonation, even mimicked the regretful voice of her husband and spoke to Jiyon.

While all the attendees, and particularly Jiyon, were enchanted and absorbed in the ritual momentum, Kang monk shaman serenely but casually, intending not to miss the opportunity to reinforce his hypothetical precept to me, somehow stepped aside from the ritual and once again instructed me:

> This is shamanism, as I emphasized before. Shamanism is not a theory, but a practice. It is not about the ritual or the items represented in the ritual, but about the spirits that you have to physically experience.

Granted, we search for the cultural canon or historical documents in order to better understand each distinct cultural reference and the wider tradition, particularly the kind of collectiveness involved in the individual cognitive system of a certain society. In analyzing the cognitive system, the linguistic pattern, and the explicit behavioral pattern, we find a means to understand the specific ritual references in each distinctive cultural locus (McGee and Warms 2003, 385). In brief, the rituals or religious particularities represented in each cultural tradition can be more clearly comprehended by the analysis of cultural specifics and particular social relations. Accordingly, an integrative study of traditional records and empirical data, or at least a balance between theory and practice, may be requisite in the social scientific study. In other words, empirical data alone, without a theoretical framework, has limited value.

Nonetheless, the spiritual presence of Jiyon's husband in the sending-off ritual at the *seonangdang* altar and the generally accurate description of the deceased given by both Lee Bosal and Kang monk shaman, neither of whom had ever met him, was difficult to explain in terms of the usual scientific disciplines, such as cognitive analysis or historicism. More similar illustrations of enigmatic experiences of spirits can also be found in other traditional religious practices as discussed in chapter 6, including the experience of Turner who reports her mystifying experience of spirits in the Ihamba healing ritual (E. Turner, 2006, 21). Inexplicable ritual anecdotes derived from the practice of underground Korean immigrant shamanism used to be met by public condemnation or discarded as superstition, and are not only unacceptable to the predominantly protestantized Korean immigrant community but also implausible by logical explanation.

While Jiyon's mind was still concentrating on the mystery of both shamans' descriptions during the séance, Lee Bosal resumed her *pison* and bowing to the *seonangdang* altar. Kang monk shaman attempted to reestablish his position by taking up again the gong and the wand. The metallic beats from gong playing and the tuned chanting suddenly again shattered the crisp and somewhat chilly air, and even overcame the darkness. The serene forest was again shaken by the loud noise that trailed echoes through the trees, ceaselessly rustling in the wind. The ritual continued until dawn.

Observing Kang monk shaman's banging the gong and chanting with all his might, as if he were completely unaware of the specific time line at which his neighbors deeply fell asleep, it was puzzling as to what the neighbors thought of the activities of Lee Bosal and Kang monk shaman; how they might respond to the *seonangdang* altar and the five colored fabric strips tied around the trunks of the big, tall oak tree, which were quite visible whenever they passed by the entrance to Lee Bosal's mansion shrine; and what they imagined from the strange noises of the ritual enactments within Lee Bosal's mansion. Surely, they were aware of something unusual. Indeed, Lee Bosal once responded to my question about her relations with the neighbors by saying that one neighbor who was not that distant, a retired Caucasian man, thought that Lee Bosal and Kang monk shaman were devotees of a kind of Asian religion which did not bother him.

The location of Lee Bosal's mansion was within a wealthy, forested community, in which some of the mansions belonged to state judges or company CEOs, often serving as weekend or holiday houses. The area itself, in the forest, was surrounded by popular resorts and attractions such as creeks and ski runs. Each residential house was, surrounded by tall trees and was at least a hundred feet or so from any adjacent house, which seemed to provide a sufficient environment for privacy. Once, about midnight, when a loud ritual was underway as usual at the *seonangdang* altar, heavy metal music was being blasted forth from a nearby house located up on the hill, a house that was distant but slightly visible from the *seonangdang* altar, indicating that sound could travel quite a distance in the area. As the loud, harsh-sounding heavy metal music went on, Kang monk shaman came to be irritated and cynically remarked during the ritual break, nodding toward the source of the noise:

> See, these ritual chanting and gonging sounds are much better than that ugly, crazy music. So, I don't have to mind whether or not I create loud noises during the ritual. I like to chant and play at the top of my voice. If anyone complains or feels offended by these ritual sounds, they should come and talk to me.

But no single complaint was ever communicated to Lee Bosal about the loud noises of the rituals during the time that I was staying at the shrine, even though the loudness and late-hour rituals often seemed to very much break the serenity of the forest.

Returning to Jiyon's sending-off ritual at the *seonangdang* altar, the ritual seemed to reach its peak. After a while, Lee Bosal took the *go* ("knot") for a *puri* ("untying") out of the *seonangdang* altar, as she ceased *pison* and bowing (R. Hwang 1996, 204; Bruno 1995; Bruno 2007a, 340). The *go* had been prepared by Jiyon prior to the beginning of the ritual, as she spent over an hour correctly tying the knots, in accordance with Lee Bosal's instructions. The *go* was made out of a lengthy section of rectangular black hemp that had ten ribbon-shaped knots tied in sequence. It is a ritual symbol in Korean shamanic tradition, symbolizing the hardships and agonies, *han*, that the deceased has undergone and within which, in some fashion, it is believed that the deceased is still entangled. If left entangled, the *go* will continue to produce misfortune for the living as the result of the vindictive actions by the restless spirits. In this regard, the *go*, the tied knots, need to be ritually *puri*, disentangled, to free the spirits from all those ties of hardships and agonies, for which the living can expect therapeutic remedies for their lives and good fortune brought from the release of the resentment of the restless spirits.

The *gopuri* is one of the most elaborately symbolic enactments in the ritual for *han-puri*, disentangling the distressed or resentful psyche, in the ritual tradition of Korean shamanism (R. Hwang 1996; U. Kim and Choi 1995). Victor Turner highlights the symbols as a quintessential part of the meaning of rituals, as he insists that the ritual symbols function as texts and mediums to identify the particular inter- and intra-references within each particular social context (V. Turner 1967, 28–31). The ritual segment of *gopuri* might be a critical part of the understanding of Korean shamanism as a folk religious tradition in this regard. The main reason is that the symbolic reference to the *go* is representatively joined with the Korean collective sense of distressed psyche, *han* (U. Kim and Choi 1995), that appears to be a perpetual ritual subject to be freed, *puri*, in the practice of traditional Korean shamanism. In other words, the manifestation of *go* or *han-puri* in the shamanic ritual represents the cultural collective consciousness, as to the particular ways that Koreans define human existential realities such as pain and sufferings and then ritually resolve them. It is unclear as to just how the primary thrust came to have specific reference to the collective consciousness of *han*. Yet, it may be noted that the sense of *han* is a culturally located common awareness within the Korean collectiveness, a shared impression that comes from the flow of human life: birth, aging, illness, and death. Ronald L. Grimes takes notice of ritual symbols, in keeping with the perspective of Victor Turner: "Ritual symbols are not simply expressive, but epistemologically and sociologically constitutive" (Grimes 1995, 157). Borrowing from Grimes's precept, the reference to *go* and *puri* may provide the core epistemological tools to comprehend the collective consciousness of Koreanness ritualized in the practice of Korean shamanism, as in the union of a cultural nut and bolt. In the presumption of Korean shamanism, all the momenta of life anomalies are identified as knots, as causing *han* that needs to be released or untied. So, when they are ritually *puri*, untied, the restless spirits are believed to be appeased and satisfied, which is also believed to eliminate unfortunate situations from the lives of living kin.

However, the general sense of *han* seems to be fading away from the collective consciousness of the Korean community, as the younger generation experiences a distinctly different cultural ethos from that of the first-generation Korean diaspora in the U.S. Perhaps, this factor may be one of the reasons to explain the current trend toward ritualless

or summary shamanic practices in public, in that the younger generation no longer shares common compassion for the traditional collective
consciousness of *han-puri*, as they are moving away from the enduring
cultural nostalgia of their parents and grandparents.

Returning to the ritual, now Lee Bosal put the lengthy set of tied *go*
around her shoulders, while she slowly and gently stepped back and forth
in her dance. It was unclear whether or not she still stayed in spirit possession. Her two hands lightly held the entangled *go* as they were untied
and streamed down her chest, while she was constantly moving her steps
in a small circle in front of the *seonangdang* altar. At a certain moment,
the knotted *go* began to feebly run down, one after another, from the top,
becoming free from the tender touch of Lee Bosal. Kang monk shaman
banged the gong as hard as he could, as if he were excited by responding
to each movement of the *gopuri*. Ten ribbon-shaped *go* were completely
unknotted in some minutes, leaving only a lengthy plain piece of black
hemp running off to the ground. Everything was completed and ceased
in minutes. It was, therefore, time for a divination. Lee Bosal snatched the
pack of *ohbang-gi* from the *seonangdang* altar and asked Jiyon to pick two
strips with her left hand. Jiyon picked a white and a yellow. In response,
Lee Bosal spoke a *gongsu* to the effect that the *seonang* had gratefully accepted the ritual. Jiyon was again asked to pick another pair of *ohbang-gi*.
This time, she picked a white and a light green, which indicated that her
ancestral spirits were also satisfied with the ritual that Jiyon had offered
that night.

The divination for Jiyon was the finale of the night's sending-off
ritual. The female attendees' footsteps were heard suddenly and busily
moving around, awakened from the drowsiness just before dawn. The
food placed on the altar was collected in a big container and carried away
to be thrown out as food for the wild animals, among the trees adjoin-
ing the creek where the *yongshin* altar (Y. Harvey 1979, 296; Jung Y. Lee
1981, 168), the dragon king or the water spirit, was located. At Lee Bosal's
shrine, the food served in the rituals was all collected and scattered in
the forest to feed and pay respect to the natural world, according to Lee
Bosal. No food, once placed on the altar, went to the refrigerator to be
preserved or shared on the meal table after the ritual. This was a matter
that Lee Bosal constantly emphasized in her shamanic practice, by saying
that her ritual deities were part of the natural world, Mother Nature. So,
she insured that her ritual and the deities were supportive of conserving
the ecosystem. Also, any liquor that had been already placed upon the

altar or poured out into the cups on the altar was thrown around the trees. All the attendees returned to the indoor connection room after the ritual utensils and the empty bowls and plates were taken back to the kitchen to be washed. Finally, Kang monk shaman expressed gratitude to everyone involved in the ritual at the closing: "Good job."

The sending-off ritual for Jiyon's deceased husband was completed at about 5:30 the following morning, as it began at the indoor altar room the previous night and moved on to the outdoor *seonangdang* altar. An additional particular instruction was delivered to Jiyon before entire dismissal by Kang monk shaman. It was for another ritual in sequence for her son. Expressing some flattery, Kang monk shaman spoke to Jiyon before he retreated to his bedroom, noting that the sending-off ritual had been originally planned for about two hours but had turned out be an overnight enactment. He then added to his remark:

> I don't know why, but I have done too much for you by such a comparatively small amount of ritual compensation you paid. This sending-off ritual should actually have been charged for about twenty thousand dollars by the usual scale, if I were to officially price it. As the *gongsu* about your son was unexpectedly delivered to me, it also caused the extension of the ritual duration until this morning. But, honestly, your tearful eyes from the beginning have softened my heart. I am telling you.

Kang monk shaman and Lee Bosal, then, went into the bedroom to rest after giving a brief comment to Jiyon. The Yi couple and Mr. Jeon often left right after the ritual, so as to drive the long distance back to their home, though sometimes they stayed for a short nap before leaving as the sun rose. Others rested in the guest room, a well-furnished, big space on the third floor.

The Indoor Altar for the *Myeongdari* Ritual

Due to the complex schedules for both Jiyon and Lee Bosal's shrine, the *myeongdari* ritual for Jiyon's son took place about two weeks after the main sending-off ritual that was offered for the spirit of her deceased husband. On the very day of the ritual itself, when Jiyon handed over the remaining costs for the *myeongdari* ritual, except for the five-hundred-dollar deposit that had already been given to Kang monk shaman shortly after the sending-off ritual for her husband's spirit, Kang monk shaman instantly instructed the ritual preparation. The ritual was to proceed in three steps in a sequence, which no one actually fully understood except Kang monk shaman. As usual, shopping for foods, whiskey, and cigarettes took place prior to the ritual performance, which on this occasion created a much smaller shopping trip than that for the preceding sending-off ritual The *myeongdari* ritual itself did not seem to require a separate big food table, but instead, the bountiful plates of fruits and rice bowls were placed on the shelves of the indoor shamanic altar. Nonetheless, the ritual expenses already exceeded the original budget, and this made Jiyon financially stressed and anxious about the unexpected extra cost additionally paid out.

The indoor main shamanic altar was set up in a room across the hallway from the kitchen, which allowed an easy flow for the ritual preparation. Also, a large dining space, extending from the shamanic altar room into the kitchen, served to simplify the ritual process by utilizing the space that was also used for ritual breaks. The sizable sliding drapes that served to cover the entrance into the shamanic altar room were often firmly closed when no ritual was in progress. The drapes were left open during the most of the daytime otherwise. The altar for the spirits was set up clockwise from the left end and extended towards the center wall of the room, as viewed from the front entrance of the shrine room. The side wall on the right had a double sliding door that gave access to an outside porch, a cozy, second-floor wood deck.

Various deities were served on the same altar extended from the left end of the wall: the *dongjashin*, *sanshin*, and *chilseong* deities along the left wall, and the *jang gun shin*, *josang shin*, and *youngwang* deities along the center wall (Covell 1986, 42–115).[9] To serve the *dongja* spirit, the child spirit, packs of candies, toys, and dolls were piled on the far left corner of the altar. The image of *sanshin*, the mountain deity, was elegantly displayed by a square copper etching that covered two-thirds of the left wall. The image, as engraved in the etching, was of an elderly man in the lotus posture, holding a fan over his belly with his right hand. An attractive, square, reddish silk sitting-mat had been added, covering the *sanshin*'s knees, as if the elderly man in the etching were actually present and sitting on the altar. The image of the *sanshin* seemed to

9. To review the terms, the *Dongja shin* refers to the child spirit, regardless of gender; the *sanshin* is the mountain deity; the *chilseong* is the deity of seven stars associated with life span; the *jang-gun shin* is the military general deity; the *yongwang* is the dragon king or the water deity; and the *josang shin* is the ancestral spirit.

parallel that of a bearded Daoist man with a large hair knot on the top of his head, wearing a lengthy robe. A seated tiger with a menacingly open mouth was to the left of the *sanshin*, as if it were guarding the deity. Two fairies standing to the right of the *sanshin* deity were meekly watching him. Clockwise from the *sanshin* deity on the altar, a painting of the *chilseongshin*, the seven stars deity, was hung on the wall. It represented a trace of Buddhist influence, as the painting included the Bodhisattva of sunlight and moonlight (Covell 1986, 85). Under the *sanshin* etching and the *chilseong* painting that were hung on the wall, three-level tiered shelves were filled with various ritual items. At the very left of the second shelf were a small, thick-walled iron bell and a big bouquet of artificial flowers. On the bottom shelf, just beneath the flowers, various candy bags were piled up high. Also on the second level of the shelf, in front of the *sanshin* etching, there was a big brass basin brimming with raw rice. On the bottom level, in front of the *sanshin* etching, was a pair of tall bronze candle stands holding two thick, white candles. A bronze incense burner was also placed between the two candle stands. Just under the *chilseong* deity, on the top shelf, there was a white triangular paper hat, such as formerly was exclusively a symbol of the *sambul*, three Buddhas, or the *samsin*, the three deities (Covell 1986, 83).[10] On the bottom shelf, in front of the *chilseong* painting, a sizable watermelon had been placed on a legged plate between a pair of candle holders with candles. Moving clockwise from the left wall, the entire center wall was covered by another copper etching with multiple images, including representations of a group of military general deities, wearing costumes that dated back to the time of the Joseon society.

Etchings of shamanic deities are rarely found in any shamanic shrines, as shamanic deities are usually represented through paintings, mostly done on the now-antiquated Korean traditional paper. In this regard, Lee Bosal told an anecdotal story to me, as to how she acquired the unique copper etchings in her shrine. As her story went, when Lee Bosal was busily seeking artists to help decorate her new shrine in the forest, she came across, by accident, an engraver who volunteered to do some artwork for her shamanic shrine. It was a great surprise to her. According to Lee Bosal, an elderly Korean gentleman, an etching artist who at the time was a professor in Canada, had been inspired by a spirit that had directed him to find a female shaman who was looking

10. The *samsin* or *shambul* deity is identified with the *cheseok* Buddha, as the deity of fertility.

for an artist to do some shamanic artwork for her. So, he had traveled about, looking particularly for a female shaman, as he had been directed in a state of spirit possession. Lee Bosal herself, meanwhile, had been in the midst of a word-of-mouth search for a professional shamanic artist. While the two of them were simultaneously engaged in searches, they finally met each other through an unidentified person's mediation in the city. When they shared their stories at their first encounter, they both were overwhelmed but appreciated meeting each other. In so doing, they were quickly connected and began the etchings at Lee Bosal's shamanic shrine. The etching artist completed both pieces of the *sanshin* deity and the military general deities within eighteen months from the start of his work in 2000. According to Lee Bosal, the conjoined searches that finally led to the beautiful etchings were a marvelous work of spirits.

On the top shelf, beneath the etching of the military general deities on the center wall, a miniature set of three Japanese samurai swords had been placed. They were hierarchically placed on black wood pedestals, as if proudly displaying militaristic power and authority through the representation of weaponry. Boxes containing Johnnie Walker scotch and Marlboro cigarettes were placed to the right and the left, respectively, of the second-level shelf, beneath the miniature set of swords. The bottom-level shelf, below the military general deities, was filled with a set of candle holders, with thick white candles, and two incense burners. Fresh Fuji apples were piled on the legged plate, and a sizable watermelon was also placed on both sides of the candle holders. At the far right of the bottom shelf, beneath the etching of the military general deities, a *jaesangdae* (R. Hwang 1996), the spirit stick, had been placed on the covered top of a large bronze basin; "the spirit enters the shaman through the spirit stick" (C. Kim 2003, 59–60). On the right wall, toward its left side, a *yongshin* painting, the dragon king or the water spirit (Covell 1986, 56–72), was hung. The painting portrayed an elderly man who stood in the midst of high ocean waves in a long red robe and accompanying two large playful fish, one on each side of him. A small Korean national flag displayed in a gold, metal, rectangular frame was hung next to the *yongwang* painting on the wall.

Through the flow of shamanic presentation on the altar from the left, clockwise to the right wall, the final touch of the Korean national flag seemed to summarize the altar and the arrangements overall as belonging to the culturally specific Korean shamanic tradition. Whereas the Korean national flag is commonly displayed together with the American flag near the pulpit in most Korean immigrant Christian churches, it is also displayed by itself in Lee Bosal's shrine and in many other Korean immigrant shamanic shrines in the U.S. The display of the Korean national flag by itself at Lee Bosal's shamanic shrine symbolizes not only the ethnic identity of the individual shaman in the immigrant context but also the cultural practice as representing traditional Korean collectiveness, even though Lee Bosal's clientele included some non-Koreans. Actually, the hearsay about Lee Bosal had indicated that she had some American, English-speaking shamanic disciples from among some spiritual musicians or professors connected with prominent U.S. universities.[11]

Under the three levels of the hierarchical shamanic altar, there was a storage space. Taking up the entire bottom level from the left to the center, the wooded storage closet supported the entirely framed-in upper altar area. This storage closet had locks on its doors, inside which Lee Bosal kept all the ritual vessels and items. On the outside of the closet, the traditional Korean drums and a gong, a *jang-gu*, a *buk*, and a *kkwaeng-gwari*, sat next to a red silk sitting-mat on the floor. They looked ready to be played and were mostly used by Kang monk shaman. A *jakdu* set (Jung Y. Lee 1981, 149; Covell 1986, 154–58; 1983, 49), the shamanic blades, was placed on the covered top of a brass basin concealed under a rectangular red fabric. The *jakdu* was to be kept firmly covered, unless there was a specific reason for using it, according to Lee Bosal. It would spurt forth a strong power that could afflict people, should it be inappropriately opened. On top of the *jakdu* set, there was a package of a crescent-shaped sword, a long-handled sword, and a trident, all rolled up and hidden in a dark brown-colored fabric wrapper. Finally, next to the *jakdu* set and the sword set placed on the covered top of the large brass basin, a rectangular brown wooden table was holding a neatly packed set of ritual props, including a shamanic folding fan, a bundle of charms, and a small brown ceramic jar.

This was a rather elaborate setting for the immigrant shamanic pantheon with which Lee Bosal and Kang monk shaman routinely engaged as they performed the shamanic rituals. Each deity, each ritual item, and even each bag of candy on the altar should be reverently and carefully arranged and handled, so as to give the deities appropriate respect and pleasant service. Nonetheless, when no ritual was underway, the altar room was kept carefully closed off behind the drapes, which produced

11. However, I myself had never had any chance to meet such persons physically present at her shrine.

a dark and spooky atmosphere by leaving the deities represented in the lively paintings and etchings totally in the dark with neither candlelight nor burning incense. The bronze bowls that held the steamed rice sat empty on the altar. The only ongoing service was that the water in the bowls was replenished and ceremonially changed when no ritual took place.

Meanwhile, there seemed to be a cultural blend in the altar presentation of Lee Bosal's shamanic pantheon, as drawing upon other Korean religious traditions, such as Buddhism, neo-Confucianism, and Daoism. This cultural mesh was obvious in the contents of the etchings and paintings that portrayed various shamanic deities. The shamanic pantheon seemed to also reflect a microcosmic world, through the presentation of symbolic interactions and social relations between deities/spirits and the human world. It reflected a constant hierarchy, lining up the ancestors and the living, life and death, mystery and reality, male and female, religion and religions, fixed money and bargaining, the professional identity and physical being of the shaman, *go* and *puri*, tears and joy, fortune and misfortune, and so forth. This curiously mixed world was summarized by Geertz's phrase:

> In ritual, the world as lived and the world as imagined, fused under the agency of a single set of symbolic forms, turn out to be the same world, producing thus that idiosyncratic transformation in one's sense of reality. (Geertz 1973, 112)

Following this, some intriguing questions could be raised in regard to the shamanic deities or spirits. How was the neo-Confucian figure ranked as one of the most important shamanic deities? How did it happen that the spirit representing a Buddhist devotee had been associated with the power to control the human life span? What made it possible for the military personnel and the upper-class authoritative masculine figure of the Joseon society to sit in the shamanic pantheon? These questions are certainly important to pursue in observing how people make access to meanings in connection with real-life situations, and thus further research may be necessary to answer those questions.

The Ritual for *Myeongdari*

As for the food setting, instead of a big, separate food table, the altar in the room was served with a large plate of fresh Fuji apples and Asian pears, some California Sunkist oranges, and a sizable watermelon, alongside the bowls of steamed rice and rice cakes, raw rice, and rice wine. Once the candles and the incense were lit on the altar, the ritual for *myeong-dari* was about to begin. Lee Bosal was facing the *sanshin*, the mountain deity, and began with *pison*, praying with rubbing the palms, whereas Jiyon placed herself for kowtowing at the corner of the altar room. Kang monk shaman started banging the drum, a *buk*, and striking the gong while also chanting, which created a sudden loudness in the altar space. Kim and Mrs. Yi joined in kowtowing, while staying in the connection room outside the altar room. While everyone ardently concentrated on their individual role, the *myeongdari* ritual was getting more organized, moving smoothly into a prototype of effervescence at the shrine, which included a very lively mixture of rhythmic loudness and repetitive movements, together with sweat, heat, and the strong incense odor. Even the unexpectedly abrupt cessation of the chanting, drumming, and gonging on the part of Kang monk shaman, after about two and a half hours, seemed to deepen the ritual with the sudden stillness. All the attendees continued being occupied in their actions with expressionless faces.

It was puzzling as to whether Kang monk shaman was engaged with the spirits by this time. He seemed to be in a stable mode, somewhat different from the usual ritual occasions. He looked likely to call it quits, having ceased his triple roles. He left the altar room and walked into the connection room, sitting down at the table. Meanwhile, all the other ritual attendees paused, cautiously trying to read his countenance. Taking a cigarette out of the red Marlboro carton, Kang monk shaman called for a divination from Lee Bosal, although she did not give the impression of being invigorated by the spirit, for some reason, at the particular moment. Nonetheless, being receptive to his request, Lee Bosal silently took the pack of *ohbang-gi* out of the ceramic jar that stood at a corner of the altar room. She shuffled them in her two hands and took the pack first to Jiyon to pick two with her left hand, as usual. In Jiyon's first turn, she picked a white and a yellow, for which Lee Bosal instantly gave her a divinatory message by interpreting that the *chilseong* deity, the deity of seven stars in charge of the life span, had gratefully accepted the *myeongdari* ritual. Jiyon, then, was instructed to pick another set and Lee Bosal gave for her the meaning of her second pick, a white and a light green: "Your ancestral spirits have also significantly accepted the ritual you offered to them."

Immediately after her announcement, Kang monk shaman made an additional comment concerning Lee Bosal's analysis:

> Your son was almost possessed by the spirits, but I removed them all for you. You should keep in mind that you need to be initiated within the next two months at least. It will be the last chance for you to survive.

The added account by Kang monk shaman indicated that Jiyon and her son's lives were both at stake and would be very difficult to retrieve, unless Jiyon followed up quickly with the initiation ritual so as to accept the spirits. It sounded like another dreadful alert, and it turned Jiyon's face quite pale, as her eyes filled with tears. The reality was that Jiyon had to face one greatly disturbing moment after another, beginning with the *gongsu* about the wandering spirit of her deceased husband. The subsequent divination about the potential illness of her son broke her heart. Furthermore, the divination had been significantly expanded to her son's short life expectancy, which itself had led to this night's ritual. So, she was then pressed hard to move on quickly to her own initiation ritual. She was getting more and more confused, feeling exhausted and frustrated. She was even experiencing deep anguish from the number of sequential demands. Jiyon just flopped down, a terrified look on her face, in response to the seemingly endless surprises dropped on her by the series of *gongsu*, particularly those given by Kang monk shaman. However, regardless of Jiyon's obvious emotional overload at the moment, both Kang monk shaman and Lee Bosal continued emphasizing that the *myeongdari* ritual had satisfied the spirits. As a final step, the fruits and foods arrayed on the altar were all taken out, as usual, to the nearby groves of trees close to the creek and offered as a feast to the wild animals.

A few days later, a phone call came from Jiyon who had temporarily departed from the shrine on the day following the ritual, so as to take care of her son and her personal matters. Jiyon's voice could be heard on the speaker phone to Lee Bosal, reporting on her son's physical symptoms. Jiyon's son had suddenly developed a severe headache, a stomachache, and even nausea, since the *myeongdari* ritual had taken place. According to Jiyon's account, her son's symptoms had begun from the very day of the ritual and thereafter worsened to a more painful condition in his stomach and elbows, as if being wrenched by someone. So, Jiyon was wondering if there was any connection between the ritual and her son's symptoms.

Lee Bosal replied that Jiyon's son was experiencing effects from the ritual. Jiyon was given an instruction to be attentive about his food, avoiding any kind of fish for at least two weeks. In addition, Lee Bosal instructed Jiyon to herself perform a ritual alternative at home that could help her son release the pains. Lee Bosal advised Jiyon: "Burn some newspaper and draw circles three times over your son's head with the ashes. Perform the same for yourself as well. If the symptoms still bother your son even after this enactment, you should let me know."

Jiyon later told Lee Bosal that her son's symptoms disappeared a couple of days after the suggested ritual alternative.

The *myeongdari* ritual was performed in the absence of Jiyon's son. More than that, according to Jiyon's account, her son knew nothing about the ritual and the detailed information about him obtained from the *gongsu* of Kang monk shaman. Accordingly, the effectiveness of the *myeongdari* ritual was still unknown. Moreover, it was difficult to explain just how the sudden symptoms of Jiyon's son were related to the *myeongdari* ritual and how the suggested ritual alternative that Jiyon performed at home contributed to removing her son's symptoms. Mysteries seemed to be added to mysteries.

2. Females in Low Regard

Mrs. Yang

Death accompanies life in the belief of Korean shamanism, particularly at times of misfortunes and the associated sense of apprehension. A similar interconnection is found in many, if not most, of the traditional folk religions of the world. Reigning over the realm of life and sanctified through the experience of the superhuman power of spirits, death in the world of the Korean diaspora in the U.S. comes into play as key not only to connection with good fortune but also for misfortune. Death, perceived as the counter-reality to life, tends to be sensed as lively yet meek in the diaspora's reaction to fear, anguish, or spiritual afflictions. In this sense, the spirits are viewed as vividly animated in the service of the living, such as for negotiation and pacification with food, money, and physical reverence. The spirits are respectfully served by the living in respect to the neo-Confucian virtues of fidelity and loyalty expressed in the manner of Korean shamanism, so as to engage in communication with the spirits.

Meanwhile, death is also identified as a potentially polluting occurrence that requires purification or cleansing, because it is perceived as the source of negative energy that is able to bring about disorder and even destruction to individual or familial life, negative energy that derives from the restless or dissatisfied spirits that are wandering about in the world of the living kin or related individuals. On occasions when negative impulses or misfortunes impact the life of the living, a Korean shaman finds the significance of death manifested in the sense of danger, fear, dirt, pollution, or contamination. In this regard, the subject of death has a central site in the interplay of the spirits with the shaman, which is rooted in the conviction that the otherwise invisible spirits have the power to control lives and circumstances in the physical world. Mary Douglas has offered an insightful remark in respect to this situation: "Reflection on dirt involves reflection on the relation of order to disorder, being to non-being, form to formlessness, and life to death" (Douglas 2002, 6–7). So then, how shall we grasp the character and significance of the comparative mechanism or the symbolic relation between the visible and the invisible, between order and disorder, as expressed in the practice of Korean shamanism?

Mrs. Yang, a first-generation Korean immigrant woman in her early sixties, arrived at Lee Bosal's shrine about 10 a.m. She had flown all the way from Los Angeles, from the largest Korean immigrant community in the U.S., to the East Coast, in order to visit Lee Bosal's shrine. Her trip was solely for divination and the supposed rituals related to issues relative to her property holdings.

After Lee Bosal had welcomed her with a big greeting, they sat around the table in the connection room. Lee Bosal, at the start, introduced Kang monk shaman to Mrs. Yang, stressing that his gifts for divination were remarkably sharp and accurate, instantly targeting the appropriate remedies or naming good fortune in any occasion. Brief greetings were shared with each other between Mrs. Yang and Kang monk shaman. Lee Bosal then quickly shifted the subject, inquiring about Mrs. Yang's daughter, stating that her daughter would play an important role in her family and would probably continue in strong leadership, like a "big man." At this time, Mrs. Yang's daughter was considering proposals of medical partnership that had been encouraged by other medical practitioners to lead a consortium, so as to establish a new hospital.

Mrs. Yang, however, having briefly replied to Lee Bosal's comment, attempted to quickly change the subject. She asked Lee Bosal's thought about the potential sale of some buildings that she owned by intimating that the matter of what to do about her buildings was her primary interest for divination. And, indeed, Mrs. Yang emphasized to Lee Bosal that she wanted a divination concerning the properties: "Do you think that they will be sold for a fair price?"

Lee Bosal calmly but briefly responded to her: "Let's see. We need to serve a nice ritual first and then we can ask the deities about this matter."

Mrs. Yang seemingly ignored Lee Bosal's brief reply and pressed ahead with her own comment: "At least two of the seven buildings should be sold at a fair price. I have had trouble enough with them."

Mrs. Yang was a wealthy real-estate investor who owned seven separate buildings around the Los Angeles area. Since she had experienced a good growth in her real estate wealth while following Lee Bosal's divinations and advice, she often flew out to visit Lee Bosal in cases when there were troubling issues with her holdings. In spite of the great distance, she had become one of the most reliable supporters of Lee Bosal's shamanic practice. For example, Mrs. Yang had financially sponsored a three-month ritual trip to Korea for Lee Bosal and two of her shamanic disciples in 2005, according to Lee Bosal. With two grown-up children who were popular plastic surgeons in the area of Beverly Hills, California, Mrs. Yang had been a widow since the time of her husband's death about five years prior to her visit that time.

Although Mrs. Yang attempted to keep the conversation solely focused on the possible sale of some of her buildings, Kang monk shaman attempted to change the subject by finally breaking his silence. He questioned Mrs. Yang about her deceased husband, insisting that her husband's spirit was restless and had put her at a disadvantage in her business and disrupted the lives of her children. He told her that she needed to offer a ritual sacrifice for the spirit of her deceased husband. He continued questioning: "Your husband was a very greedy and domineering person, right?"

Mrs. Yang responded to him with a few slow nods, as if she concurred with his description of her deceased husband's personality.

"He wants you to serve a sending-off *gut*, the shamanic ritual, for him," continued Kang monk shaman.

But Mrs. Yang, with a quizzical look, replied that a nice sending-off ritual had been offered for her deceased husband right after he passed away.

Kang monk shaman continued to pester Mrs. Yang: "Where did you serve the ritual and who performed it?"

"It was performed by a female Buddhist monk in California," answered Mrs. Yang.

While listening to her, he all of sudden raised his voice, saying:

> Why did you give the ritual charge to the female Buddhist monk? The deity does not like rituals served by a female monk. Female monks are held in low regard in the world of the spirits. How could you expect the sending-off ritual to be properly accomplished by the female monk? Since the female performer is downplayed by the spirits, I am suspicious about the effectiveness of the ritual.

Mrs. Yang seemed very dubious of Kang monk shaman's utterance, as she stared at Lee Bosal, looking for her comment about the unexpected moment.

Lee Bosal, however, quietly endorsed Kang monk shaman's assertion, saying: "I agree with him that the ritual served by the female monk was not a good idea."

Mrs. Yang became quiet, with no immediate reaction, but she seemed to be rather puzzled, unconvinced by the remark from Lee Bosal in support of Kang monk shaman.

Meanwhile, Kang monk shaman insisted that the ritual performed by the female Buddhist monk probably failed to achieve its purpose and had not been able to send off the spirit of her deceased husband to rest in the other world.

Mrs. Yang looked very uncomfortable after hearing such negative remarks about the ritual practice of female Buddhist monks. Mrs. Yang was a long-term Buddhist who routinely respected the performances of female Buddhist monks. Finally, Mrs. Yang began to wonder what then should be done in the face of the supposedly unfulfilled sending-off ritual for her deceased husband. Doubtless, an "appropriate" sending-off ritual needed to be offered by the male Kang monk shaman. Mrs. Yang, finally, showed her willingness to commission a "proper" sending-off ritual for the spirit of her deceased husband, without hesitance or confrontation.

However, as soon as Mrs. Yang indicated her agreement to the proposed redoing of the ritual, Kang monk shaman brought up another subject to her, asking a question: "Have you recently visited a funeral home or house of the deceased person?"

"Yes," she promptly replied. "I went to the house of one of my friends who had recently lost her husband." Mrs. Yang, puzzled again, asked him why he had asked this question.

Kang monk shaman emphatically asserted:

> You are haunted by the *sangmunsal*[12] because of visiting the house of the deceased person. That matter should be cleansed first of all, before offering the sending-off ritual for your deceased husband. Unless you do that, it will impair your business, the ritual we will serve, and everything else.

"So, what should I do?" Mrs. Yang asked, seemingly quite embarrassed by the reference to the *sangmunsal*.

Kang monk shaman advised that a brief ritual to get rid of the *sangmunsal* should be performed that very evening.

Mrs. Yang approved the suggestion, so the ritual preparations, as specified by Kang monk shaman, were soon underway. The various foods and ritual items were quickly obtained from local stores and the Korean grocery, and soon Kim, Mrs. Yi, and Jiyon were busily working in the kitchen preparing the items for the small food table. That evening, Hee Kyung joined the other female ritual attendees in the preparations.

Lee Bosal in general had been a supporter of the hierarchy in the world of spirits that ranked the male Buddhist monk as superior to the female shaman. Thus, she was willing to subordinate herself to the Buddhist monk on any occasion. She also differentiated her faith as a Buddhist from her calling to be a shaman, as was manifested in her self-subordination to the Buddhist monk shaman whom she treated as her superior. Lee Bosal's high regard of Buddhism also impacted her shamanic practice. But this was a more personal matter for Lee Bosal. Surely, situations in which a Korean immigrant shaman also owned a separate Buddhist altar space next to her shamanic altar room, as did Lee Bosal, are rather unusual. It was also a curious instance of differentiation between faith and practice.

---

12. *Sangmunsal* refers to a combination of *sangmun*, which implies visiting the funeral or home of the deceased, and *sal*, which acknowledges the destructive impulses of spirits. It means potential affliction in connection with a visit to a place connected with a recently deceased person, a threat of being hooked in or possessed by the spirits. Thus, the ritual for *sangmunsal* is a kind of exorcism, in which the *sal* should be cleansed and cleared away, in order to avoid potential affliction by the spirits (Jung Y. Lee 1981, 116, 121, 129).

Hee Kyung

Hee Kyung showed up occasionally at Lee Bosal's shrine, comforting herself from the routine hardship of operating a massage parlor in the city. In her late fifties, Hee Kyung, a college-educated, divorced, single mom, had migrated to the U.S. from Korea with her daughter after attending an English language institute, a so-called ESL school. However, her life as a single mother and in the Korean diaspora in the East Coast had never met her expectations but had contained many difficulties. She had undergone multiple problems. She had borrowed money in order to open a massage parlor, but her debts were only increasing. Her status as a temporary resident in the U.S. constantly threatened the security and safety of herself and her daughter. In addition, her relationship with a younger boyfriend also led her to anguish and suffering. She had not been able to properly assist and support her daughter's preparation for life as an adult. In acknowledgement of the unyielding hardships that she had experienced, Kang monk shaman had given her a brief shamanic diagnosis: "It is because of spirit possession, though not to the extent that it requires initiation as a professional shaman, but sufficient that it needs to be appeased in order for your life to become settled." Hee Kyung, who had become an on-and-off visitor to Lee Bosal's shrine, as well as being a longtime Buddhist, was inclined to listen to Kang monk shaman. However, she remained unconvinced by his divination and the associated instruction about a ritual.

On that evening in the guest room, where she usually stayed over after the nighttime ritual when she visited Lee Bosal's shrine, she somewhat sarcastically shared with me her personal perception of religion, saying that there was neither good nor bad religion. Referring to her aunt, an elder in a Protestant church in Korea, and her cousin, a *manshin* in Korea,[13] she allowed that sincerity in religious devotion could earn blessings from the deities, regardless of the particular religious tradition that was followed. She said that she persisted with her visits to Lee Bosal's shrine because she was impressed by Lee Bosal, but she felt rather uneasy with Kang monk shaman who seemed to be too demanding to associate with his instruction. More than that, his divinations verbally delivered to her had been mostly incongruent with her situation. Hee Kyung went back to the city the following morning and never again showed up during my time at the shrine.

13. *Manshin* refers to an expert practitioner of Korean shamanism.

3. The Ritual to Cleanse the *Sangmunsal*

The U.S. *Sanshin* Altar

Mrs. Yang's ritual started at about 11 p.m., once the altar and the small, separate food table had been set up. Kang monk shaman signaled the beginning of the ritual by banging the drum and the gong in the indoor shamanic altar room. As usual, Lee Bosal stood facing the altar and engaging in *pison*, praying with rubbing the palms. Mrs. Yang, next to Lee Bosal, began kowtowing constantly up and down, whereas all the other attendees also joined in kowtowing while facing the altar, though remaining within the connection room. After the loudness and the persistent motion of kowtows had filled the space for about an hour, Kang monk shaman stopped his playing and chanting and announced that all the ritual attendees should move on to the U.S. sanshin altar, the altar honoring the local mountain deity.

The U.S. sanshin altar was located entirely separately from the main shamanic altar room. This altar served particularly the spirits of local mountains near Lee Bosal's shrine. Distinct from the traditional *shanshin*, the mountain deity, who was served at the main shamanic altar and who was one of the prototypical deities in traditional Korean shamanism, the U.S. sanshin was served separately at Lee Bosal's shrine, as a new addition to the immigrant practice of Korean shamanism. Lee Bosal frequently indicated that the *qi*, the spiritual energy, in the local mountains was very strong, and thus no ritual could fully reach its objective without the approval of the U.S. sanshin.

The U.S. sanshin altar was placed against the wall of the living room that was on the other side of the rear, center wall of the main indoor shamanic altar. On the right-hand side from the top of the stairs, the wall that separated the living room from the area at the top of the stairway was the backdrop of the U.S. sanshin altar. Covering half of the wall was a painting of an elderly Daoist man standing alongside a tiger that had a frightful look. Although the local mountains and any image of their spirit should be expected to acknowledge a certain foreignness, the image of the U.S. mountain deity in the painting was presented as parallel to the traditional image of the *sanshin* that was shown in the etching in the main shamanic altar room. Nonetheless, the addition of the U.S. sanshin into the pantheon of Korean immigrant shamanism served as a recognition of the altered footprint of the shamanic practice, now geographically re-located to a very nontraditional context.

The U.S. sanshin altar was set around the living room fireplace. The extensive mantel above the fireplace and beneath the painting of the U.S. sanshin was incorporated in the setup as accommodating a pair of candlesticks, two candlesticks at each end, with the incense burner in the center. On a separately set four-legged table in front of the fireplace, a pair of bronze cups for rice wine and a bronze raw rice bowl were placed. Kim and Jiyon were busily carrying out the plates of Fuji apples, California oranges, and a sizable watermelon to be added to the separate food table of the U.S. sanshin altar. Hee Kyung brought over the bottle of Korean rice wine from the main shamanic altar room, while Mrs. Yi served a set of bowls with the steamed rice.

When the U.S. sanshin altar was ready, Lee Bosal lit the candles and the incense. Kang monk shaman instructed all the attendees to begin kowtowing as he assumed his role of chanting and gong playing. The attendees stood in three rows, facing the U.S. sanshin altar. The living room space itself was nicely decorated with pieces of furniture: a grand piano, three bookcases, a glass-topped table, and a pair of couches, whose dimensions made it rather difficult for the attendees to sit there unobtrusively while yet continuing to kowtow. Lee Bosal stood in the first row, between the back of a long couch and the altar, whereas Kang monk shaman placed himself at Lee Bosal's immediate right. Mrs. Yang stood on the immediate left of Lee Bosal. The second row included Kim, Jiyon, and Mrs. Yi, between the rectangular glass table and the couches, while the last row consisted of Hee Kyung and Mr. Yi in the open space remaining on the window side.

The ritual at the U.S. sanshin altar proceeded smoothly, with no particular intervention or extra divination being added. Lee Bosal persistently served *pison* in front of the altar. Mrs. Yang and all the other attendees continually kowtowed by alternating their postures by kneeling down and getting back up, while concentrating on their own prayers and actions. They were all sweating profusely, and their shirts were getting saturated. The space was now filled with musty air, creating an effervescent aura for the ritual.

Lee Bosal once stated that the rituals at the U.S. sanshin altar were offered as one-time rituals seeking approval just for that day's ritual. That is, approval by the U.S. sanshin was separately required on each ritual occasion. However, the ritual for Mrs. Yang that night was the first opportunity for me to experience the ritual in the U.S. sanshin altar during my stay.

Cleansing the *Sangmunsal* at the Outdoor *Seonangdang* Altar

After about an hour and a half of serving the ritual at the U.S. sanshin altar, Kang monk shaman ceased chanting and playing, as he called for a short break before moving out for the following ritual at the outdoor *seonangdang* altar for a tutelary deity (D. Im 1996). Kang monk shaman quickly lit a cigarette as he sat down for the break, whereas Lee Bosal requested tea for the female attendees as she sat down next to him. Mr. Yi joined them at the table to have some tea. Mrs. Yang seemed calm but was carefully watching everything, while following the instructions given to her. The other female attendees were standing around by the kitchen counter, drinking tea and chatting. When the teacups had been emptied, Kang monk shaman, hastily stubbing out the cigarette in the ashtray, called all the attendees back to move on to the outdoor *seonangdang* altar.

Food, ritual props, and some large containers were brought out to set on the *seonangdang* altar, using the steep stairway that linked the entrance door. A group of three ritual props, consisting of the trident, the crescent-shaped sword, and the long-handled sword, each wrapped in the dark brown fabric and kept on the top of the *jakdu* set, was also taken out to the *seonangdang* altar by Lee Bosal. A large, portable, rectangular mat was laid over the bare ground near the shrine's entrance door and apparently was intended for someone to sit on. A separate table was placed in front of the door, distant from the *seonangdang* altar. Some bowls and a pack of ritual props were laid on the table. The various stainless steel bowls on the table contained each different elements of ritual food, such as water, salt, or red bean. The pack of three swords was also arranged next to the bowls on the table. The ritual representation of the separate outdoor table setting for the *sangmunsal* had a very different appearance from that of the usual food table. The ritual properly began once the foods and the rice wine had been set up on the *seonangdang* altar, and the candles and the incense had been lit. At that point, Lee Bosal, as usual, stood for *pison*, facing the front center of the *seonangdang* altar. Mrs. Yang was instructed by Lee Bosal to kowtow three times to the *seonangdang* deity and one time to each deity of the four directions. Kang monk shaman, standing next to Lee Bosal, was chanting, alongside playing the gong. All these sounds began resonating from the yard of the *seonangdang* altar, spreading out through the crisp air and disturbing the serenity of the midnight forest.

The brief but intense atmosphere at the *seonangdang* altar, produced primarily by the three major performers, Kang monk shaman, Lee Bosal, and Mrs. Yang, ceased when Lee Bosal walked over to the small, separate side table. She took a handful of salt crystals from one of the bowls and began forcefully scattering them around the table. She asked Mrs. Yang to kneel on the mat and lower her face to the mat. As Mrs. Yang followed Lee Bosal's instruction and thus docilely remained in that specific posture, Lee Bosal thrust a thin, white vinyl covering over her body as she knelt on the mat. The background chanting and gong playing were resumed, even louder than before, as Lee Bosal threw handful after handful of salt crystals and red beans on top of and at the sides of Mrs. Yang who managed to remain still while kneeling, facing the ground under the vinyl cover. As the bowls emptied, Kim, who stayed nearby so as to instantly assist Lee Bosal in the ritual, instantly refilled them. The continuing shower of water, salt crystals, and red beans forcibly poured down over the vinyl that covered the body of Mrs. Yang.

The salt crystals, red beans, and water are common ritual elements in Korean traditional religious practice, particularly in the shamanic rituals (C. Im 1996, 34). Keeping or scattering these items is regarded as a means of protection from or cleansing of pollutions, negative spirits, or spiritual afflictions. Therefore, these elements are commonly used, within and outside ritual settings, as part of folk remedies for households or businesses, so as to drive out the negative impulses or energies.

Lee Bosal took the crescent-shaped sword out of the sword pack that was laid on the small, separate table and began brandishing it about, in a series of cuts through the air, around and over Mrs. Yang's covered body. Her actions were like cutting or killing various invisible forces, all the while rhythmically moving around Mrs. Yang's kneeling body. Moreover, she would take mouthfuls of water from the water bowl and then furiously spit out the water, spraying the sword before and after brandishing it, as if sharpening the sword. Then, Lee Bosal abandoned the crescent-shaped sword and took up the trident from the sword pack, thrusting it about as if she were poking or piercing invisible, negative spirits. Lee Bosal asked Jiyon to bring the kitchen knife, which she also took up, making all sorts of cuts and pokes through the air around Mrs. Yang's body and concurrently spraying water out of her mouth onto the swords. After a while, Lee Bosal again picked up the crescent-shaped sword with her left hand, while keeping the kitchen knife in her right hand. It seemed that she was about to reach the climax of the ritual for *sangmunsal*. She appeared to be almost totally unconscious but at the highest level of activity during the segment of her sword ritual that had gone on for almost thirty minutes.

Everything instantly came to a halt when Lee Bosal threw the sword and the knife on the ground, and Kang monk shaman also stopped chanting and gong playing. Lee Bosal just stood there with a blank look and empty hands, as if she were awaiting a return to consciousness. Both Lee Bosal and Kang monk shaman were dripping wet. Kim, Mrs. Yi, and Hee Kyung immediately moved to lift the vinyl cover off from Mrs. Yang and to help the wriggling client stand up. After a few minutes, Lee Bosal slowly began to restart the ritual so as to move toward closure. She picked up the thrown-away swords and placed them back on the small table, but then she took them up again and forcibly threw the swords and the kitchen knife, one by one, back onto the ground, as if she were checking something. Then, she did it again, putting them back on the table but then throwing them down yet again. And each time, after she had thrown down one of the swords, she exclaimed, "*Jo-tta*," meaning "good" in Korean. Later on, she described these symbolic actions and her exclamation as the final ritual step, checking on the ritual satisfaction. According to her, the ritual could be regarded as successful when the thrown swords and kitchen knife ended up vertically aligned from her viewing point. Mrs. Yang, observing all this sword divination, smiled at Lee Bosal in spite of being covered with dirt, water, salt crystals, and red beans.

In the next ritual step, following the sword divination, Lee Bosal finally picked the *ohbang-gi* from the *seonangdang* altar for a divination. As the pack was shuffled and then deployed out to Mrs. Yang, her first set of selections was a white and a yellow. Lee Bosal interpreted that to mean the *sangmunsal* was cleansed from her. As her second selection, Mrs. Yang picked the white and the red with her left hand, and Lee Bosal delightfully divined that the deity would give her good fortune. Quickly responding to Lee Bosal's divinatory message, Mrs. Yang immediately asked her if the good fortune would be related to the buildings she owned and wanted to sell soon at a fair price. Lee Bosal simply responded to her by saying: "The deities will take care of them."

Thus was the ritual for the *sangmunsal* ended successfully. All the female attendees quickly shifted to clearing up the ritual aftermath. The scattered red beans and salt were swept up. The food was put into the big containers, to be thrown out later into the groves of trees near the creek. Kim took charge of cleaning the swords and reassembling them into a pack. Jiyon cleaned up and rearranged the *seonangdang* altar. Meanwhile, Kang monk shaman and Mr. Yi went back into the connection room to rest, whereas all the female attendees were still working outside in the dark, trying to clean the ritual area and restore the post-ritual environment to normal.

4. Closure

Ritual in the practice of Korean immigrant shamanism is a dialectical and dialogical reaction of the shaman to the encounter with mysterious, uncertain powers that are regarded as rooted in the world of death, a world of the spirits. In engaging the difficulties of life and inescapable death, the unpleasant forces and realities of life that seem so powerful against the desired good and healthy life are perceived as encounters with the malevolent actions of spirits in the tradition of Korean shamanism. In order to preserve a good and healthy life, the resentful spirits need to be appeased and satisfied in a respectful manner, including the material presentation and the behavioral reverence of kowtows. The spirits are personified as parallel to the superior or senior human powers of the everyday world of traditional Korean society. In this regard, ancestral spirits are consecrated as masters who have the power to control and condition the lives of servants, so that living kin serve them with a kind of entertainment and recognition that would please the masters, so as to help the living kin to acquire well-being, remedies, or good fortune. In this hierarchical mechanism, the lives of living servants can be harmed whenever the entrenched morality of filial piety and loyal service of the spirits is not made manifest. The troubled lives of the living, accordingly, can be improved through begging, offering bribes, and expressing subordination to the spirits. In brief, ritual in the practice of Korean immigrant shamanism embodies a microcosm of the social relations and the dialectical relationship between the inexplicable power of the spirits and the irrational difficulties of the living, a world in which there is no easy answer to the question "Why me?" Therein, the shamanic rituals and negotiations represent a means of bringing about transformation through "idiosyncrasy" in the lives of the Korean diaspora, as therapeutically exchanging unpleasant life realities for good fortune, in accord with the belief of Korean immigrant shamanism (Geertz 1973, 112).

8

Conclusion

Korean Diasporic Shamanism in Transition

1. The Alternative Remedial Mechanism

In the New Cultural Context

KOREAN IMMIGRANT SHAMANISM REPRESENTS part of the cultural endowment that has accompanied the call of the Korean diaspora, supporting a new life in the U.S. by way of reinventing part of the traditionally collective ethos through the presentation in its rituals of authoritative images, military costumes, weapon-like ritual props, and the central moral virtues of the early Joseon society (Jung Y. Lee 1981, 31–34; Haeoe Gongbo-Gwan 1996, 65). In this light, the practice of Korean immigrant shamanism can be identified as "the return of a form of institutional repression" dating back to the past regime of the early Joseon society (Spiro 1967, 141), one that has continued to be present in Korean society and has made the journey across the sea with immigrants.[1] Hence, the immigrant shamanic ritual functions as a culturally alternative

---

1. I am indebted to Melford Spiro for the insightful remark in his research, *Burmese Supernaturalism*, in which he identifies Burmese Buddhism as "an institutionalized form of repression" and the "nat festival" as "an institutionalized form of the return of the repressed." Nonetheless, I borrow here only the literal implication of his insightful remark, the repression of traditional culture. My research is in a much more individualized form of diasporic shamanic practice, whereas Spiro's work is in institutionalized Burmese Buddhism.

remedial mechanism in the Christianized immigrant community by mediating between the culturally attributed power of spirits and the currently "othered" life of the Korean diaspora in the U.S.

Migration, in general, involves the potential for changes in significance and function of religious life in the transfer to a new cultural context. Some scholars have taken special note of this religious dimension in the process of globalization, for which Ronald Robertson has coined a new term, glocalization (Robertson 1992, 66, 173–74; Clarke 2006, 6, 126, 357). In this particular process, the common experiences shared in a mainstream religious tradition may be modified in response to the limits set by various local cultural conditions encountered in the course of immigration. Also, certain relocated religious practices may develop distinctive characters, due to moving from one cultural location to another. As indicated, the trajectory of the religious dimension also importantly affects the transnational relocation of Korean shamanism that is involved in the experience of Korean diaspora, struggling to sustain itself in the acculturation process to the nontraditional cultural context in the U.S. (Min and Kim 2002, 66; Williams 2004, 178). Encountering an incongruous environment, the Korean immigrant shaman interacts with the "glocal" condition of not only the broader immigrant society but also of the shared Koreanness of the immigrant community in the U.S.

Shamans are regarded as a very insignificant presence, if not totally negative, within the Korean immigrant community that has been substantially constituted by Evangelical Protestantism since the earliest migration history in the U.S. (Guillermo 1991, 40; H. Kim and Patterson 1974, 57–58).[2] Korean immigrant churches have provided a home for the Korean diaspora, not only by sheltering the sense of cultural resistance in keeping with a shared experience of traditional ethnic culture but also by assisting the everyday immigrant life to be adequately Americanized in the new social environment through networking, reassurance of communal belonging, and facilitation of various cultural and legal services for positive survival. Functionally, the Protestant immigrant church provides the heart of Korean life in the U.S., which by itself represents a holistic web of cultural, spiritual, psychological, and physical resources and helps to support the Korean diaspora within varied contextual challenges in the immigrant life. So, it is perhaps adequate to say, in this regard, that having affiliation with the immigrant church means not only having access to

---

2. See ch. 3 about the first Korean diasporic group in 1903.

various resources to acquire manifold benefits but also reaffirming self-identity by belonging to their distinctive ethnic community. In contrast, Korean immigrant shamans are considered as a counter-presence for this culturally Christianized community. Unlike the immigrant church, immigrant shamanism represents no shared system or community at all and is thus unable to assist the imminent needs of the Korean diaspora. Korean immigrant shamans themselves are neither welcomed as part of the community, nor do they have access to those resources to help themselves, a contrast to shamans in Korea who exist in a religiously plural context, in which shamanism is more accepted. In other distinction, the clients of shamans in the U.S. are more likely to be Christians. The practice of Korean immigrant shamanism is thus culturally secluded and religiously disregarded within the shamans' own immigrant community. Yet many within the same dismissive community seek out their help, replicating a binary existence.

Being culturally deviant and communally isolated, however, Korean immigrant shamans find ways to fill "the little space for alternative practice" (Sorensen 1989, 163), continuing to reinvent the collectively conventional homeland ethos in the life of Korean diaspora. The shamanic clientele is predominantly first-generation Korean diaspora, including regular churchgoers and others who are directly or indirectly involved in the Protestant immigrant church. Wrestling with troubled life situations and the pressure to succeed materially in the immigrant life, many Korean immigrants privately and confidentially search for the shaman to consult about acquiring quick resolutions. Reflecting on my fieldwork with the three main shaman informants shows that the shamanic clients came from the local community, as well as from a distance, even from distant states.[3] Some of the Christian shamanic clients were reluctant to physically show up to consult with the shaman. The clients, some of whom were actively involved in evangelical Christian churches, rather preferred having phone consultations, so that they could still protect their privacy and restrict venerability. Phone consultations probably also helped those who were related to Evangelical Protestantism to lessen their sense of guilt through not having fully engaged in so-called idolatry; they were not in the presence of the idols themselves or exposed to the spirits physically.[4]

3. Lee Bosal asserted that she maintained a global network of her own clients. She often had phone calls for divinations or ritual requests from New Zealand or Australia. Meanwhile, M. Doryeong claimed that he also had statewide clients in the U.S.

4. As an anecdotal illustration by Lee Bosal about her Christian clients, she cited

Even when the client was physically present at the consultation or ritual, and once the temporary dynamic between the shaman and the client had been completed with the designated solution, the consultation/ritual conclusion generally constituted the complete relational closure in most cases. Not much developed to any extended form of networking or group activity, except for some of the clients. Regardless of the client participating physically or seeking virtual anonymity, Korean immigrant shamanism operates as a functionally alternative remedial mechanism, so as to help promote the client's individual or familial concerns, particularly this-worldly, materialistic success in the immigrant context. Meanwhile, the Protestant immigrant church functions more for conserving collective values and culturally communal practices in keeping with "ethnization" or "traditionization" as community (Williams 2004, 34).

Individualized Ritual Settings

In terms of my informants' practice, the practice of Korean immigrant shamanism is quite individualized, meaning that each shaman decorates altar settings differently; performs rituals distinctively by using individually different ritual props; and obtains a different life story. Although the shamanic deities were similarly named, the shamanic paintings and altar settings with the arrangement of various ritual items varied. The images of deities represented in the shamanic paintings were even dissimilar from altar to altar. The only shared condition among the various immigrant altar settings of my informants was, in general, the coupled presentation of the shamanic paintings that hung on the wall as the background and the shamanic altar that was placed in front of them. Although this is from observation in the immigrant shamanic practice of my informants, this variation in individual altar environments may not be different from the homeland practice of Korean shamanism.

---

a first-generation pastor's wife at a small, beginning church, in her fifties, who called her for a phone consultation about the church situation of having no new members, although it had opened a year before. As the story went, Lee Bosal divined for her that a big tree at the entrance of the church building was blocking new people coming to the church and that the tree should be chopped down to assist church growth. The pastor's wife agreed that there was a big tree entirely blocking the view of the façade and the entrance door of the church. In another illustration, a first-generation Korean diasporic female church deacon, the owner of a dry cleaning store in Texas, often called to request a ritual about her marriage, since she routinely experienced domestic violence from her husband.

The most prominent feature of individualization in the immigrant shamanic practice may well be related to the character of the spirit possession of each shaman, considering that each shaman serves each different *momju*, the bodily governing spirit, and therefore each one receives her or his distinctive shamanic gift from each particular possessing spirit. In this regard, although all of my shaman informants were similarly charismatic shamans, they served distinctive spirits, which led to ultimate differentiation in their ritual performances and altar settings. My female informant, Lee Bosal, primarily served a male spirit as her *momju*, whereas the two male shamans were each possessed by different female spirits. In the altar setting of M. Doryeong, the shamanic painting of a female spirit wearing traditional Korean female attire, *chima* and *jeogoree*, was placed at the center on the wall right above the altar. This indicated the central significance of the female deity or spirit in his shamanic practice. Meanwhile, none of the main female spirits was represented in the shamanic paintings or etchings displayed in Lee Bosal's altar.[5] That altar setting exuded a rather masculine mood, being predominantly decorated with male-figured paintings together with a set of three Japanese samurai swords, both quite unlike what was arranged on M. Doryeong's flowery altar. So, the shamanic altar settings looked ostensibly as visible aspects of the cross-gender impersonations represented by the occasion of cross-gender spirit possession.

In turning to additional details of the shamanic altar settings, the altar at Lee Bosal's shrine was routinely arranged with more food than other materials, such as raw and cooked rice, fruits, rice wine, etc. Since Lee Bosal's altar was shared with Kang monk shaman as her husband, it also routinely displayed his favorite items, such as a few cartons of Johnnie Walker whisky and Marlboro cigarettes. However, M. Doryeong's altar was covered mostly with silk or plastic flowers, along with miscellaneous items that were not perishable, but not predominantly with food. Johnnie Walker whisky or Marlboro cigarettes were not to be seen on M. Doryeong's shamanic altar, but instead, a modestly priced bottle of Korean rice wine was placed at the corner of the altar. It could be possible that this difference of materialistic display in the altar setting was mainly

5. Kang monk shaman preserved a small covered white ceramic jar as his own ritual symbol placed on the tiered shelf, sharing the altar setting with Lee Bosal as her husband. The covered jar was never opened, and none of the attendees at Lee Bosal's shrine, definitely, had any idea of what was contained in it. Furthermore, I never heard his elaborated description about his female *momju* in any occasion in the shrine.

a reflection of the contrasting financial condition of each shaman's eco-nomic sustainability. Lee Bosal and Kang monk shaman asserted that their shamanic deities helped them earn reasonably in their shamanic practices, and their displays in the shrine reflected its material prosperity. Meanwhile, M. Doryeong insisted, in contrast, that his female *momju* did not want him to be materialistically greedy. So, he did not have a fortune for economic prosperity was working part-time at a Korean-owned nail salon.[6]

However, it is also questionable to interpret these two contrasting shamanic situations solely as an aspect of "the thinly disguised sex-war" in the occasion of cross-sexual spirit possession (Lewis 1986, 35; Brian Wilson 1985, 32). I. M. Lewis illustrates, in this regard, a wide range of "sex-war" examples that represent female susceptibility to spirit posses-sion in the male-dominant society (1986, 35–38). In other words, women as the socially confined are prone to be possessed by the spirits, and they help reassure and empower themselves through the experience of spirit possession, particularly within the patriarchy. My interest, in this regard, is to hypothesize that possession by a female spirit brings about disad-vantages and impoverishment to the current life of the possessed sha-man in the form of a return of culturally repressed, conventional gender disparity in the cross-sexual spirit possession. The suggestion is that the female spirit as a social minor in the traditionally male-dominant Korean society can lead to moral and economic discrepancy in the current prac-tice of Korean immigrant shaman.[7]

This "disguised sex-war" is best illustrated by the ritual food table that shows up in shamanic practice, reflecting the conventional space and gender dichotomy that prevailed in the old Korean society. A rich food table is always favored as a means of pleasing the shamanic deities or spir-its, which also prevails in the practice of Korean immigrant shamanism.

---

6. M. Doryeong seemed to enjoy his part-time work at the nail salon. His indi-vidual persona and behavior was rather feminized, as manifested through his male body. Although it is somewhat speculative to say so, the cross-sexual spirit possession of his *momju* presumably contributed to the feminization of his persona.

7. Kang monk shaman remained a dominant male figure, despite being himself guided by a female *momju*, which sharply contrasts with M. Doryeong who seemed submissive to his female *momju*. He asserted that he had an ability to control the world of the spirits, not just the ability to communicate with them. Kang monk shaman's situation was rather unique, presumably because of his long career as a Buddhist monk prior to his shamanic call. His ritual performances appeared very impressive, differing from many other traditional shamans'.

However, the accompanied proceedings associated with the ritual food table, such as washing, cleaning, cooking, and setting up, are all women's work even in the practice of male shamans. Laurel Kendall identifies the role of shamans as analogous to that of Korean housewives in traditional Korean society: "Korean shamanism is a professional elaboration upon Korean household religion" (Kendall 1985, 166). This remark goes together with the general presumption of the female gender specificity of Korean shamans.

However, reminiscent of the priestly role of the shaman in the rituals, my male shaman informants avoid the domestic roles associated with the ritual food table, keeping women in the kitchen. So, preparation of the ritual food table invokes the traditional dichotomy between men and women, dividing the space and role for males from those for females. Kang monk shaman strictly separated the space and role of women from men within and beyond the ritual setting at Lee Bosal's shrine. That is, men were resting and being served with drink or food while women were at work in the kitchen. M. Doryeong was fully reliant upon his female apprentice, when he had one, to set up the ritual food table. The Korean immigrant male shamans were not only encompassed by their own cultural male-dominant ethos but also unable to manage the traditional housewife's role associated with their shamanic practice. Yet, in the precept of Lee Bosal, *jaeju* (Y. Harvey 1979, 263; C. Choi 1989, 236), the talent, should be given by the deities, but *uishik*, the ritual and the food setting, should be learned from the shamanic teacher. In this regard, even the male shaman should have learned how to manage the ritual food table within the period of his shamanic apprenticeship. Associated with the ritual food table, the cultural reproduction of stereotypical maleness was pervasive in the immigrant shamanic practice, particularly in the practice of my informants. This "disguised sex-war" will continue in the immigrant shamanic practice, as long as the food table is ritually relevant to serving the shamanic deities.

In addition, with reference to the ritual props used in divination, my female shaman informant, Lee Bosal, used only *obhang-gi* for divination, whereas M. Doryeong, the male shaman, used various props, such as charms, a folding fan, and a gong, together with an extensive ritual performance, including chanting for a divination. Kang monk shaman, the husband of Lee Bosal, randomly spoke *gongsu*, the divinatory message, to the clients and the ritual attendees, but he did not perform any particular enactments or utilize any ritual props solely for a divination.

Instead, he attempted to collaborate with Lee Bosal in the enactment of divination, becoming complementary to her divinatory message. Identified as charismatic shamans, my three informants all relied upon the invisible power of spirits in divination, as well as in rituals. However, as for achieving exquisite ritual efficacy, distinctiveness prevailed in each ritual performance of each shaman, in terms of ritual segments and the use of ritual props (C. Choi 1989, 26).[8]

From Tradition to Change

Korean shamanic ritual in the practice of the East Coast is undergoing slow change in the process of cross-cultural adaptation. In terms of Annemarie de Waal Malefijt's notion of internal and external variables that impact cultural change, the character of cultural receptivity may be a very important aspect for understanding the impact of a change in the religious landscape, together with the associated change in ritual practice in the new cultural context (Malefijt 1968, 329). Receptivity is imperative for the diaspora, but the nature of cultural receptivity often involves an encounter with counter-impulses from the new cultural contact, causing tension, as people seek a balance between the old and new, between confrontation and adaptation. In the encounter with many limits set by new legal and environmental codes in the immigrant context, Korean shamans on the East Coast are, on the one hand, resolutely resisting influences from the new cultural context, in keeping with their traditionized shamanic practice in the immigrant cultural environment. On the other hand, the immigrant shamans have already partially opened the door to cultural negotiation with Western Christianity, which used to be considered one of the most unpleasant encounters in their traditional shamanic practice, by accepting clients from the Christianized community in the U.S. In addition, some foreign, local spirits also begin to be part of the immigrant shamanic pantheon, which reflects changes of the landscape in the practice of Korean immigrant shamanism.

The performance of traditional Korean shamanic rituals has often been compared to theatrical plays or human dramas, due to the inclusion of various art forms, colorful costumes, dance, emotionally driven

8. As to the differentiated forms of enactment and the following ritual efficacy, the difference of residential environment in their practice might also be of importance, in comparison between M. Doryeong's tiny shrine and Lee Bosal's spacious indoor shrine and outdoor altars.

narratives; the ritual can be viewed as a multifaceted entertainment (Kendall 1983, 166; C. Choi 1989, 246). Most of all, the ritual impersonations enacted by the shaman, of spirit figures who appear in connection with real-life stories that arouse the sympathy of the audience, can easily lead outsiders to the given ritual context to view the rituals as theatrical drama. Actually, in providing the appearance of a show, shamanic rituals performed in the public arena in Korea have been a great attraction for villagers and visitors (Brian Wilson 1985, 26).

However, the full-coursed, dramatized, enjoyable "show" performed by Korean charismatic shamans in multicolored costumes may no longer be part of the scene in the immigrant cultural context in the East Coast of the U.S.[9] As mentioned, the ever-present legal and environmental limitations serve to eliminate the very visible, audible, non-Western, Korean native rituals from the public arena or from residential neighborhoods in the immigrant cultural arena. Even Korean immigrants themselves do not welcome the public performance of Korean shamanism in the U.S. Furthermore, as for the immigrant clients' confidentiality, assigned high priority in the discreet search for a shaman, the rituals performed for their life remedies and/or good fortune are incompatible with public disclosure within the Christianized immigrant community.

Meanwhile, the restricted availability of appropriate time and location for both shaman and client also contributes to inventing reduced forms of summary ritual in the immigrant shamanic practice. In other words, from the perspective of both shaman and client, there exists a virtue in effective quickness in the ritual, as opposed to a lengthy, time-consuming, conventional shamanic ritual, due to the less flexible circumstances of time and space in the life of the immigrant world. Moreover, particularly on the part of shamans, uninterrupted time and protected spaces for ritual performance should be a requisite condition, so as to achieve ritual efficacy even with the virtue of quickness.

My female immigrant shaman informant was able to secure a relatively large space separate from her consultation office, which provided her with considerable flexibility in her shamanic practice. Whereas other shamans have to travel about seeking appropriate creeks or forests for freely performing rituals, she no longer has to spend time searching for

9. The East Coast shamanic setting may be different in some ways than the West Coast of the U.S. On the tenth anniversary of the L.A. Rodney King riots, Kumhwa Kim, joined by twelve others, publicly performed shamanic rituals and had come back to perform at UCLA (*Yonhap News* 2002; *Maeil Economy* 2002).

a reasonably protected ritual space and is even able to obtain outdoor altars for the *yongshin*, the water spirit, and the *seonangdang*, the village tutelary spirit. Her forest mansion even included a sizable guest room for clients who may need to stay over after a lengthy nighttime ritual, though most clients leave fairly quickly after ritual consultations or ritual performances. Meanwhile, in the situation of the male immigrant shaman informant M. Doryeong, there was insufficient space and residential freedom to have lengthy consultation and/or rituals at the "office" where M. Doryeong combined his professional and personal space in a small rental unit that was even shared with a housemate. Maintaining a tiny apartment room in a built-up urban area for his shamanic altar and engaged in part-time work at a nail salon, he could not afford an appropriate space for a lengthy ritual. Accordingly, for some expansive rituals, he had to search for a safe outdoor space near some running water or a mountain, quite far from his urban residence. This search was also difficult for him because he did not have a driver's license or means of transport.

In general, shamanic clients appeared quickly and left fairly soon after achieving the purposes of their visits to the shaman. Some clients showed up together with their own ritual offerings, but others did not attend their own ritual proceedings, leaving the ritual process solely in the hands of the shaman. On either occasion, a basic desire of the clients was to have "quick" resolutions for their problems or instant good fortune. This demand for the quickness is associated with the clients' awareness of the tainted reputation of shamanism, regarded as demonic superstition, and involves their vulnerability as the emotional response to it in the predominantly Christianized immigrant context.

The demand of quickness seemed to be also a factor in the marked reduction of the colorful representation of shamanic costumes in the immigrant shamanic rituals, as compared with the homeland practice in Korea. Tae-gon Kim asserts that the charismatic shamanic costume is a ritual symbol, representing the state of the shaman controlled by the ego of a deity or spirit (T. Kim 1988, 128). Recognizing the quintessential aspect of spirit possession in traditional Korean shamanism, his remark denotes that the shamanic costumes as a means of shamanic manifestation symbolically represent the presence of the shamanic deities. However, the immigrant shamans whom I observed in my fieldwork on the East Coast seldom put on traditional colorful garments during their rituals. Kang monk shaman often wore the gray, baggy pants and the traditional Buddhist robe over them that looked similar to part of the traditional Kendo uniform. Lee Bosal sometimes wore the gray, baggy pants that were commonly used by female Buddhist devotees in Korea. But, for most other ritual occasions, she used to be in casual clothing. M. Doryeong was always in casual clothing within and beyond the ritual setting, usually in a pair of dark-colored sports pants or baggy pants and a random T-shirt. Overall, this situation simply but apparently meant that the traditional, ceremonial proceeding, with colorful presentation of costumes and charismatic shamanic deities, was gradually replaced by summary forms of ritual by corresponding to the contextual limit and following the client's desire for a quick resolution in the immigrant shamanic practice.

The emphasis on quickness also seemed to contribute to eliminating the dramatic momenta richly portrayed in ritual episodes. The dramatic and symbolic moments with cries, laughs, or sarcastic narratives being exchanged between the shaman and the possessing spirits, often involving even the clients, were apparently seldom observed in the immigrant shamanic ritual. Instead, the shaman-centered divinations and the associated rituals that focused on problems and questions in search of resolutions took precedence and bypassed the dramatic elements in the yearning for a quick remedy. The atmosphere of immigrant shamanic ritual, therefore, mostly seemed rather serious and tense, less entertaining.

Once the ritual proceeding was completed, acquiring certain types of shamanic remedies or promises for good fortune, the shamanic clients quickly went back to their routine life in the mainstream, Christianized immigrant community. The experience with the shamans would be set aside for some time, as they were back in their everyday life. However, their experience of the checkered life will lead them again to contemplate a traditional, culturally established, common-sense *"Jeom-ina-chireo-gal-gga?"* (Shall I go for a divination?). So, the shaman will seek out for another quick remedy that creates "a third space," an alternative space ethnized by traditional Korean collective consciousness but secluded from the Christianized immigrant community and the broader society in the U.S.

2. Evolving toward a New Religion

If newness is identified by the notion of "different, albeit converging" practice with traditional practice, Korean immigrant shamanism in the U.S. is evolving toward a new religion (Clarke 2006, 9). The probative analysis of immigrant shamanism as "engaged with the modern society from the one which they originated," may be fairly pertinent to understanding the significance of the "new" practice of Korean shamanism in the U.S. (Arweck 2002, 265). Considering the scholarly discussion in the rise of a new religious movement, I do not attempt either to speculate about Korean immigrant shamanic practice as an "option for spirituality" that can enrich an individual's true self or to degrade it as a kind of "cult" or "sect" that, properly or not, seems to disperse a negative nuance (Clarke 2006, 7, 9; Hunter 1983, 45; Bryan Wilson 1981, 217). However, concerning the trace of something new within the Korean immigrant shamanic realm that deviates from the traditional form in Korea itself, it seems useful to examine the trend of shamanic subjectivization in the new cultural context (Hunter 2009, 92). James Davison Hunter, citing Arnold Gehlen, refers to subjectivization as "a corollary process to de-institutionalization" (Hunter 2009, 4). According to Hunter, subjective cultural choices, apart from institutional routines, assist to promote a kind of newness in the subjectively empirical arena that is liable to change (Hunter 2009, 4). In this regard, the trace of something new observed in the practice of Korean immigrant shamanism, including new deities, signifies a subjective induction that deviates from the traditional practice and that is caused by the individual shaman's encounter with the new culture and by the geographical relocation.

Note, inter alia, the common appearance of the American national flag on the altars of the immigrant shamans I encountered, the altar of Lee Bosal and Kang monk shaman and that of M. Doryeong. This may seem insignificant at first glance but it is regarded as rather significant in its association with the ethnic immigrant shaman's experience of spirit possession. Considering that culturally identified, specific markers found in each traditional religion are limited by a cultural location, involving the American national flag in the Korean immigrant shamanic pantheon is something not taken for granted. Apart from the American flag, the Korean shamanic altar has representations only of culturally constituted traditional shamanic deities and the associated offerings to them. In that each national flag is an emblem that represents the pride, culture, and identity of a particular country, the appearance of the American national flag on the traditional Korean shamanic altar seems quite foreign. With the display of this flag on the altar, the Korean immigrant shamanic practice is culturally located, but its cultural identity is no longer indicated as strictly Korean. Instead, it has become an in-between cultural practice, both Korean and American, as manifested by the symbolic presence of two national flags in conjunction with the immigrant shamanic altar. Also, keeping with the presence of two flags, a cultural negotiation with the foreign spirits is potentiated, involving local, American spirits in the immigrant shamanic practice. In this regard, Lee Bosal simply remarked that the display of American national flag on her altar was a symbolic recognition of the current location of her shrine and shamanic practice in the U.S. Considering that her first husband was a Native American and that the current area of her shrine property had been a local Native American residence in the past, the presence of the American national flag on Lee Bosal's altar might also symbolize her particular openness to the local Native American spirits. Moreover, M. Doryeong seemingly provided a very compatible and realistic comment about the small set of three American flags placed on his altar. He asserted that the specific number three was the shamanic deities' favorite number in the presence of the American national flag on his altar, which signified reverence given to the local American spirits whom he did not want to offend. These illustrations point to the shamans' acknowledgment of traditional practice in a new geographical and cultural context.

This comment of M. Doryeong was reflected in the physical appearance of a new altar at Lee Bosal's shamanic shrine, named "the U.S. *sanshin*," the U.S. mountain deity. Negotiating not to offend a local mountain spirit in the area of her shrine, Lee Bosal offered honor and gained initial authorization by the U.S. *sanshin* prior to any scheduled ritual performance.

This symbolic reaction as part of the cultural negotiation with the nontraditional, local spirits of the foreign country comes by way of the recognition of a new deity and invitation to the pantheon of Korean immigrant shamanism. This reaction to the foreign locale's spirit, furthermore, signifies possible differentiation from altar to altar and from ritual to ritual, reliant upon each specific local environment in which each individual shaman resides and practices in the U.S. As local U.S. spirits are included in their practice, creating a distinctive title and inventing a new altar, the subjectivized choice of each shaman can greatly contribute to the production of variation or change in the ritual construction of shamanic deities, altar settings, ritual forms, etc.

Given these points, it may be noteworthy as to how the individual Kang monk shaman creates an immense impact upon the differentiation of ritualization in the immigrant shamanic practice at Lee Bosal's shrine.

Drawing upon his long-term Buddhist transition from fairly traditional Buddhist monkhood to becoming a charismatic shaman, his Buddhist formation and his presumption of traditional male dominance played a major role in his transformation of the ritual practice at Lee Bosal's shrine. Kang monk shaman's Buddhist formation was markedly strong, so as to affect changes in the blending avenue of shamanic rituals.

The ritual in traditional Korean shamanism is, in general, the shaman-led, dialogical proceeding interactively with the spirits. Comparing the performance of Korean shamanic ritual to traditional theatrical plays staged in a dialogical interplay between the actor/actress and audience, the shamanic audience stays on the observer's side, in general, rather than participating in the other's ritual proceeding. In contrast, traditional Buddhist ritual invites all the devotees to partake in the ritual kowtows and to engage in contemplation in the practice. Buddhist ritual seeks more to enrich the spirituality of the devotees who are present, whereas Korean shamanic ritual is appropriated for remedies. In this regard, a personal remark by Lee Bosal is quite illuminating: "My belief is in Buddhism, whereas my calling is to shamanism." In this context, then, Kang monk shaman involved all of the audience in the ritual, creating his own "Buddhist" congregation at Lee Bosal's shrine. He invited all the attendees to the shamanic-Buddhist seance and to join in the associated spirituality by accentuating particularly extended kowtowing and producing a Buddhist-shamanic effervescence during the ritual at the shamanic shrine in the forest. In this, his Buddhist ethos immensely contributed to the shamanic ritual, leading to gradual deviation at Lee Bosal's shamanic shrine in the personal relationship with Lee Bosal, as husband and wife. Taken overall, it emphasizes the malleability of the ritual practice in the immigrant context, alerting to potential changes and adjustments ranging from shamanic subjectivized choices and/or cultural shifts to the immigrant life.

Current Korean immigrant shamanic practice appears still very similar to the traditional forms of practice, in the ritual placements of altar setting, the deities invoked, the foot table, and the reasons that clients come. But its potential for change with some new inclusions is already underway. In my observations, each Korean immigrant shaman is learning to respond differently to the question of how to Americanize one's own practice of shamanism. The overwhelming Christian context of the Korean immigrant community is one of the biggest differences from the homeland of Korea, where Christians are only about a quarter of the population. Immigrant shamans struggle to settle into a new cultural condition, even by opening negotiation with the local, foreign spirits and somewhat with other established Korean religious traditions, in order to prevent conflicts from the representation of traditional native Korean spirits in her or his immigrant pantheon. Calling forth the traditional deities to the othered life in the U.S., the Korean immigrant shaman helps acquire quick remedies and/or good fortune for the preponderantly Christianized, first-generation, nostalgic immigrant clients. The immigrant shamans still repeatedly enact what they have learned from their shaman teachers, but they will gradually change their ritual fashions correspondingly to their experiences of new, foreign spirits in the cross-cultural context in the U.S. They may deviate from traditional practice, but this process is neither rapid nor radical. Assuming that the immigrant shamanic practice survives, even if only on the fringes, it will take on new forms, not only contributing to further deviations from traditional forms of practice in Korea but also leading to innovations of varied ritual forms in the domain of diasporic shamanic practice, including various foreign spirits in the pantheon of Korean immigrant shamanic practice.

GLOSSARY

The Romanized Korean word/s appears first, followed by the Korean, then by the English translation of each term.

An: 안   inside or interior

Anche: 안채   the inside or women's quarter

Anchal-gido: 안찰기도   a prayer by the laying on of hands

Baekdu-san: 백두산   Baekdu Mountain

Baekjung: 백중   a Buddhist day of all spirits

Bak: 밖   outside or exterior

Bakache: 바깥채   the outside or men's quarter

Baksu: 박수   a male shaman

Beopsa: 법사   a Buddhist monk

Binyeo: 비녀   traditional ornamental hair pin for the married women

Bok: 복   fortune

Bokchae: 복채   the fortune-telling fee

Bosal: 보살   Bodhisattva, a female Buddhist devotee

Bujeong-tanda: 부정탄다   touched or polluted by unclean spirits

Bukbang-gye: 북방계   the northern system

Bulgong-deurrida: 불공드리다   offering a Buddhist prayer

Byeolsang: 별상   the special messenger spirit

Byeolshin gut: 별신굿   an ocean village ritual

Chacha-ung: 차차웅   the shamanic sovereignty

Cheokshinje: 척신제   a ritual for greeting deities

Cheolip: 철립 a warrior's helmet

Cheonbok: 천복 the long indigo vest

Cheon-in/Cheon-min: 천인 the lowest class

Cheop: 첩 concubine

Chilseong: 칠성 the seven stars deity of the Big Dipper

Chilseong-dang: 칠성당 the hall of the seven stars deity

Chima: 치마 traditional Korean female skirt

Chungseong: 충성 loyalty

Daegam-shin: 대감신 the elite male power deity, a title of governmental office

Dan-gun: 단군 the founder of the first kingdom of Korea, Gojoseon

Dang-gut: 당굿 an agricultural village ritual

Dongja-shin: 동자신 the child spirit

Do-reul-dakda: 도를 닦다 training oneself spiritually

Eonni: 언니 a big sister

Eop: 업 karma

Eoshik: 의식 the ritual and food setting

Gabuja: 가부좌 a lotus posture

Gang-shin-mu: 강신무 a charismatic shaman

Gibok: 기복 praying for luck or fortune

Gidowon: 기도원 a prayer garden

Gojoseon: 고조선 the first nation of Korea

Gongsu: 공수 a divinatory message

Gopuri: 고풀이 untying the knots, meaning untying the distress of the restless spirits

Gori: 거리 a ritual segment

Gung-mu: 궁무 a royal shaman

Gut: 굿 the shamanic ritual

Gut-gori: 굿거리 an episodic segment in the shamanic ritual

Gwan-jaesu: 관재수 misfortunes related to public authorities

Gwan-mu: 관무　a governmental shaman

Halla-san: 한라산　Halla Mountain

Han: 한　a culturally collective sense of depressed feeling

Hanji: 한지　traditional Korean paper

Han-puri: 한풀이　disentangling the resentful psyche

Hanyang gut: 한양굿　the shamanic ritual regionally originated from Hanyang

Hwan-in: 환인　the heavenly king

Hwan-wung: 환웅　the heavenly son of Hwan-in

Hwa-rang: 화랑　the national youth institution in the Silla kingdom

Hyo: 효　filial piety

Ilgwang Bosal: 일광보살　the sunshine Bodhisattva

Iseung: 이승　this world

Jaeju: 재주　the shamanic talent

Jaesangdae: 재상대　the spirit stick

Jageun-manura: 작은마누라　a little wife or concubine

Jakdu: 작두　the sharp double-edged blade

Jang-gu: 장구　double-headed traditional Korean drum

Jang-gun-shin: 장군신　the military general deity

Japshin: 잡신　the miscellaneous spirit

Jeogori: 저고리　traditional Korean female jacket

Jeom-ina-chireo-galgga?: 점이나 치러갈까?　Shall I go for a divination?

Jeoseung: 저승　the world of the dead

Jeseok: 제석　the deity of fertility, identified with *samsin* or *sambul*

Jijang Bosal: 지장보살　Ksitigarbha, Bodhisattva of suffering

Jinogwi-gut: 진오기굿　the *honnyeong-gut*, a ritual for a deceased unmarried adult

Jiri-san: 지리산　Jiri Mountain

Josang-shin: 조상신　the ancestral spirit

Jotta: 좋다 good

Jung-in: 중인 the middle class

Keun-manura: 큰마누라 a big or major wife

Kkwaeng-gwari: 꽹과리 traditional Korean gong

Manshin: 만신 an expert, skillful, senior female shaman

Minjung: 민중 common people

Mireuk Bosal: 미륵보살 the Buddha of the future

Momju: 몸주 the bodily governing spirit

Mu-byeong-jang-su: 무병장수 longevity and health

Mudang: 무당 a female shaman

Mungwan: 문관 a military official

Myeongdari: 명다리 a ritual to lengthen the life span

Naerim-gut: 내림굿 *immuje*, 임무제 *shin-gut*, 신굿 the initiation ritual

Nae: 내 inside or interior

Nambang-gye: 남방계 the southern system

Namcheolik: 남철릭 a blue dress

Nam-jon-yeo-bi: 남존여비 men as superior to women

Nunchi: 눈치 a sense to quickly perceive the context

Oei: 외 outside or exterior

Ogwigut: 오귀굿 *neokgut*, 넋굿 a memorial ritual performed right after death

Ohbang-gi: 오방기 the five colored, rectangular fabric strips

Palgwan-hoe: 팔관회 a national harvest festival as the special observance of Buddhist precepts in the Goryeo dynasty

Pison: 피선 praying with rubbing the palms

Pung-eo-je: 풍어제 a ritual for a big catch of fish

Saju: 사주 an individual's data of birth year, month, day, and time

Sam-guk-yusa: 삼국유사 memorabilia of the three kingdoms

Sam-jong-ji-deog: 삼종지덕 a woman's lifetime servitude to father, husband, and son

Samsin-halmeonni: 삼신할머니   the birth or three spirits of grandmother

Sang-min: 상민   the lower class

Sang-mun-sal: 상문살   a destructive impulse of spirits emanating from visiting a funeral or the home of the deceased

Sanshin: 산신   the mountain deity

Sasi: 사시   9 to 11 a.m. with the snake symbol in accord with the ancient Chinese zodiac

Seol-ik-da: 설익다   not so well cooked

Seon-gwan: 선관   a governmentally assigned ritual leader

Seonnang: 서낭   the village tutelage deity

Seunim: 스님   a Buddhist monk

Shin-abeoji: 신아버지   a shamanic father

Shin-adeul: 신아들   a shamanic son

Shin-byeong: 신병   a shamanic illness

Shin-eomeoni: 신어머니   a shamanic mother

Shin-eul-bullida: 신을 불리다   calling out the spirits

Shin-jeom: 신점   a divination based on spirit possession

Shin-narim: 신내림   initiation

Shin-ryeong-nim: 신령님   dear deity

Shin-ryeong-nim-deul Neo-greob-ge Yong-seo-hae Juseyo: 신령님 들 너그럽게 용서해 주세요   dear deities, generously forgive me

Shin-ttal: 신딸   a shamanic daughter

Sipjangsang: 십장생   ten traditional symbols of longevity

Taebek-san: 태백산   Taebek Mountain

Tanda: 탄다   riding, burning

Tongseong-gido: 통성기도   a loud prayer

Uishik 의식   the ritual and food setting

Umsa: 음사   a secretive, licentious sacrifice

Wolgwang Bosal: 월광보살   the moonlight Bodhisattva

Yaksa Bosal: 약사보살   the medicine Bodhisattva

Yangban: 양반   the ruling class, two parties of civil and military officials

Yang-in: 양인   the upper class

Ye: 예   propriety

Yeon-deung-hoe: 연등회   a spring festival, lighting lanterns in celebration of the Buddha's birthday

Yong-shin: 용신   the dragon or water deity

Yongwang-nim: 용왕님   dear dragon king deity

Young-hum: 영험   the spiritual power

Bibliography

Andreski, Stanislav. 1984. *Max Weber's Insights and Errors*. Boston: Routledge & Kegan Paul.

Arweck, Elisabeth. 2002. "New Religious Movements." In *Religions in the Modern World*, edited by Linda Woodhead et al., 264–84. New York: Routledge.

Ashcroft, Bill, et al., eds. 1998. *Post-Colonial Studies*. London: Routledge.

Atkinson, Paul, and Martyn Hammersley. 1994. "Ethnography and Participant Observation." In *Handbook of Qualitative Research*, edited by Norman K. Denzin and Yvonna S. Lincoln, 248–61. Thousand Oaks, CA: Sage.

Babcock, Barbara. 1978. *The Reversible World: Symbolic Inversion in Art and Society*. Ithaca, NY: Cornell University Press.

Badger, R. B. "Shamanism and Korean Protestantism." The News from Wabu-eup, Oct. 26, 2009. https://rbbadger.wordpress.com/2009/10/26/shamanism-and-korean-protestantism/.

Bell, Catherine. 1992. *Ritual Theory, Ritual Practice*. New York: Oxford University Press.

Bendix, Reinhard. 1960. *Max Weber: An Intellectual Portrait*. Berkeley: University of California Press.

Berktay, Fatmagül. 1998. *Women and Religion*. Buffalo: Black Rose.

Berreman, Gerald D. 1972. "Raw, Caste, and Other Invidious Distinctions in Social Stratification." *Race Class* 13:385–414.

Bhabha, Homi K. 1994. *The Location of Culture*. New York: Routledge.

Blain, Jenny. 2001. *Nine Worlds of Seid-Magic*. New York: Routledge,

Boddy, Janice. 1988a. "Spirits and Selves in Northern Sudan." In *A Reader in the Anthropology of Religion*, edited by Michael Lambek, 398–418. Oxford: Blackwell.

———. 1988b. "Spirits and Selves in Northern Sudan: The Cultural Therapeutics of Possession and Trance." *Medical Anthropology* 15:4–17.

———. 1989. *Wombs and Alien Spirits*. Madison: University of Wisconsin Press.

Bonnefoy, Yves. 1991. *Mythologies*. 2 vols. Translated by Gerald Honigsblum. Chicago: University of Chicago Press.

Bourdieu, Pierre. 1979. *Distinction: A Social Critique of the Judgement of Taste*. Translated by Richard Nice. Cambridge: Harvard University Press.

Bourguignon, Erika. 1973a. *Possession*. San Francisco: Chandler & Sharp.

———. 1973b. *Religion, Altered States of Consciousness, and Social Change*. Columbus: Ohio State University Press.

———. 1979. *Psychological Anthropology: An Introduction to Human Nature and Cultural Differences*. New York: Holt, Rinehart & Winston.

Brown, Karen McCarthy. 1991. *Mama Lola: A Vodou Priestess in Brooklyn*. Los Angeles: University of California Press.

Bruno, Antonetta Lucia. 1995. "Purification Ritual in Chindo Island." In *Korean Cultural Roots: Religion and Social Thought*, edited by Ho-Youn Kwon, 45–65. Chicago: Integrated Technical Resources.

———. 2007a. "A Shamanic Ritual for Sending on the Dead." In *Religions of Korea in Practice*, edited by Robert E. Buswell Jr., 325–52. Princeton Readings in Religions. Princeton: Princeton University Press.

———. 2007b. "Transactions with the Realm of Spirits in Modern Korea." *Journal of Academy of East Asian Studies* 7:47–67.

Buck, Peter Henry. 1939. *Anthropology and Religion*. New Haven: Yale University Press.

Budiman, Abby. 2021. "Koreans in the U.S. Fact Sheet." Pew Research, Apr. 29. https://www.pewresearch.org/social-trends/fact-sheet/asian-americans-koreans-in-the-u-s/.

Bullock, Alan, and Stephen Trombley, eds. 1999. *The New Fontana Dictionary of Modern Thought*. 3rd ed. Waukegan, IL: Fontana.

Canda, Edward R. 1995. "Bodhisattva, Sage, and Shaman: Exemplars of Compassion and Service in Traditional Korean Religions." In *Korean Cultural Roots: Religion and Social Thought*, edited by Ho-Youn Kwon, 31–44. Chicago: Integrated Technical Resources.

Chen, Carolyn. 2002. "The Religious Varieties of Ethnic Presence." *Sociology of Religion* 63:215–38.

Chilson, Clark, and Peter Knecht, eds. 2003. *Shamans in Asia*. New York: Routledge Curzon.

Cho, HungYoon. 2004. *Han'guk Mu ui Segye* [The world of Korean shamanism]. Seoul: Han'gukhaksuljeongbo.

Ch'oe, Kilsong. 1984. "Male and Female in Korean Folk Belief." *Asian Folklore Studies* 43:227–33.

———. 1989. "The Symbolic Meaning of Shamanic Ritual in Korean Folk Life." *Journal of Ritual Studies* 3: 217–33.

Choe, Sang-Hun. 2007. "Shamanism Enjoys Revival in Techno-Savvy South Korea." *Asia Pacific News*, July 7.

Choi, Choongmoo. 1989. "The Artistry and Ritual Aesthetics of Urban Korean Shamans." *Journal of Ritual Studies* 3:235–49.

Choi, Jongseong. 2006. *Joseon Jeonki ui Jonggyo Munhwa wa Moosok* [Religious culture and shamanism in the Early Joseon]. Seoul: Hanguk Musokhakhoi.

Choi, Manja. 1991a. "A Feminist Theological Analysis of Korean Shamanism." *Hanguk Gidoggyo Shinhak Nonchong* 7 (8):231–66.

———. 1991b. "A Feminist Theology of the Korean Goddess." *Faith Renewal II: A Report on the Second Asian Women's Consultation on Interfaith Dialogue, Nov. 1–7, 1991, Colombo, Sri Lanka* 1 (7):180–90.

Chosun Ilbo. 2022. "More Than a Million Shamans and Fortunetellers in Korea: Doubled during the Last Ten Years." [In Korean.] *Chosun*, May 25. https://www.chosun.com/site/data/html_dir/2017/11/24/2017112402043.html.

Chung, Byung-jo. 1996. "Korean Buddhism Harmonizing the Contradictory." In *Korean Cultural Heritage: Thought and Religion*, edited by Joungwon Kim, *Koreana* 2:44–53. Seoul: Korea Foundation.

Chung, Hyun Kyung. 1990. *Struggle to Be the Sun Again: Introducing Asian Women's Theology.* Maryknoll, NY: Orbis.

Chung, Myung-sub, et al. 2013. *Encyclopedia of Korean Folk Beliefs.* Vol. 2 of *Encyclopedia of Korean Folklore and Traditional Culture.* Seoul: National Folk Museum of Korea.

Clark, Charles Allen. 1961. *Religions of Old Korea.* Seoul: Christian Literature Society of Korea.

Clarke, Peter B. 2006. *New Religions in Global Perspective.* New York: Routledge.

Covell, Alan Carter. 1983. *Ecstasy: Shamanism in Korea.* Elizabeth, NJ: Hollym.

———. 1986. *Folk Art and Magic: Shamanism in Korea.* Elizabeth, NJ: Hollym.

Czaplicka, Maria A. 1914. *Aboriginal Siberia: A Study in Social Anthropology.* Oxford: Clarendon.

Dennis, Philip A. 2004. *The Miskitu People of Awastara.* Austin: University of Texas Press.

Dongguk University. www.dongguk.edu. Accessed Aug. 2009.

Donovan, Josephine. 1985. *Feminist Theory: The Intellectual Traditions.* New York: Continuum.

Douglas, Mary. 2002. *Purity and Danger: An Analysis of Concepts of Pollution and Taboo.* New York: Routledge.

DuBois, Thomas A. 2009. *An Introduction to Shamanism.* New York: Cambridge University Press.

Durkheim, Emile. 1933. *The Division of Labor in Society.* Translated by George Simpson. New York: Macmillan.

———. 1982. *The Rules of Sociological Method and Selected Texts on Sociology and Its Method.* Translated by Steven Lukes. New York: Macmillan.

———. 1995. *The Elementary Forms of Religious Life.* Translated by Karen E. Fields. New York: Free.

Eliade, Mircea. 1964. *Shamanism: Archaic Techniques of Ecstasy.* Translated by Willard R. Trask. New York: Pantheon.

Encyclopedia of Korean Folk Culture. N.d. "Seonangdang." www.folkency.nfm.go.fr.

Ferrarotti, Franco. 1977. *Toward the Social Production of the Sacred: Durkheim, Weber, Freud.* La Jolla, CA: Essay Press.

Foundation for Shamanic Studies, The. www.shamanism.org.

Geertz, Clifford. 1973. *The Interpretation of Culture.* New York: Basic Books.

———. 2002. "Religion as a Cultural System." In *The Reader in the Anthropology of Religion,* edited by Michael Lambek, 61–82. Oxford: Blackwell.

Giddens, Anthony. 1978. *Emile Durkheim.* New York: Penguin.

Gold, R. L. 1958. "Roles in Sociological Field Observations." *Social Forces* 36:217–23.

Governor-General of Chosen. 1932. "Chosen no mugeki" [Korean shamanism]. *Chyosa siryo* 36:10–12.

Gowan, John Curtis. 1975. *Trance, Art, and Creativity: A Psychological Analysis of the Relationship between the Individual Ego and the Numinous Element in Three Modes—Prototaxic, Parataxic, and Syntaxic.* Buffalo, NY: Creative Education Foundation, State University College.

Grim, John A. 1983. *The Shaman: Patterns of Religious Healing among the Ojibway Indians.* Norman: University of Oklahoma Press.

———. 1984. "Chasu Kut: A Korean Shamanistic Performance." *Asian Folklore Studies* 43:235–59.

Grimes, Ronald L. 1995. *Readings in Ritual Studies.* London: Pearson.

————. 2000. *Deeply into the Bone: Re-inventing Rites of Passage*. Berkeley: University of California Press.

Guest, Kenneth J. 2003. *God in Chinatown*. New York: New York University Press.

Guillemoz, Alexandre. 1993. "The Naerim Kut of Mister Kim." In *Shamans and Cultures*, edited by Mihály Hoppál and Keith D. Howard, 27–32. Istor 5. Los Angeles: International Society for Trans-Oceanic Research.

Guillermo, Artemio R. 1991. *Churches Aflame: Asian Americans and United Methodism*. Nashville: Abingdon.

Guksa Pyunchan Uiwon Hoe. 1994. *Hangooksa: Joseon choki ui Sahoe wa Shinbun goojo* [Korean history: society and class structure during the Early Joseon Period]. Edited by TaeYoung Kim et al. Seoul: Tamgoodang.

Ha, Sen Hea. 1996. "Korean American Shamanism in Los Angeles." MA thesis, University of California, Los Angeles.

Haeoe Gongbo-Gwan. 1996. *Korean Heritage*. Elizabeth, NJ: Hollym.

————. 1997. *Religious Culture in Korea*. Elizabeth, NJ: Hollym.

Hahm, Pyong-choon. 1988. "Shamanism and the Korean World-view, Family Life-Cycle, Society and Social Life." In *Shamanism: The Spirit World of Korea*, edited by Richard W. L. Guisso and Chai-shin Yu, 60–97. Studies in Korean Religions and Culture 1. Berkeley, CA: Asian Humanities.

Halifax, Joan. 1982. *Shaman: The Wounded Healer*. New York: Crossroad.

Han, Suzanne Crowder. 1995. *Notes on Things Korean*. Elizabeth, NJ: Hollym.

Harner, Michael J. 1968. "The Sound of Rushing Water." *Natural History* 77 (6):28–33, 60–61.

————. 1972. *The Jivaro: People of the Sacred Waterfalls*. Garden City, NY: Doubleday.

————. 1973. "The Sound of Rushing Water." In *Hallucinogens and Shamanism*, edited by Michael J. Harner, 15–27. New York: Oxford University Press.

Harvey, Graham, ed. 2003. *Shamanism: A Reader*. New York: Routledge.

Harvey, Youngsook Kim. 1979. *Six Korean Women: The Socialization of Shamans*. Monographs of the American Ethnological Society 65. St. Paul: West.

Hoskins, Janet. 2002. "Blood Mysteries: Beyond Menstruation as Pollution." *Ethnology* 41:299–390.

Huhm, Halla Pai. 1980. *Kut: Korean Shamanist Rituals*. Elizabeth, NJ: Hollym.

Hunter, James Davison. 1983. *American Evangelism: Conservative Religion and the Quandary of Modernity*. NJ: Rutgers University Press.

————. 2009. "The Ethical Challenge of Our Time: Reflections on History, Ideas, and Action." Lecture at the Wheatley Conference on Ethics at Brigham Young University. 16 pages.

Hwang, Joon Yon. 1995. "The Confucian Rules of Propriety and Their Influences on the Korean People." In *Korean Cultural Roots: Religion and Social Thought*, edited by Ho-Youn Kwon, 122–36. Chicago: Integrated Technical Resources.

Hwang, Rushi. 1992. "The Role of *Kut* in Contemporary Shamanism." *Koreana* 6 (2):15–21.

————. 1996. "The *Kut* in Contemporary Shamanism." *Korean Cultural Heritage: Thought and Religion*, edited by Joungwon Kim, *Koreana* 2:198–205. Seoul: Korea Foundation.

Hwang, Sun-myung. 1996. "The Origins of Korean Religious Beliefs." In *Korean Cultural Heritage: Thought and Religion*, edited by Joungwon Kim, *Koreana* 2:20–27. Seoul: Korea Foundation.

Ilyon. 1972. *Samguk Yusa: Legends and History of the Three Kingdoms of Ancient Korea.* Translated by Ha Tae-Hung and Grafton K. Mintz. Seoul: Yonsei University Press.

Im, Chae hae. 1996. "Meaning of Water in Korean Folk Religion." *Koreana* 10 (3):32–39.

Im, Dong-kwon. 1996. "Village Rites: A Rich Communal Heritage." In *Korean Cultural Heritage: Thought and Religion*, edited by Joungwon Kim, *Koreana* 2:156–65. Seoul: Korea Foundation.

Institute of Korean Church History Studies, ed. 1989. *A History of Korean Church.* Seoul: Christian Literature.

Jackman, Tom. 2009. "Fairfax Police Suspect Teen May Have Died in Korean Exorcism." *Washington Post*, Oct. 22. https://www.washingtonpost.com/wp-dyn/content/article/2009/10/21/AR2009102104110.html.

Jacobson, Matthew Frye. 2000. *Barbarian Virtues: The United States Encounters Foreign Peoples at Home and Abroad, 1876–1917.* New York: Hill & Wang.

Janelli, Roger L., and Dawnhee Yim Janelli. 1982. *Ancestor Worship and Korean Society.* Stanford: Stanford University Press.

Jeon, Hyungtaek. 1994. "Cheon-in." In *Hangooksa: Joseon choki ui Sahoe wa Shinbun goojo* [Korean history: society and class structure during the Early Joseon Period], edited by TaeYoung Kim et al., 195–244. Seoul: Tamgoodang.

Jogye Order of Korean Buddhism. http://www.koreanbuddhism.net.

Jung-Ang Ilbo Yellow Book 2010. http://us.koreanworld.net. Site discontinued.

Junker, Buford H. 1960. *Field Work: An Introduction to the Social Sciences.* Chicago: University of Chicago Press.

Kavan, Heather. 2007. "The Korean Exorcist Meets the New Zealand Justice System." *Aotearoa Ethnic Network Journal* 2 (2):53–58.

Kendall, Laurel. 1983. "A Kut for the Chon Family." In *Traditional Thoughts and Practices in Korea*, edited by Eui-Young Yu and Earl H. Phillips, 141–69. Korean-American and Korean Studies 3. Los Angeles: Center for Korean-American and Korean Studies, California State University.

———. 1984. "Wives, Lesser Wives, and Ghosts: Supernatural Conflict in a Korean Village." *Asian Folklore Studies* 43 (2):215–25.

———.1985. *Shamans, Housewives, and Other Restless Spirits: Women in Korean Ritual Life.* Honolulu: University of Hawaii Press.

———. 1993. "Chini's Ambiguous Initiation." In *Shamans and Cultures*, edited by Mihály Hoppál and Keith D. Howard, 15–26. Istor 5. Los Angeles: International Society for Trans-Oceanic Research.

———.1996a. "Initiating Performance: The Story of Chini, A Korean Shaman." In *The Performance of Healing*, edited by Carol Laderman and Marina Roseman, 17–58. New York: Routledge.

———. 1996b. "Korean Shamans and the Spirits of Capitalism." *American Anthropologist*, n.s., 98 (3): 512–27.

———. 2007. *Shamans, Nostaligias, and the IMF: South Korean Popular Religion in Motion.* Honolulu: University of Hawaii Press.

———. 2013. "Exorcism Death in Virginia: On the Misrepresentation of Korean Shamans." In *Shamanism and Violence*, edited by Diana Riboli and David Torni, 89–102. Burlington, VT: Ashgate.

Kibria, Nazli. 2002. *Becoming Asian American.* Baltimore: Johns Hopkins University Press.

Kim, Ai Ra. 1996. *Women Struggling for a New Life.* Albany: New York University Press.

Kim, Chongho. 2003. *Korean Shamanism: The Cultural Paradox*. Vitality of Indigenous Religions. Burlington, VT: Ashgate.

Kim, Hyung-chan, and Wayne Patterson. 1974. *The Koreans in America 1882–1974: A Chronology & Fact Book*. Ethnic Chronology Series 16. New York: Oceana.

Kim, Joungwon, ed. 1996. *Korean Cultural Heritage: Thought and Religion*. Koreana 2. Seoul: Korea Foundation.

Kim, Kumja Paik. 2011. "Re-evaluating Court and Folk Painting of Korea." In *A Companion to Asian Art and Architecture*, edited by Rebecca M. Brown and Deborah S. Hutton, 341–64. Oxford: Wiley-Blackwell.

Kim, Kwang-on. 1992. "The Implements and Costumes of the Shaman." *Koreana* 6 (2): 48–53.

Kim, Matthew D. 2007. *Preaching to Second Generation Korean Americans: Towards a Possible Selves Contextual Homiletic*. American University Studies. New York: Lang.

Kim, Rebecca Y. 2006. *God's New Whiz Kids? Korean American Evangelicals on Campus*. New Brunswick, NJ: Rutgers University Press.

Kim, Seong Nae. 1998. "Problems in Defining Shaman Types and Local Variations." In *Korean Shamanism: Revivals, Survivals, and Change*, edited by Keith Howard, 33–43. Seoul: Royal Asiatic Society.

Kim, Seung-Kyung. 1995. "Fieldwork with a 'Disguised' Worker: In a South Korean Export Processing Zone." *Anthropology Today* 11 (3):6–9.

Kim, Sharon. 2010. *A Faith of Our Own: Second Generation Spirituality in Korean American Cultures*. Los Angeles: British Library.

Kim, Tae-gon. 1988. "Regional Characteristics of Shamanism in Korea." *Shamanism: The Spirit World of Korea*, edited by Chae-shin Yu and R. Guisso, 119–30. Berkeley: Asian Humanities Press.

———. 1996a. "The Concept of Gods in Korean Shamanism." In *Shamanism and Northern Ecology*, edited by Juha Pentikäinen, 235–48. Religion and Society 36. New York: Mouton de Gruyter.

———. 1996b. "Shamanism's Influence on Traditional Society and the Arts." In *Korean Cultural Heritage: Thought and Religion*, edited by Joungwon Kim, *Koreana* 2:206–11. Seoul: Korea Foundation.

———, and Soo-kyung Chang. 1998. *Korean Shamanism-Muism*. Seoul: Jimoondang.

Kim, Uichol, and Sang-Chin Choi. 1995. "Indigenous Form of Lamentation, Han: Conceptual and Philosophical Analysis." In *Korean Cultural Roots: Religion and Social Thought*, edited by Ho-Youn Kwon, 245–66. Chicago: Integrated Technical Resources.

Kim, Won Ryong. 1994. *Hanguk misul munhwa ui ihae* [Understanding Korean artistic culture]. Edited by Won Ryong Kim and Kyong-hui Chang. Seoul: Yekyung.

Kim, Yulkyu. 1992. "Shamanistic Images in Korean Mythology." *Koreana* 6 (2):24–29.

Kim, Yung-Chung. 1982. *Women of Korea: A History from Ancient Times to 1945*. Seoul: Ewha Womans University Press.

Kister, Daniel A. 1993. "Comic Play in a Korean Shaman Rite." In *Shamans and Cultures*, edited by Mihály Hoppál and Keith D. Howard, 40–46. Budapest: International Society for Trans-Oceanic Research.

———. 1997. *Korean Shamanist Ritual*. Budapest: Akadémiai Kiadó.

Kock, Leon de. 1992. "Interview With Gayatri Chakravorty Spivak: New Nation Writers Conference in South Africa." *ARIEL: A Review of International English Literature* 23 (3):29–67.

Korea Foundation. 1996. *Religious Culture in Korea.* Elizabeth, NJ: Hollym.

Korea Daily. "JoongAng Korean Directory." [In Korean.] *Korea Daily*, n.d. http://yp.koreadaily.com/main.asp?bra_code=NY.

Korea Times. "Directory." [In Korean.] *Korea Times*, n.d. http://yp.koreatimes.com/.

Korean Statistical Information Service. Kosis.kr/eng.

Kurien, Prima. 1988. "Becoming American by Becoming Hindu." In *Gatherings in Diaspora*, edited by R. Stephen Warner and Judith G. Wittner, 37–70. Philadelphia: Temple Univesity Press.

———. 2002. "We Are Better Hindus Here": Religion and Ethnicity among Indian Americans." In *Religions in Asian America*, edited by Pyong Gap Min and Jung Ha Kim, 99–120. Walnut Creek, CA: Altamira.

Kwok, Pui-Lan. 2000. *Introducing Asian Feminist Theology.* Introductions in Feminist Theology. Cleveland: Pilgrim.

Kwon, Soo-Young. 2004. "How Do Korean Rituals Heal?: Healing of Han as Cognitive Property." *Journal of Pastoral Theology* 14:31–45.

Lambek, Michael. 1981. *Human Spirits: A Cultural Account of Trance in Mayotte.* New York: Cambridge University Press.

Langer, Susanne K. 2002. "The Logic of Signs and Symbols." In *A Reader in the Anthropology of Religion*, edited by Michael Lambek, 136–44. Malden, MA: Blackwell.

Laufer, Berthold. 1917. "Origin of the Word Shaman." *American Anthropologist*, n.s., 19: 361–71. https://www.jstor.org/stable/660223?seq=1.

Lee, Ha-Jung, and Sang-Eun Lee. 2010. "Formal Characteristics of the Ten Traditional Longevity on Relics of the Latter Part of the Joseon Dynasty: With a Focus on Embroideries." *Journal of the Korean Fashion & Costume Design Association* 12 (1):131–39.

Lee, Henry K. 1995. "Five Women Accused of Murder in East Bay Exorcism Death." *Chronicle East Bay Bureau*, Mar. 17.

Lee, Jeong A. 2010. "Narim Kut Concealed, Sexually Abusing and Blackmailing Shaman Arrested." [In Korean.] *Maeil Daily Newspaper*, Aug. 21.

Lee, Jonghun. 2010. "From Incarceration to Assults." [In Korean.] *SBS*, Aug. 9. https://news.sbs.co.kr/news/endPage.do?news_id=N1000780177&plink=SEARCH&cooper=SBSNEWSSEARCH.

Lee, Jonghyun. 2009. "Shamanism and Its Emancipatory Power for Korean Women." *Affilia* 24:186–98.

Lee, Joung Young, and Keith D. Howard. 1993. "Without Ecstasy, Is There Shamanism in South-West Korea?" In *Shamanism and Cultures*, edited by Mihály Hoppál and Keith D. Howard, 3–14. Los Angeles: International Society for Trans-Oceanic Research.

Lee, Jung Young. 1973. "Concerning The Origin and Formation of Korean Shamanism." *Numen* 20 (2):135–60.

———. 1981. *Korean Shamanistic Rituals.* Religion and Society 12. The Hague: Mouton.

———. 1994. *Embracing Change: Postmodern Interpretation of the I-Ching from a Christian Perspective.* Cranbury, NJ: Associated University Presses.

Lee, Ki-baik. 1984. *A New History of Korea*. Translated by Edward W. Wagner and Edward J. Shultz. Seoul: Il-Cho-Gak.

Lee, Kwang Eun. 2005. "Oebuwa chadan . . . Woorineon Jimseungcheorum Salatta" [We lived like caged animals in a vacuum]. *Segye Ilbo*, June 5.

Lee, Neunghwa, and Young Dae Seo. 2008. *Joseon Moosok Go* [Korean shamanic thought]. Seoul: Changjak gua Bipyungsa.

Lee, Pylyoung. 1993. "Joseon Hoogi Mudang goa Gut" [Shaman and ritual in the Late Joseon]. *Jeongsin Moonhwa Yeongoo* 16 (4):3–39.

Lee, SooKeun. 1994. "Introduction." In *Hangooksa: Joseon choki ui Sahoe wa Shinbun goojo* [Korean history: society and class structure during the Early Joseon Period], edited by TaeYoung Kim et al., 1–12. Seoul: Tamgoodang.

Lee, Sookjin. 2001. "Yŏsŏng iu Jongyo rosŏ iu Musok" [Shamanism as the women's religion]. *Shinhaksasang* 112: 210–39.

Lee, Sung Moo. 1994. "Yangban." In *Hangooksa: Joseon choki ui Sahoe wa Shinbun goojo* [Korean history: society and class structure during the Early Joseon Period], edited by TaeYoung Kim et al., 55–110. Seoul: Tamgoodang.

Lehmann, Jennifer M. 1993. *Deconstructing Durkheim: A Post-structuralist Critique*. New York: Routledge.

Lewis, I. M. 1986. *Religion in Context: Cults and Charisma*. New York: Cambridge University Press.

Lien, Pei-te, and Tony Carnes. 2004. "The Religious Demography of Asian American Boundary Crossing." In *Asian American Religions: The Making and Remaking of Borders and Boundaries*, edited by Tony Carnes and Fenggang Yang, 38–51. New York: New York University Press.

Loomba, Ania. 1998. *Colonialism/Postcolonialism*. New Critical Idiom. New York: Routledge.

Lukes, Steven. 1973. *Emile Durkheim: His Life and Work: A Historical and Critical Study*. New York: Penguin.

Maeil Economy. 2002. "Racial Integrity in the Tenth Anniversary of the LA Riots." [In Korean.] *Maeil Economy*, Apr. 21. https://www.mk.co.kr/news/home/view/2002/04/104226/.

Malefijt, Annemarie de Waal. 1968. *Religion and Culture: An Introduction to Anthropology of Religion*. New York: Macmillan.

Matsuoka, Fumitaka. 1995. *Out of Silence*. Cleveland: United Church.

McAlister, Elizabeth. 2002. *Rara! Vodou, Power, and Performance in Haiti and Its Diaspora*. Berkeley: University of California Press.

McBride, Richard D., II. 2007. "Yi Kyubo's 'Lay of the Old Shaman.'" In *Religions of Korea in Practice*, edited by Robert E. Buswell Jr., 233–43. Princeton Readings in Religions. Princeton: Princeton University Press.

McCauley, Robert N., and E. Thomas Lawson. 2002. *Bringing Ritual to Mind: Psychological Foundations of Cultural Forms*. Cambridge: Cambridge University Press.

McGee, R. Jon, and Richard L. Warms. 2003. *Anthropological Theory: An Introductory History*. 3rd ed. New York: McGraw-Hill.

Mead, Sidney M. *The Nation with the Soul of a Church*. New York: Harper & Row, 1975.

Meštrović, Stjepan G. 1992. *Durkheim and Postmodern Culture*. Communication and Social Order. New York: Aldine de Gruyter.

Michael, Henry N., ed. 1963. *Studies in Siberian Shamnaism*. Heritage 4. Toronto: University of Toronto Press.

Min, Pyong Gap. 1996. *Caught in the Middle: Korean Merchants in America's Multiethnic Cities*. Berkeley: University of California Press.

———, and Jung Ha Kim, eds. 2002. *Religions in Asian America: Building Faith Communities*. Critical Perspectives on Asian Pacific Americans Series. New York: Rowman & Littlefield.

Ministry of Culture and Sports. 1996. *Religious Culture in Korea*. Elizabeth, NJ: Hollym.

Mintz, Barbara R. 1992. "Korean Shamanism: From the Outside." *Koreana* 3 (2):62–63.

Moore, Robert L., and Frank E. Reynold, eds. 1984. *Anthropology and the Study of Religion*. Studies in Religion and Society. Chicago: Center for the Scientific Study of Religion.

Morris, Brian. 1987. *Anthropological Studies of Religion: An Introductory Text*. New York: Cambridge University Press.

National Folk Arts Contest, The. http://www.kfaf.or.kr/bbs/introduction.php.

National Institute of the Korean Language, The. www.korean.go.kr.

Nisbet, Robert A. 1965. *Emile Durkheim*. Makers of Modern Social Science. Englewood Cliffs, NJ: Prentice-Hall.

Noel, Daniel C. 1997. *The Soul of Shamanism: Western Fantasies, Imaginal Realities*. New York: Continuum.

O'Connor, Aanhad. 2007. "Virginia Tech Shooting Leaves 33 Dead." *New York Times*, Apr. 16.

O'Neill, Ann W. 1997. "Judge Rules Exorcism Death Manslaughter." *Los Angeles Times*, Apr. 17. https://www.latimes.com/archives/la-xpm-1997-04-17-mn-49709-story.html.

Pai, Hyung Il. 2000. *Constructing "Korean" Origins: A Critical Review of Archaeology, Historiography, and Racial Myth in Korean State-Formation Theories*. Harvard East Asian Monographs 187. Cambridge: Harvard University Press.

Park, Andrew Sung. 2004. *From Hurt to Healing: A Theology of the Wounded*. Nashville: Abingdon.

Park, Ju-min. 2004. "Korean Shamanism Finds New Life in Modern Era." *Reuters News*, June 29.

Peek, Philip M. 1991. "African Divination Systems: Non-Normal Modes of Cognition." In *African Divination Systems: Ways of Knowing*, edited by Philip M. Peek, 193–212. Bloomington: Indiana University Press.

Popchong, The Ven. 1996. "Buddhist Thought as Revealed in Temple Architecture." In *Korean Cultural Heritage: Thought and Religion*, edited by Joungwon Kim, *Koreana* 2:76–85. Seoul: Korea Foundation.

Ro, Young-chan. 2012. "Korean Shamanism and Indegenous Spirituality." In *Dreaming A New Earth: Raimon Panikkar and Indigenous Spiritualities*, edited by Gerard Hall and Joan Hendriks, 81–92. Melbourne: Mosaic.

———. 2014. "Minjung Theology, Liberation and Contextual Theologies." Presentation at Theological Forum, Yonsei University, Songdo, Korea, Oct. 23–25.

Robertson, Ronald. 1992. *Globalization: Social Theory and Global Culture*. London: Sage.

Rudolph, Lloyd I., and Susanne Hoeber Rudolph. 1967. *The Modernity of Tradition: Political Development in India*. Reprint, Chicago: University of Chicago Press.

Saliba, John A. 1974. "The New Ethnography and the Study of Religion." *Journal for the Scientific Study of Religion* 13 (2):145–59.

Salopek, Paul. 1996. "Korean Exorcism, Bare-Knuckle Style." *Chicago Tribune News*, Aug. 8.

Seo, Hyun seon. 1991. "Giddokyo Yeoksa ae isuseo ui Moonyu Bakhae wa Hangook Moosok" [Shamanic persecution and Korean shamanism in the history of Christianity]. *YeonGoo NonJip* 20:99–124.

Seo, Jeongbum. 2003. "Hangook Musok ui Hyundaijeok uimi" [Modern understanding of Korean shamanism]. *Energy* (May):169–87.

Seo, Youngbo. 1972. *ManGiYoRam*. Edited by Minjok Moonhwa Yeongooso. Seoul: goreyo University Press.

Song, YoungHoon. 2020. "The Fortuneteller Market Is More Active Than the Movie Market in Korea." [In Korean.] *Newstof*, Jan. 6. http://www.newstof.com/news/articleView.html?idxno=10161.

Smith, Jonathan Z. 1982. "The Bare Facts of Ritual." In *Imagining Religion: From Babylon to Jonestown*, 53–65. Chicago Studies in the History of Judaism. Chicago: University of Chicago Press.

———. 1998. "Religion, Religious, Religions." In *Critical Terms for Religious Studies*, edited by Mark Taylor, 269–84. Chicago: University of Chicago Press.

Sorensen, Clark W. 1989. "Introduction: Ritual and Modernization in Contemporary Korea." *Journal of Ritual Studies* 3 (2):155–65.

Spiro, Melford E. 1967. *Burmese Supernaturalism: A Study in the Explanation and Reduction of Suffering*. Englewood Cliffs, NJ: Prentice-Hall.

———. 1987. *Culture and Human Nature: Theoretical Papers of Melford E. Spiro*. Edited by Benjamin Kilborne and L. L. Langness. Chicago: University of Chicago Press.

Strauss, Claudia. 2004. "What Makes Tony Run? Schemas as Motives Reconsidered." In *Anthropological Theory: An Introductory History*, 3rd ed., edited by R. Jon McGee and Richard L. Warms, 409–30. New York: McGraw Hill.

Suh, Hyun-sun. 1991. "The Persecution of Witches in Christian History and Korean Shamanism." *Yeongunonjip* 20:1–11.

Suh, Nam-dong. 1983. "Towards a Theology of Han." In *Minjung Theology: People as the Subjects of History*, edited by the Commission on Theological Concerns of the Christian Conferences of Asia, 55–69. Third World Studies. Maryknoll, NY: Orbis.

Suh, Youngji. 2015. "In an Era When Anyone Can Learn the *Gut* Ritual at Shamanic Academies." [In Korean.] *Hankyoreh News*, April 2.

Sun, Soon-Hwa. 1991. "Women, Religion, and Power: A Comparative Study of Korean Shamans and Women Ministers." PhD diss., Drew University.

Task Force on Korean American Ministries. 2000. "United Methodist Ministries among Korean Americans." *New World Outlook* (Mar.–Apr.):20–22. https://archives.gcah.org/handle/10516/8839.

Taussig, Michael. 1987. *Shamanism, Colonialism, and the Wild Man: A Study in Terror and Healing*. Chicago: University of Chicago Press.

Thandeka. 2000. *Learning to Be White: Money, Race, and God in America*. New York: Continuum.

Thompson, Ken. 1982. *Emile Durkheim*. New York: Routledge.

Turner, Edith. 2006. *Among the Healers: Stories of Spiritual and Ritual Healing around the World*. Religion, Health, and Healing. Westport, CT: Praeger.

Turner, Victor. 1967. *The Forest of Symbols: Aspects of Ndembu Ritual*. Ithaca, NY: Cornell University Press.

———. 1983. *On the Edge of the Bush: Anthropology as Experience*. Edited by Edith L. B. Turner. Tucson: University of Arizona Press.

———. 1995. *The Ritual Process: Structure and Anti-structure*. Lewis Henry Morgan Lectures 1966. New York: Aldine de Gruyter.

———. 2004. "Symbols in Ndembu Ritual." *Anthropological Theory: An Introductory History*, edited by R. Jon McGee and Richard L. Warms, 536–53. 3rd ed. New York: McGraw-Hill.

———, and Edward M. Bruner, eds. 1986. *The Anthropology of Experience*. Chicago: University of Illinois Press.

Tylor, Edward Burnett. 1958. *Primitive Culture*. New York: Holt.

Van Gennep, Arnold. 1960. *The Rites of Passage*. Translated by Monika B. Vizedom and Gabrielle L. Caffee. Chicago: University of Chicago Press.

Vermeersch, Sem. 2007. "The Palgwanhoe: From Buddhist Penance to Religious Festival." In *Religions of Korea in Practice*, edited by Robert E. Buswell Jr., 86–99. Princeton Readings in Religions. Princeton: Princeton University Press.

Võ, Linda Trinh, and Rick Bonus, eds. 2002. *Contemporary Asian American Communities: Intersections and Divergences*. Asian American History and Culture. Philadelphia: Temple University Press.

Walraven, Boudewijn. 1999. "Popular Religion in a Confucianized Society." In *Culture and the State in Late Chosŏn Korea*, edited by JaHyung Kim Haboush and Martina Deuchler, 160–98. Cambridge: Harvard University Asia Center.

———. 2007. "Shamans, the Family, and Women." In *Religions of Korea in Practice*, edited by Robert E. Buswell Jr., 306–24. Princeton Readings in Religions. Princeton: Princeton University Press.

Weber, Max. 1946. *From Max Weber: Essays in Sociology*. Edited and translated by H. H. Gerth and C. Wright Mills. New York: Oxford University Press.

———. 1947. *Max Weber: The Theory of Social and Economic Organization*. Translated by A. M. Henderson and Talcott Parsons. New York: Oxford University Press.

———. 1968. *Max Weber: On Charisma and Institution Building*. Edited by S. N. Eisenstadt. Chicago: University of Chicago Press.

———. 1971. *Max Weber: The Interpretation of Social Reality*. Edited by J. E. T. Eldridge. New York: Scribner.

———. 1993. *The Sociology of Religion*. Translated by Ephraim Fischoff. Boston: Beacon.

West, Cornel. 1994. "The New Cultural Politics of Difference." In *The Post-Modern Turn: New Perspectives on Social Theories*, edited by Steven Seidman, 65–80. Cambridge: Cambridge University Press.

Williams, Raymond Brady. 2004. *Williams on South Asian Religions and Immigration*. Collected Works. London: Ashgate.

Wilson, Brian Alden. 1985. "Power to Powerless: Shamanism and the Korean Woman." PhD diss., University of Wisconsin.

Wilson, Bryan. 1981. "Time, Generations, and Sectarianism." *The Social Impact of New Religious Movements*, edited by Bryan Wilson, 217–34. New York: Rose of Sharon.

Yang, Fenggang, and Helen Rose Ebaugh. 2001. "Transformation in New Immigrant Religions and Their Global Implications." *American Sociological Review* 66 (4): 269–88.

Yi, Nŭng-hwa. 1977. *Joseon Musokgo* [A study of Joseon Shamanism]. Seoul: Hangukhak Yeonguso.

Yi, Sung-nam. 1992. "An Interview with Kim Kum-hwa." *Koreana* 6 (2):50–55.

Yon, Il. 1986. *Samguk Yusa.* Translated by Tae-Hung Ha and Grafton K. Mintz. Seoul: Yonsei University Press.

Yonhap News. 2002. "Racial Integrity in the Tenth Anniversary of the LA Riots." [In Korean.] *Yonhap News,* Apr. 21. https://www.yna.co.kr/view/AKR20020421000300075.

Yoon, Hong-key. 2007. "Confucianism and the Practice of Geomancy." In *Religions of Korea in Practice,* edited by Robert E. Buswell Jr., 205–22. Princeton Readings in Religions. Princeton: Princeton University Press.

Yoon, Sungbum. 1964. *Gidokkyo wa Hangooksasang* [Christian religion and Korean thought]. Seoul: Christian Literature Society of Korea.

Yoon, Yee-Heum. 1996. "The Role of Shamanism in Korean Culture." In *Korean Cultural Heritage: Thought and Religion,* edited by Joungwon Kim, *Koreana* 2:188–91. Seoul: Korea Foundation.

———. 2000. "The Current State of and Issues Related to Research on Korean Religion." *Korean Journal* (Spring):190–240.

Young, Robert J. C. 1999. *White Mythologies: Writing History and the West.* New York: Routledge.

Yu, Eui-Young, and Earl H. Phillips. 1983. *Traditional Thoughts and Practices in Korea.* Los Angeles: Korean-American and Korean Studies.

Yun, Sa-soon. 1996. "Confucian Thought and Korean Culture." In *Korean Cultural Heritage: Thought and Religion,* edited by Joungwon Kim, *Koreana* 2:108–13. Seoul: Korea Foundation.

Business Directory

Kwon, Young-dae, ed. 2011. *Korean Business Directory.* Flushing, NY: Art Plan Communication. Phone: (718) 358–9300; fax: (718)460–2379; address: 136–56 39th Ave. #400, Flushing, NY 11354.

Sejong Sillok [Joseon dynasty chronicles]

Vol. 2. Dec. 22, fifth year of *Sejong: Chongmyo-jo.*

Vol. 28. June 28, twenty-eighth year of *Sejong: Imja-jo.*

Vol. 32. April, thirty-second year of *Sejong: Yonsangun Ilgi.*

Vol. 49. Ninth year of *Yonsangun, Pyonin-jo: Yi Ik. Songhosaseol,* 1:114 (*Songhwangmyo*), 1:217 (*Mu*). *Sejong Silok,* 72: May 12 (*JeongChook*), 1436.

Index

income for shamans, 14
indigeneity, 17n31
individual charisma, 143, 144–55,
    160
individualization in the immigrant
    shamanic practice, 238–39
initiation rituals, 5–6, 14n24, 15n28,
    103n8, 163–65, 184–86, 221
inland Korea, 33n48, 51n12, 71–72,
    149, 151n23, 157
insanity, 142
instantaneousness, 180, 244–45
institutional religion, 176–80
interconvertibility, 17–18
inter-gender subjectivity, 96–97
intra- and interchurch networking,
    73
Islam, 110
Israel, 145
Iwa in traditional Vodou practice,
    103n7

Jacobson, Matthew Fyre, 20n34
jaeju (shamanic talent), 14, 143–55,
    143n13, 241
jaesangdae (spirit stick), 217
jageun manura (little wife or
    concubine), 153n26
jakdu (sharp double-edged blade),
    13n23, 218, 230
Janelli, Roger and Dawnhee, 155–57
jang-gu (double-headed traditional
    Korean drum), 218
jang-gun shin (military general
    deity), 65, 215, 215n9
Japanese annexation, 46n1, 51n9,
    67, 107
Japanese colonization of Korea,
    46n1, 49n4, 50–51n9, 107
Japanese samurai swords, 217, 239
japshin (miscellaneous spirit), 86
jeoseung (world of the dead), 132,
    165, 165n6
jeseog Buddha, 110
Ji-jang Bosal (Ksitigarbha,
    Bodhisattva of suffering),
    133, 133n7

jinogwigut or *honnyeong-gut* (ritual
    for a deceased unmarried
    adult), 6
Jiyon (shamanic trainee), 163–69,
    163n4, 165n5, 172–73, 176,
    184–85, 190, 202–22, 226,
    229, 231–33
Jogye Buddhism, 36n51
josang gut, 139
josang shin (ancestral spirit), 215,
    215n9
Joseon dynasty, 4, 4n3, 10, 18,
    46–48, 52n15, 53–67, 53n17,
    60n23, 61n26, 66n32, 67n33,
    88, 137, 194, 196, 197–98,
    235–36
jungin (middle-ranking group),
    54n17
Jung Lee, Young, 51n12, 96, 103,
    103n8

Kang monk shaman, 36–40, 36n52,
    39n54, 190n23, 239–42, 244,
    246–48
    baekjung ceremony, 132, 137,
        140
    and Buddhism, 137
    bujeong tanda (ritual pollution),
        13
    costs of rituals, 14n24
    deviant gender role, 17
    as dominant male figure, 240n7
    gendered shrines, 199
    Hee Kyung, 227
    initiation ritual, 184–86
    interruption of marriage, 186–93
    Jiyon, 163–69, 163n4, 202–22
    and Kim, 130
    lawsuits by female clients,
        187n21
    menstrual period, 180–84
    Mrs. Yang, 223–26
    Mr. Yi and Mr. Jeon, 176–80
    ritual symbol, 239n5
    seonangdang altar, 230–33
    shamanic costumes, 201n2
    U.S. sanshin altar, 228–30
    yongshin altar, 169–76

www.ingramcontent.com/pod-product-compliance
Lightning Source LLC
Chambersburg PA
CBHW071844270326
41929CB00013B/2092